U0443068

[英]雷蒙德·瓦克斯 著　谭宇生 译

牛津通识读本·

隐私

Privacy

A Very Short Introduction

译林出版社

图书在版编目（CIP）数据

隐私／（英）雷蒙德·瓦克斯（Raymond Wacks）著；谭宇生译.
—南京：译林出版社，2020.10
（牛津通识读本）
书名原文：Privacy: A Very Short Introduction
ISBN 978-7-5447-8352-1

I.①隐⋯ II.①雷⋯ ②谭⋯ III.①隐私权－研究 IV.①D912.7

中国版本图书馆 CIP 数据核字（2020）第 134835 号

Privacy: A Very Short Introduction, First Edition by Raymond Wacks
Copyright © Raymond Wacks 2010
Privacy: A Very Short Introduction was originally published in English in 2010. This licensed edition is published by arrangement with Oxford University Press. Yilin Press, Ltd is solely responsible for this bilingual edition from the original work and Oxford University Press shall have no liability for any errors, omissions or inaccuracies or ambiguities in such bilingual edition or for any losses caused by reliance thereon.
Chinese and English edition copyright © 2020 by Yilin Press, Ltd
All rights reserved.

著作权合同登记号　图字：10-2019-263 号

审图号：GS（2020）3392号
书中插图系原书插图

隐私　[英国] 雷蒙德·瓦克斯　／著　谭宇生　／译

责任编辑　陈　锐
特约编辑　石业青
装帧设计　景秋萍
校　　对　王　敏
责任印制　董　虎

原文出版　Oxford University Press, 2010
出版发行　译林出版社
地　　址　南京市湖南路 1 号 A 楼
邮　　箱　yilin@yilin.com
网　　址　www.yilin.com
市场热线　025-86633278
排　　版　南京展望文化发展有限公司
印　　刷　江苏扬中印刷有限公司
开　　本　635 毫米 × 889 毫米　1/16
印　　张　20.75
插　　页　4
版　　次　2020 年 10 月第 1 版
印　　次　2020 年 10 月第 1 次印刷
书　　号　ISBN 978-7-5447-8352-1
定　　价　39.00 元

版权所有·侵权必究

译林版图书若有印装错误可向出版社调换。质量热线：025-83658316

序 言

程 啸

在1890年12月15日出版的《哈佛法律评论》中,两位美国律师沃伦(Samuel D. Warren)与布兰代斯(Louis D. Brandeis)合作发表了一篇名为"隐私权"(the right to privacy)的文章。他们在文中写道:"文明的前行使人们的生活日渐紧张且复杂,适时地远离世事纷扰,极有必要。随着文化修养的提高,人们对公共场合更为敏感,独处隐私之于人更是必不可少。但如今的新闻报刊和各类发明,侵害个人隐私,使人遭受精神上的痛苦与困扰,较之纯粹身体上的伤害,有过之而无不及。"正是这篇著名文章,首次提出了"隐私权"的概念。

经历了一百多年的发展,隐私权在世界各国法律中已经成为一项重要的权利,被认为是一项基本人权。无论是各国法律还是国际公约,都明确要求对自然人的隐私加以保护。例如,1948年联合国通过的《世界人权宣言》第12条规定:"任何人的私生活、家庭、住宅和通信不得任意干涉,他的荣誉和名誉不得加以攻击。人人有权享受法律保护,以免受这种干涉或攻击。"

1966年的联合国《公民权利和政治权利国际公约》第17条规定："任何人的隐私、家庭、住址和通信不得加以任意或非法干涉,他的名誉和声誉不得加以非法攻击。"

隐私权之所以受到如此重视,是因为保护隐私、尊重隐私权,对于维护人性的尊严和促进个人人格的发展极为重要。每个人都生活在一个需要对自己和对他人尽职尽责的社会中。在这个忙忙碌碌、纷纷扰扰的世界中,如果没有私人生活的安宁,无法安心地休息,如果没有私密的空间,可以无须顾虑地进行私密活动,如果缺少一块只保留给自己的心灵家园,那么,个人将很难履行他(她)的职责。无论是为了促进自决与自主的个人人格的发展,还是促进有责任感的家庭成员和更为广泛的社区的发展,隐私的保护都是非常重要的。如果说传统侵害隐私权的行为主要表现为跟踪、窥视、偷拍、偷录、进入等行为,那么,随着网络信息科技尤其是大数据和人工智能技术的发展,在高度数字化的现代社会中,侵害隐私权的行为则主要表现为,通过人脸识别、闭路电视监测、无线射频识别系统、Cookie技术,以及各种传感器未经权利人同意而对私密信息进行大规模、自动化、低成本的收集、存储、加工和使用。因此,现代社会对隐私的保护,不仅仅是防止利用垃圾短信、垃圾邮件、骚扰电话侵害私人生活的安宁,以及通过进入、窃听、窥视、拍摄住宅等行为侵害自然人的私密空间和私密活动,更重要的是,通过个人信息保护制度来防止自然人的各种私密信息免受非法处理。

正因如此,现代各国法律,或是在隐私权之外提出个人信息权益的概念,以实现对个人信息的保护,如欧盟;或者扩张隐私权的概念,通过"信息隐私"(information privacy)的概念来实现对个人信息的保护，如美国。我国采取的是前一种模式。2020年5月28日，第十三届全国人民代表大会第三次会议审议通过了《中华人民共和国民法典》，在第四编"人格权"中，专章对"隐私权和个人信息保护"做出了详细的规定。该章既规定了隐私权，明确将隐私规定为"自然人的私人生活安宁和不愿为他人知晓的私密空间、私密活动、私密信息"；同时又规定了自然人对个人信息的权益，明确了个人信息中的私密信息适用有关隐私权的规定（没有规定的，适用有关个人信息保护的规定）。尽管我国《民法典》采用八个条文对隐私权和个人信息保护做出了规定，但如何处理隐私权和个人信息保护的关系，在隐私权和个人信息保护中，应当怎样协调信息自由、言论自由与权益保护等相互冲突的价值等问题，还存在很大的争论。

就广大非法律专业人士而言，虽然他们也很关注隐私权和个人信息的保护，但是限于专业知识，对于什么是隐私，保护隐私有何利弊，现代网络科技对于隐私究竟有什么威胁，何为私密信息与敏感信息，个人信息与个人数据是什么关系等问题，往往一头雾水，难以理解。如果能有一部由隐私权研究领域的权威专家撰写的，既系统全面、精确严谨又高屋建瓴、深入浅出的著作，则无疑能够极大地帮助他们理解这些问题。译林出版社即将出版的这本由英国法学家雷蒙德·瓦克斯教授撰写的《隐私》，正是这样一本值得推荐给广大读者的好书。通读全书后，我认为本书的特点可归纳为以下三方面：

首先，大家小书，作者权威。秉持"大家"写"小书"的原则，牛津通识读本系列中每一本著作的作者都是该领域的顶尖、权威专家，本书亦不例外。《隐私》一书的作者雷蒙德·瓦克斯教授,是香港大学法学与法理学的荣休教授,对隐私权和个人信息保护领域有长达数十年的研究,曾先后出版了《隐私保护》《个人信息：隐私与法律》《隐私与新闻自由》《隐私与媒体自由》等多部该领域的重要著作,乃是隐私权和个人信息保护领域的权威专家。不仅如此,瓦克斯教授还积极参与隐私和个人信息保护的相关立法实践活动,如作为香港法律改革委员会下属的隐私权分委员会的成员。故此,书中对相关内容的分析始终能够做到理论知识与实践问题的紧密结合。

其次,系统全面,要言不烦。本书不仅回顾了隐私保护的历史起源与发展历程,更密切关注现代网络信息科技发展对隐私造成的各种侵害,如生物识别技术、信息记录程序、黑客、身份盗用、DNA数据库等中隐私权及其他人身财产权益被侵害的问题。作者在书中不仅阐释了隐私权保护的积极价值,也提醒读者注意到隐私保护对女性的压迫、妨碍信息的流动、影响商业效率和可能构成对公众的欺诈等消极作用。据此,作者也对隐私权保护中各种利益的权衡,特别是隐私权与言论自由的关系问题进行了专门的、精彩的论述。瓦克斯教授虽然是一位普通法教授,但在讨论隐私问题时,并不完全以普通法为中心,而是很注重比较法的研究,如对德国、法国、意大利等大陆法系国家隐私权与个人信息保护也时不时加以对比分析。这就使得本书也具有相当程度上的比较法研究的价值。

再次,图文并茂,生动有趣。一方面,书中在介绍到相关问题时时常使用各种对应的图片,既生动清晰地说明了问题,又增加了阅读的乐趣,增长了读者的见识。例如,在讨论隐私权保护的价值时,国内不少学者喜欢提及英国功利主义法学家杰里米·边沁所谓的"圆形监狱",但圆形监狱是什么样子,我却一直不清楚,直至看到瓦克斯教授这本书中的图片才解答了这个疑惑。另一方面,作者博览群书,旁征博引,虽然书中引用了很多经典参考文献,但作者采取了专栏与正文加以区分的方式。这既使得有兴趣的读者能够按图索骥,拓展阅读;也使得那些希望快速了解本书内容的读者可以跳过专栏而只阅读正文,从而减轻了阅读的负担。

总之,雷蒙德·瓦克斯教授撰写的《隐私》一书,无论对于从事隐私权和个人信息保护研究的法律专业人士来说,还是对于广大对隐私问题有兴趣的非法律界人士而言,都是一部非常值得推荐的好书!相信广大读者在读完本书之后一定会有所收获,也会引起对隐私和个人信息保护问题更深入、更持久的思考!

2020 年 9 月 5 日

目 录

前言 1

第一章 对隐私的侵袭 1

第二章 一种经久不衰的价值 30

第三章 一种法定权利 51

第四章 隐私权和言论自由 79

第五章 数据保护 107

第六章 隐私的消亡? 128

附录 136

索引 139

英文原文 149

前　言

　　几乎每天都有报道说我们的隐私又受到了侵犯。差不多就在三十年前，我出版了另一本关于这一争议性题材的小书。现在读起《保护隐私权》，我们不可避免地会被技术进步带来的结构性变化所震撼。当然，最引人瞩目的是网上个人信息的脆弱性。数字世界产生的其他威胁还有很多：生物识别技术、闭路电视监测、无线射频识别（RFID）系统、智能身份证，以及多重反恐措施的创新，都对这一基本价值产生了威胁，甚至在民主社会中也是如此。然而，与此同时，通过博客、社交网站（如MySpace、Facebook、YouTube、Twitter）和信息时代的其他发明所带来的私人数据的爆炸性增长也令人不安，这都使得简单的概括隐私权的重要性成为棘手的问题。Web2.0的出现使互联网从信息提供者升级为社区创建者。对八卦新闻的贪得无厌继续助长了追求轰动效应的媒体，这些媒体常常贬低私人领域的概念，而私人领域是我们合法主张的，知名人士被理所当然地侵扰，这令他们百口莫辩。

收集、储存、交换和使用信息的方式已经改变了,并且威胁个人隐私的特征也随之改变了。然而,尽管电子革命几乎触及我们生活的方方面面,但罪魁祸首不是技术本身,而是它的用途。就在本周,我在菲律宾了解到一项使用RFID芯片的提案,该芯片被广泛用于跟踪货物和患者的医疗数据及保护学生免受绑架。在皮肤下面植入芯片(像跟随主人的小狗一样)在追踪失踪人员(包括那些患有痴呆症的人)方面,显然有一定的优势。但这个代价是否太高?当我们听任自己的权利被视而不见——即使其目的是有益的,我们的社会还能是一个自由的社会吗?

尽管有这些非凡的技术发展,我在1980年思考的许多问题并没有根本改变。确实,在对这本书和过去三十年中其他著作所讨论的隐私权核心问题的分析中,我现在几乎找不到任何持异议之处!这一发现让人稍感宽慰。当然,我可能是错的。但是,尽管过了三十多年,我仍然认为,将隐私权扩展到"决策"问题(堕胎、节育、性偏好)并导致其与自由和自主权混为一谈(这种混为一谈是可以理解的)是错误的。我还从这样一个事实中得到些许安慰,那就是,虽然对隐私权减少的反乌托邦式预测甚嚣尘上,但很少提及这些和其他常常渗透在隐私权领域的"决策"问题。当隐私权倡导者警告说我们的信息社会带来了无数的危险时,他们却很少为这些问题伤脑筋,尽管这些问题很重要。这是否默认了隐私权的真正含义与我们对这个概念的直觉理解和使用是一致的?隐私权难道不是主要保护敏感信息的一种利益吗?当我们哀叹它的消亡时,难道我们不为失去对个人隐私的控制而感到悲痛吗?这种控制的本质是对我们最私密的细节明确行使自主权,不管这些细节是被窥探到的还是被无偿公布的。

也许这种路径是错误的?为什么各种截然不同的隐私权不能作为同一基本理念的不同但相关的维度而共存?何不允许"信息隐私权"与"决策隐私权"和平共处呢? 我觉得讽刺的是,美国最高法院原先片面忽视前者,而加强宪法对后者的保护,但现在可能风水轮流转了。而且有一些细微的迹象表明,如后文所述,人们承认迫切需要根据欧洲的思路来依法保护个人信息。我之所以抵触将隐私权等同于自主权,并不是因为否认权利的重要性,甚至也不是因为宽泛的表述这些权利易于获得法律上的认同,澄清这一点非常重要。相反,它所基于的信念是,通过将这一问题作为个人信息保护来处理,总是勉为其难地硬塞入隐私权这件紧身衣所造成的各种难题可能更容易得到解决。隐私权的概念已变得过于模糊和臃肿,难以对其进行有用的分析。这种含糊不清实际上削弱了隐私权价值的重要性,也阻碍了对其进行有效保护。

我对隐私和数据保护的论述主要是从法律的角度出发的。但是,尽管法律是保护隐私不可或缺的工具,这个主题显然还蕴含其他一些层面——社会、文化、政治、心理和哲学。此处我试图考虑这些和其他几种力量,它们塑造了我们对这个富有挑战性的概念的理解。

我研究隐私权的历程始于多年以前,当时我还是牛津大学的一名研究生。那时无论是文献(主要是美国人写的)还是立法(主要是斯堪的纳维亚地区的),都很少。第一代数据保护法律还处于萌芽阶段。当然,自那以后,情况发生了令人难以置信的变化。把这种现象描述为爆炸并不夸张。我涉足这个领域源于从学术上去努力阐明隐私权这个难以解释的概念。这种日益脆弱的权利的实际层面从未远离我们,它们也不可能远离,因为信息时代近在眼前。二元宇宙和它的多重数字形式,加上新的精密的电子监视装置和厚颜无耻的侵入性媒体,使人们对个人信息安全的任何自满都显得天真无邪。此外,我很幸运地参加了关于法律改革和其他的若干委员会,这些委员会致力于阐明隐私权千变万化的性质,并制定了可据以保护隐私的措施。从这些机会中获得的经验对我理解并判断隐私和数据保护产生了巨大的影响。我很感激香港法律改革委员会下属的隐私权分委员会的成员,从他们那里我学到了很多。

捍卫和保护隐私的运动是由世界各地的公益研究和倡导团体不屈不挠地发起的。在这危险的前线巡逻的是各类杰出人士,对他们,我们亏欠了很多。这些组织,特别是美国的电子隐私信息中心(EPIC)和英国的国际隐私组织,不仅捍卫隐私权事业,而且还对该问题几乎所有可以想到的方面都进行了严谨的研究,包括通常在许多法域中危险的隐私权状况,并定期提供信息。我特别向戴维·巴尼萨、罗杰·克拉克、西蒙·戴维斯、格斯·侯赛因和马克·罗滕贝格致敬,他们与其他群体和个人的众多劳动成果之一是,来自四十多个国家的一百多个非政府组织和隐私权专家于2009年11月在马德里签署了一项隐私权未来的重要宣言。虽然这项宣言是在本书付梓后才能定稿,但仍有可能将其作为附录列入本书。

多年来,一群杰出的同事、隐私事务专员和其他研究人员以各种方式给我鼓励、建议和帮助。感谢约翰·培根—肖恩、埃里克·巴伦特、科林·本内特、马克·伯特霍尔德、乔恩·宾,已故的彼得·伯克斯、迈克尔·布赖恩、安·卡武克安、戴维·弗莱厄蒂、格雷厄姆·格林利夫、戈弗雷·卡恩、迈克尔·柯比、斯蒂芬·劳、查尔斯·拉布、梅甘·理查森、斯特凡诺·罗多塔、杰米·史密斯和奈杰尔·沃特斯。但任何人都不应因我本人在此处和别处出现的纰漏而承担责任。

牛津大学出版社的团队一如既往是这个项目的最佳合作者。我特别感谢安德列亚·基根、埃玛·马钱特、凯拉·狄金森、克斯廷·德马塔和德博拉·普罗瑟罗。卡迪戈·拉马林根和她的SPI团队做了出色的工作,将我的文本和图像转换成这么漂亮的一卷书,这已经不是第一次了。

在文稿的写作收尾时,甚至在阅读校样的时候,仍然持续涌现无数侵犯隐私的报道。请读者注意,你手中这本书的主题是非常不稳定的,对个人隐私的新挑战在等待着我们。为了保护和维系这一不可或缺的民主理想,我们需要警惕和决心。

雷蒙德·瓦克斯

第一章

对隐私的侵袭

从前,乘客无须被搜身就可以登机。"hacking①"形容咳嗽——可能是由病毒引起的;"cookies②"是拿来吃的,而不是让人担惊受怕的。

有人监视着你。无所不在的"老大哥"③不再让人震惊。无论公私部门,对交易数据的"低技术"收集都变得很普遍。除了闭路电视监控系统在公共场所的日常监视外,对移动电话、工作场所、车辆、电子通信和网络活动的监测也迅速在大多数先进社会普及。

从广义来说,隐私的含义超出了这些以个人信息为主要目标的侵犯,它将包括对私人领域的多重侵犯,特别是政府的侵犯,这体现为沃伦和布兰代斯④提出的短语——"独处的权利"。

---

① hacking(黑客攻击),原意为咳嗽的声音。——译注
② cookies(信息记录程序),原意为小甜饼。——译注
③ 英国左翼作家乔治·奥威尔著名小说《一九八四》中的独裁者,无时无刻不在监视其臣民。——译注
④ 指塞缪尔·D.沃伦和路易斯·D.布兰代斯,参见第三章。——译注

这个广义性的概念让人联想到爱德华·科克爵士17世纪的著名宣言，即"一个人的家就是他最坚固的城堡"，它包含各种侵权问题，不仅侵犯了"空间"和"地点"的隐私，而且还干扰了通常具有道德属性的"决策"问题，比如堕胎、节育和性偏好等。

就监控的情形而言，片刻的反思就会揭露出许多有讽刺意味的事，甚至诸多难题，其性质及我们对它的反应既不直接也不显明。"老大哥在看着你"是威胁？是陈述事实？还是仅仅欺骗性的恐吓？这有什么不同吗？例如，我得知自己被一台闭路电视摄像机监视，这是否侵犯了我的隐私呢？如果摄像机（现在广泛使用的）只是一个逼真地模仿闪光灯、探测镜头、恐吓性移动拍摄的仿制品，会怎么样？其实它什么都没有录下，但我不知道它没录下。我反对的理由是什么？又或者假设摄像机是真的，但由于出故障了而没有生成、存储或使用图像？我的行动没有被监控，但主观上我无法镇定。只要有一个装置出现，似乎在监控和记录我的行为，就无疑让我不安。

换句话说，我相信自己被监视使我感到不平。实际上，我是否是监视的对象，这并不重要。因此，我反对的理由并不是因为有人在监视我——因为我没被人监视，而是因为我感觉到自己被监视的这种可能性。

在这方面，被一个可见的闭路电视摄像机监控不同于其他避不开的秘密设备：电子监听装置。我的房间、办公室或者我的电话也许会被窃听，既然是窃听，顾名思义，我通常对自己的隐私被侵犯一无所知。当然，我不知情并不影响这种做法令人反感。然而，与仿制品或出故障的相机不同的是，这种秘密设备使我一直受到监视：我的私人会话被记录或截听，尽管我没有意识到，我的通信（电子邮件或普通邮件）被秘密拦截，也是如此。

在前一种情况下，没有任何个人信息被捕获；后一种情况则有，但我可能永远不会知道。这两种情况都属于"侵扰"范畴，

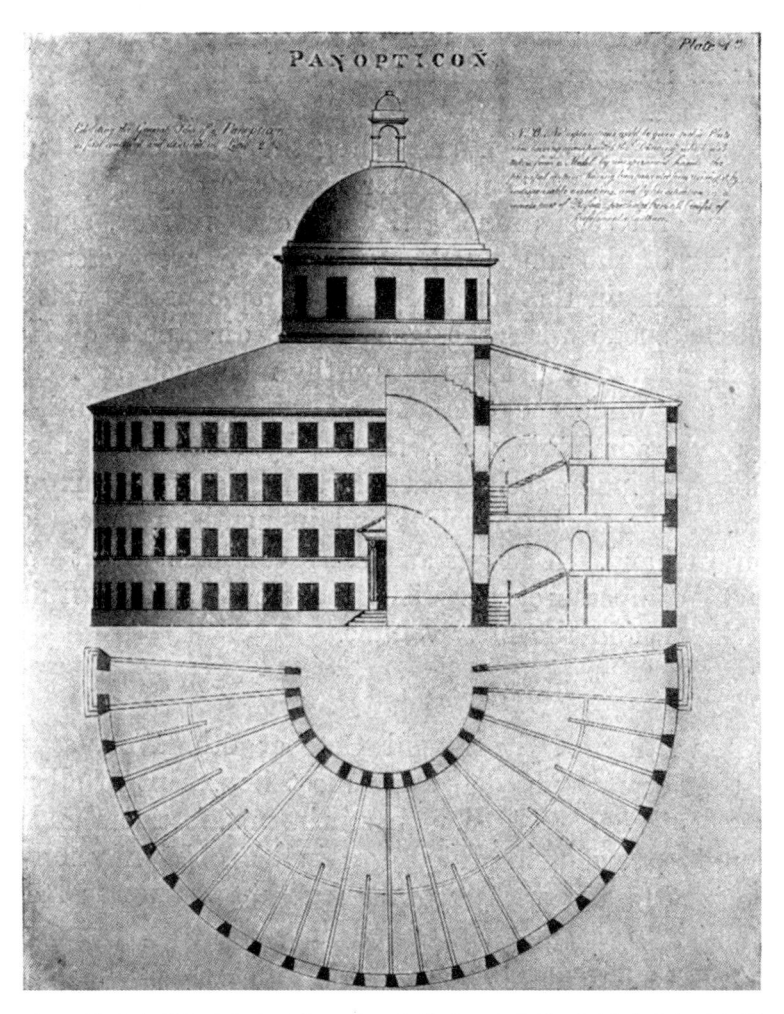

图1 英国功利主义者杰里米·边沁设计了一个监狱，方便对囚犯进行秘密观察。"圆形监狱"这个词在贬义上用来比喻对个人信息的监控，尤指对网上信息的监控。

但每一种都有不同的含义。事实上，越研究这个（被忽视的）问题，"侵扰"这个主题就变得越支离破碎。我们需要对每种行为进行单独的分析；它们都会引起一系列互不相关的令人担忧的情况，尽管这些情况都会因为人们的普遍担心而混在一起——人们担心自己的社会可能正在滑向或已经显示出奥威尔式社会严苛审查的恐怖特征。

  从根本上说，这是一个关于感觉及其后果的问题。虽然我确信闭路电视监控系统在监视我是基于明显的证据，而我对自己的通信或对话被截取不知情则显然是无证据支撑的，但这种不安是类似的。两种情况下，人们都厌恶地意识到需要调整自己的行为，因为他们推测自己的言行受到了监视。例如，在南非种族隔离最黑暗的镇压时期，反政府活动分子的电话经常被安全部门窃听。因此，人们要小心翼翼、战战兢兢地说话。这不可避免会让说话显得生硬、不自然。人们在公共场合或私人空间改变或调整自己的行为，是国家未能适当管理监视的结果，这种结果令人不安。例如，越来越多应用于工作场所的监控手段，不仅在改变这种环境的特点，而且也在改变我们所做工作的性质和我们做事的方式。我们知道自己的行为被监控，或者仅仅可能被监控，这损害了我们的心理和情感自主性：

> 自由交谈的特点通常是夸夸其谈、脏话连篇、信口开河，这种反社会的欲望或观点的表达，我们无须认真对待。

如果要保持谈话的亲密、私密和非正式的特点，谈话必须未经剪辑。确实,电子监管的趋势可能会从根本上改变人们相互间的关系和身份认同。在这样的世界里,可以说雇员更不可能有效地行使其职责。如果这种情况发生,窥探的雇主得到的结果最终会与他希望得到的完全相反。

窃 听

无论是固定电话还是移动电话,都很容易被窃听。对固定电话来说,线路只是一个长电路,由一对铜线组成,形成一个环路。通过许多交换站,电路将你的谈话从你家里传送到电话另一端的装置。在任何时候,窃听者都能将一个新的负载附加到电路板上,就像把一个额外的设备插入延长线上一样。用于电话窃听的负载是一种装置,可以将电路转换回你谈话的声音。这种原始的拦截方式的主要缺点是,窃听者需要知道窃听对象何时使用电话,他需要待在岗位上监听。一种不太方便的更复杂的方法是在线路上安装一个录音设备。就像电话应答机一样,它从电话线上接收电信号,并将其编码为磁带上的磁脉冲。这种方法的缺点是入侵者需要保持录音设备连续运行,以便监听任何谈话,但很少有磁带足够大,因此,声控录音机提供了一个更为实用的选择。尽管这样,磁带也不太可能持续足够长的时间来捕捉监听对象的对话。

答案显而易见:窃听器。窃听器接收音频信息并用无线电波传递信号。窃听器通常有小型麦克风,可以直接接收声波。电流被发送到无线电发射台,发射台传送的信号随电流变化。窃听者在附近设置一个无线电接收器,接收到这个信号并将其传输给扬声器或将其编码在磁带上。一个带有麦克风的窃听器

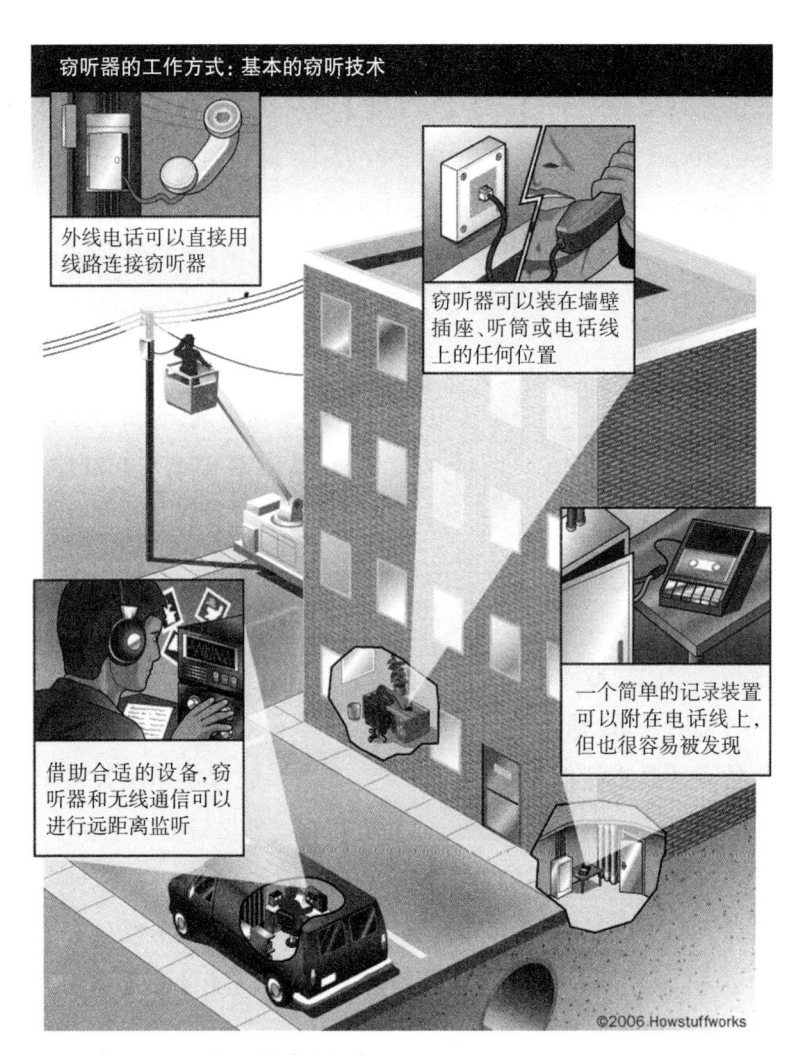

图2 窃听电话是相当简单的操作

尤其有价值，因为它可以听到房间里的任何谈话，不管窃听对象是否在通话。然而，传统的窃听器可以在没有话筒的情况下运行，因为电话有话筒。窃听者需要做的就是将电话线的任何一处连接到窃听器，因为它直接接收电流。通常情况下，窃听者会把窃听器连接到电话里面的电线上,这是传统的方法。这就免去了窃听者重返现场的必要,录音设备可能被藏在一辆面包车里,车子通常停在窃听对象的住所或办公室外。窃听移动电话需要拦截从听筒传送到听筒里的无线电信号,再将它们转换回声音。1990年代的模拟移动电话很容易被窃听,但当代数字手机的易受攻击性则要低得多。要读取这些信号,需要将数字电脑的比特转换成声音,这是一个相当复杂且昂贵的操作。不过,手机通话可能会在移动运营商的服务器上被拦截,或者在为无线通信携带加密语音数据的固定线路上被拦截。

当你用手机给别人打电话时,你的声音会被数字化,并发送到最近的基站,再通过移动运营商的交换机将其传输到接收方附近的另一个基站。在基站之间,语音数据是通过固定线路传输的,固定电话的情况也是如此。看来,如果窃听者通过固定电话线路收听这样的电话,手机就和传统的电话没有什么不同,也一样易受攻击。

对隐私的预测

监控似乎令人生畏,未来它对我们的私生活的侵入可能更精密且骇人,包括生物识别技术,诸如卫星监测、穿透墙壁和衣物等以增强搜索精准度,以及"智能尘埃"装置——微小型无线微机电传感器(MEMS)更广泛应用,可以探测从光到振动的一切现象。这些所谓的"尘粒"小如一粒粒沙子,它们将收集数据,这些数据可以通过双向波段无线电在相距一千英尺远的尘粒之间发送。

随着网络空间成为一个日益危险的领域,我们每天都在得知网民所受到的新的、令人不安的攻击。2001年9月11日之前，人们就令人不安的新技术破坏人的自由表达了越来越多的担忧，这种担忧与全方位监控的趋势同时发生。我们听闻关于隐私脆弱性的报道至少已有一个世纪。但在过去十年里，这些报道呈现出更为紧迫的形式。这里存在着一个悖论。一方面，人们抨击计算机对人的操纵力在近年来的进展是对我们最后一点隐私的天罚；另一方面，互联网又被誉为乌托邦。当陈词滥调争论不休时，期望计算机操纵力的提升所体现的问题能够被合乎情理地解决是不明智的，但在这两种夸张的说法之间，可能存在着某些类似于真相的东西。至少就隐私的未来而言，几乎毫无疑问，这类问题正在我们眼前发生变化。如果说在笨重的原子空间，我们在保护个人免受监控蹂躏方面只取得了有限的成功，那么在我们这个华丽的新二元世界里，前景会好多少呢？

当我们的安全受到围攻时，我们的自由也不可避免地受到威胁。如果在一个世界里，我们的每一个动作都被监视，这就侵蚀了我们的自由，而这种自由正是人们窥探旨在保护的目的。自然，我们要确保用于加强安全的手段的社会成本不会超出其收益。因此，在停车场、购物中心、机场和其他公共场所安装闭路电视的后果并不令人惊讶：犯罪活动转移了，犯罪分子只是去了别的地方。而且，这种侵蚀除了向极权主义敞开大门之外，一个监控社会很容易导致人与人之间产生不信任和猜疑的气氛、减少对法律及其执行者的尊重，并强化对那些容易被发现和证实的罪行的检举控诉。

其他的新情况已经全面改变了法律环境的基本特点。法律受到了无数技术进步所带来的深刻影响和挑战。计算机欺诈、身份盗用和其他"网络犯罪"将在下文述及。

诸如克隆、干细胞研究和基因工程等生物技术的发展引起了棘手的伦理问题,也使传统的法律概念面临挑战。在一些法域,采用身份证和生物鉴别技术的建议遭到了强烈反对。DNA和闭路电视证据的使用改变了刑事审判的性质。

奥威尔式的监控在一些国家似乎已经存在且很活跃。例如,英国的公共场所有超过四百万台闭路电视摄像机:大约每十四名居民中就有一台。英国还拥有世界上最大的DNA数据库,大约有五百三十万个DNA样本。由公私部门安装闭路电视摄影机的诱惑是很难抗拒的。数据保护法(在第五章中讨论)

图3　无处不在的闭路电视摄像机可能会降低其效能

表面上控制了闭路电视的使用,但这种条例并未被证明特别有效。丹麦采取了一种激进的解决办法,即禁止使用闭路电视,但有些地方例外,例如加油站。瑞典、法国和荷兰的法律比英国更为严格,这些国家实行许可证制度,法律要求在监测区外围设置警告标志。德国法律也有类似的要求。

生物识别技术

我们都是独一无二的。你的指纹是一种"生物识别":生物信息的量度。长期以来,指纹一直被用作将个人与犯罪联系起来的一种手段,但指纹也提供了一种切实的隐私保护方法:与使用(并非总是安全的)密码登录计算机相比,越来越多的人使用指纹识别器,指纹识别成为更安全的入口点。我们可能会在超市收银台和自助取款机上看到更多的指纹识别器。

没有完美的生物识别,但理想是找到一种独特的个人属性,这种个人属性是不变的,或者至少不大可能随时间流逝而改变,利用对这一特征的度量作为识别所涉个人的一种手段。通常情况下,生物识别的一些样本由识别的对象提供,这些样本被数字化并存储在数据库中。然后,可利用生物识别技术,将主体的数据与其他个人的生物特征进行比对来识别主体,或确认某个单一主体的身份。

为了应对恐怖主义的威胁,未来无疑将更多地运用生物识别技术。这包括人体生理特征和DNA的一些测量方法。生物识别技术可基于以下特征:人的外貌(有静态图像支持),例如,护照中关于身高、体重、肤色、头发、眼睛的颜色、可见的身体标记、性别、种族、面部毛发、是否戴眼镜的描述;自然的生理特征,例如，颅骨测量、牙齿和骨骼受伤情况、拇指印、一组指纹；手印、虹膜和视网膜扫描、耳垂毛细血管模式、掌型；生物动力学，例如，手写签名的方式、统计分析的语音特征、按键动力学，特别是登录ID和密码；社会行为（由录像视频支持），例如，习惯的身体信号、一般语音特征、讲话风格、可见的残障；强加的物理特征，例如，狗牌、项圈、手镯和脚链、条码、嵌入式芯片、应答器等。

人们担心的是，在专制国家，生物识别技术可能会被强加给公众。生物识别技术供应商将通过向专制政府出售技术而蓬勃发展，并通过寻求"软柿子"在相对自由的国家站稳脚跟；他们可能从动物开始，或从诸如体弱者、穷人、老年人、囚犯、雇员等受控制的人群开始。一个不那么悲观的预测是，社会将认识到威胁的严重性，并对技术及其使用施加限制。这将需要公众的

> **生物识别技术的局限性**
>
> 人们经常提到的一种识别方法是将微芯片植入人体内，以便储存和传播身份信息，但我们不能排除这种芯片可以通过手术移除和替换，或者可以通过远程访问改变信息的可能性。即使我们从婴儿身上（婴儿还在母亲肚子里的时候）提取DNA样本，在送往实验室分析的路上仍然有可能被另一个样本代替。没有绝对万无一失的方法来确证一个人的身份，即便是最精确的生物识别技术。
>
> K.奥哈拉和N.夏伯特，《咖啡机里的监控》，Oneworld，2008年，第68—69页。

支持和民选代表的勇气，他们将需要顶住来自大公司和国家安全与执法当局的压力，这些机构援引恐怖主义、非法移民与国内"法律和秩序"来证成这一技术的实施。

互联网

网上活动尤其容易受到攻击。恶意软件（或称"恶软"）的"炮兵部队"，包括病毒、蠕虫、木马、间谍软件、"网络钓鱼"、"机器人程序"、"僵尸"、漏洞和漏洞利用。

病毒是将自身的副本引入其他程序的代码块。它通常会携带一个有效负载，可能只具有滋扰价值，然而在许多情况下，其后果是严重的。为了躲避早期检测，除了执行复制功能，病毒可以延迟功能的执行。蠕虫会通过网络生成自己的副本，而不会感染其他程序。特洛伊木马是一个看似执行积极任务的程序（有时也是这样做的），但它通常是令人讨厌的，例如，它嵌入实用程序中的按键记录程序。

间谍软件是指通常隐藏在电子邮件附件中的软件，它秘密地收集设备中关于其用户或设备应用的数据。这些数据被传递给另一方，其中可能包括用户的浏览历史，记录个别按键（以

图4　网上冲浪危机四伏

获得密码），监视用户的行为以便进行消费者营销（所谓的"广告软件"），或观察受版权保护的作品的使用情况。网络钓鱼通常采取电子邮件的形式，这种电子邮件似乎是发自银行等可信任的机构。它试图诱使收件人泄露密码或信用卡详细信息等敏感数据。这些信息通常是非常不可信的，充满了拼写错误和其他明显的问题，然而这些明显的诡计成功欺骗了大量的接收者。

有些恶意软件窃取个人数据或将你的电脑转换为由第三方远程控制的"机器人"，"机器人"可用来收集电子邮件地址、发送垃圾邮件或攻击公司网站。另一种形式的攻击是"拒绝服务"（DoS），它使用一大群"机器人"或"僵尸"向公司网站铺天盖地地发送虚假的数据请求。"僵尸"在互联网上创建了大量的处理器，这些处理器被置于中央或定时控制之下（因此称之为"僵尸"）。攻击将致力于使一个网站脱机。这可能持续数天，给受害公司带来相当大的损失。这些攻击行为通常伴随着对金钱的需求。

漏洞（Bugs）是软件中的错误，特别是微软的视窗操作系统，它可能会使用户的系统容易受到所谓"解密高手"（crackers）的攻击。微软通常会发出补丁供用户下载，直到下一个漏洞出现。"漏洞利用"是对特定漏洞的一种攻击。标准技术得到了在互联网上流传的既定准则和编程代码的支持。

据报道，2009年初，欧盟各国已鼓励警察在没有搜查令的情况下行驶侵入权，这种无证侵入的手段很少使用。这使得欧洲各地的警察在警官认为"远程搜查"对于预防或侦查严重犯罪（这种犯罪会被判处三年以上徒刑）是必要且适当的情况下，能够入侵私人电脑。这可以通过多种方式实现，包括将病毒附加到电子邮件消息中,只要打开该邮件,就会秘密激活远程搜索工具。

信息记录程序

信息记录程序是网站服务器传送到访问者的浏览器并存储在他或她的计算机上的数据。这些数据使网站能够将访问者的计算机识别为与之互动过的计算机,并记住以前交易的细节,包括搜索词,以及读取某些网页所花费的时间。换句话说,缓存技术默认允许网站偷偷地将自己的标识符永久地放到我的个人计算机上,以便跟踪我的网上行为。

信息记录程序是可持久的,它们可能会显示一个特定时期内访问过的每个网站的详细列表。而且,信息记录程序文件的文本可能会显示以前提供的个人数据。亚马逊等网站认为这种做法是合理的,声称通过向顾客提供基于其浏览行为可能忽视的书籍

图5　似乎没有人不受黑客攻击的影响

链接,来帮助顾客改善购物体验。但是,这也带来了一个明显的危险,那就是我的身份可能会因为过于关注上网冲浪过程中的一些不相关的部分而被曲解,或者,另一方面,从各种来源收集起来的个人数据可能会被组合起来,从而形成一个详尽的生活方式形象。

黑　客

　　黑客曾经被认为是无害的"网络窥探者",他们坚持一种略带任性但讲道德的行为准则,要求人们不应该盗取数据,而只是报告受害者系统中的漏洞(见方框)。正如莱西希所说的那样,他们比保安更有侵略性,保安会检查办公室的门,以确保门锁上……而(黑客)不仅检查了门锁,还让自己进去了,快速地扫视了一下四周,留下了一张可爱的(或讽刺的)纸条,上面写着,"嘿,笨蛋,你把门开着"。

　　虽然这种悠闲的文化最终吸引了执法当局的兴趣——他们通过立法来反对这种文化,但现实仍然令人头疼。根据威瑞信公司的西蒙·丘奇的说法,犯罪分子用来销售用户信息的在线拍卖网站仅仅是个开始。他预计,将不同数据库组合在一起的

> **黑客的(可疑的)乐趣**
>
> 　　做一个黑客是很有趣的,但需要付出大量的努力,努力需要动力。成功运动员的动力来自一种使他们身体强健、促使他们超越其身体极限的愉悦感。同样,要想成为一名黑客,你必须从解决问题、提高技能和锻炼你的智力中获得基本的快感。如果你天生不是这样的人,你就需要先成为

这样的人，才能成为一名黑客。否则你会发现你的黑客能量会被性、金钱和社会认同等干扰所消耗……要想表现得像个黑客，你必须相信其他黑客的思考时间是宝贵的，以致分享信息、解决问题并给出解决方案几乎是你的道德责任，这样其他黑客就可以解决新的问题，而不是只得不断地重新处理旧问题……黑客（和一般的有创造力的人）永远不应该感到无聊或者总是不得不埋头于愚蠢的重复性工作，因为当这种情况发生时，意味着他们没有做只有他们能做的事情——去解决新的问题。这种浪费伤害了每一个人。因此，无聊和单调乏味的苦工不仅是令人不快的，而且实际上是罪恶……黑客自然是反独裁的。任何能命令你的人都可以阻止你去解决吸引你的任何问题，而且，考虑到独裁思想的运作方式，他们通常会找到一些愚蠢到极点的理由来这样做。所以，无论你在哪里发现独裁主义的态度，都必须与其进行斗争，以免它扼杀你和其他黑客……要成为一名黑客，你必须培养出这些态度中的某一些。但是仅仅保持一种态度并不会让你成为一名黑客，也不会让你成为一名冠军运动员或者是摇滚歌星。成为一名黑客需要智慧、实践、奉献和努力……如果你尊重能力，你就会喜欢发展自己的能力，努力工作和奉献将成为一种紧张的游戏，而不是乏味的苦差事。这种态度是成为黑客的关键。

埃里克·史蒂文·雷蒙德，《如何成为一名黑客》，http://www.catb.org/~esr/faqs/hacker-howto.html。

"混搭"网站可能会被转换为犯罪用途。想象一下，如果一个黑客把他从一家旅行社的数据库中收集到的信息与谷歌地图结合起来，他可以为一个精通技术的盗贼提供行车指南，便可在你一去度假的时候就立马到达你空无一人的房子。

身份盗用

挪用一个人的个人信息并进行欺诈或冒充是一个日益严重的问题，每年造成数十亿美元的损失。2007年，美国联邦贸易委员会的一项调查发现，2005年共有3.7%的调查参与者表示他们曾是身份盗用的受害者。这一结果表明，当年大约有八百三十万名美国人遭受某种形式的身份盗用，所有受害者中有10%的人自掏腰包支付了一千二百美元或更多的损失。占比相同的受害者至少花了五十五个小时来解决他们的问题，其中用时排名前5%的受害者至少花费了一百三十个小时。在2006年的调查中，身份盗用造成的损失总额估计为一百五十六亿美元。

身份盗用通常至少涉及三个人：受害者、冒名顶替者和一个信贷机构。信贷机构以受害者的名义为冒名顶替者开立一个新账户，新账户可包括信用卡、公用事业服务，甚至是抵押贷款。

身份盗用有多种形式。最有害的行为可能包括信用卡欺诈（盗取一个账号，以便进行未经许可的收费）、新账户欺诈（冒名顶替者以受害者的名义开一个账户或"贸易热线"，可能直到受害人申请信贷之后才被发现）、身份克隆（冒名顶替者冒充受害者的身份）和盗用身份犯罪（冒名顶替者冒充受害者，致使受害者因某种罪行被捕，或因违法而被罚款）。

部分责任必须归咎于金融服务行业本身。他们在授信发放贷款和促进电子支付方面的保密措施不严格，从而导致安全让位于便利。

身份证

乍看之下，一张包含持有人关键个人信息的强制性身份证，似乎会是解决身份盗用、税务和福利欺诈、非法移民，当然还有恐怖主义等多重问题的灵丹妙药。然而，除了在遏制有害活动方面的实际效力外，强制性身份证不可避免地会引起强烈的敌意，特别是来自隐私权倡导者的敌意，尤其在英美法系国家，例如英国、澳大利亚、加拿大、美国、爱尔兰和新西兰，在这些国家引入强制性身份证的尝试迄今为止都未成功。在斯堪的纳维亚国家的阻力也很大。文化力量显然与要求个人携带"证件"的观念背道而驰。例如，在英国，人们对任何旨在证明自己存在的民主权利的强迫行为，都有根深蒂固的反对意见！

不过，大约有一百个国家确实存在各种形式的强制性身份证，在欧洲和亚洲，反对使用各种强制性身份证的人则少得多。包括法国、德国、西班牙、葡萄牙、比利时、希腊和卢森堡在内的十一个欧盟成员国都在使用强制性身份证。在亚洲，中国香港的经验具有启发意义。自1945年以来，香港一直主要（或至少表面上）使用身份证件来管制非法入境者的拥入。事实上绝大多数香港居民对任何时候都要随身携带身份证的规定和身份证上的个人资料都不太注意，这是毫无疑问的。的确，为购买戏票、预订餐厅，以及其他类似的目的而证实自己的身份，已成为一个非常便利的方法。

最近,香港特区政府把这张卡"升级"成了现在被称为"身份智能卡"的东西,卡里有一张芯片,里面包含持卡人的出生、国籍、住址、婚姻状况、职业的详情,以及配偶或子女的详细资料。法律要求对居民进行拍照和提取指纹,居民方可获得身份智能卡。特区政府声称,使用智能卡有许多好处,包括更高的安全性(刻在卡的不同层面上并保存在芯片中的数据可以防止遗失或被盗的身份证被他人篡改或使用)、便利性(具有多种应用功能,如电子证书和图书馆借书证功能,持卡人可一卡多用)、"优质服务"(持卡人可在网上享受各种各样的公共服务),以及更方便的旅行(通过旅客自动清关系统和车辆自动清关系统,芯片内储存的指纹模板可使出入境手续的办理更加方便快捷)。

为了减轻对滥用数据的担心,特区政府坚持认为,RFID芯片中只存储了最低限度的数据。更敏感的个人信息保存在后端计算机系统中。不同用途的数据是分开的,所有的非入境用途都是自愿的。数据的收集、储存、使用和公布都必须符合《个人资料(隐私)条例》等立法的规定。只有获授权的部门才可使用有关的数据库,各政府部门之间并无共用数据库。持卡人在其身份被认证后,可以通过智能身份证读卡器查看卡上的数据,这些读卡器安装在入境自助服务站。隐私影响评估(PIA)是在智能身份证项目的不同阶段进行的。香港立法机构已修订法例,以加强保护数据的隐私性。

这听起来让人放心,而且提高效率、公平性和便利性的吸引力也不容轻率地忽视。但是在英国提议使用身份证时,这些优点就必须与"功能蠕变"、错误、私密性和身份盗用等非常

> **反对使用身份证的十二个论据**
>
> 1. 阻止不了犯罪；
> 2. 阻止不了福利欺诈；
> 3. 阻止不了非法入境；
> 4. 会助长歧视；
> 5. 会造成警察权力不必要的增强；
> 6. 将成为国内护照；
> 7. "自愿"卡会变成强制性；
> 8. 成本将会不可接受；
> 9. 遗失身份证会造成很大的不便和痛苦；
> 10. 身份证会危及个人信息的隐私性；
> 11. 身份证将使犯罪行为更加顽固并使虚假身份制度化；
> 12. 会损害国家认同感和人格完整。
>
> 西蒙·戴维斯，《老大哥》，潘书出版社，1996年，第139—151页。

现实的前景相平衡。任何政府机构出于各种目的使用这些数据、在各部门之间共享信息，以及合并数据库的诱惑可能是不可抗拒的。即使是最先进的身份证，也无法阻止欺诈者或恐怖分子。

DNA数据库

DNA证据在犯罪侦查中的应用越来越多，这就产生了对样本数据库的需求，以确定某个人的情况是否与犯罪嫌疑人的情况相匹配。英格兰和威尔士的DNA数据库（有五百三十万人的数据信息，占总人口的9%）可能是世界上最大的。它包括近一百万从未被起诉或后来被宣告无罪的嫌疑人的DNA样本和指纹。无辜的人对保留他们的基因信息感到愤愤不平并不奇怪，但滥用的可能性也是存在的，这并不是一件小事。这种令人沮丧的前景导致有两个人要求在他们自由后将他们的数据信息删除，因为无法说服英国法院，于是他们向欧洲人权法院提起上诉。欧洲人权法院在2008年底一致裁定，他们的隐私权受到了侵犯。

图6　DNA数据的各种用途对个人隐私构成相当大的风险

> **你床上的监控**
>
> 计算机变得越来越小,可以由许多新奇有趣的材料制成或装配起来。可能性是无止境的,但危险也是如此。例如,电子纺织品或"可水洗计算"领域提供了各种令人着迷的未来。可以监测生命体征、产生热量或者作为开关的布料表明了无限的可能性,从荒谬的(不断变换颜色)的衣服到实用的(可以给你的手机充电)的夹克衫。特克斯簇尼克公司的"特克斯簇聚合物"是由纤维制成的,当纤维变形时,它们的电阻就会改变,因此能检测到压力,非常方便,但是想象一下,一张床单能够探测并播报躺在上面的人数。
>
> K. 奥哈拉和 N. 夏伯特,《咖啡机里的监控》,Oneworld,2008年,第9页。

当嫌疑人被判无罪时,其他法域倾向于销毁其DNA数据信息。例如,在挪威和德国,DNA样本只有经法院批准才可以永久保存。在瑞典,只有服刑两年以上的已定罪罪犯的档案可以保留。美国允许联邦调查局(FBI)在逮捕嫌疑人时提取其DNA样本,但如果没有提出指控或嫌疑人被无罪释放,这些样本可以根据要求被销毁。在拥有DNA数据库的大约四十个州中,只有加利福尼亚州允许永久性地保存被指控但之后又被消除嫌疑的个人的数据信息。

有人建议,为了避免针对某些群体(例如黑人男性)的歧视,应将所有人的DNA数据信息收集起来并保存在数据库中。这种极端的建议不大可能得到普遍支持。但显而易见的是,为了保持系统的完整性和保护隐私,这类敏感而脆弱的基因数据需要被严格的管制。

击退对隐私的侵犯

促进隐私保护技术(PETs)旨在通过删除或减少个人数据,或者在防止不必要或不想要地处理个人数据的同时不损害数据系统的运作,来保护隐私。最初这项技术采取的形式是"化名工具":这种软件允许个人在操作电子系统时拒绝透露他们的真实身份,并且可以只在绝对必要时才予以透露。这些技术有助于减少收集到的关于个人的数据量。然而,它们的效果在很大程度上取决于那些有权撤销或废除化名保护的人的正直性。不幸的是,人们无法一直信任政府。

更强大的PETs没有采取化名方式,而是提供了更强的匿名性保护,使政府和企业无法将数据与已识别的个人联系起来。这通常是通过一系列中介运作服务实现的,每个中介都知道链条中紧邻的中介的身份,但都没有足够的信息来促进识别之前和之后的中介。它不能将通信追踪到发送方,也不能将其转发给最终的接收方。

这些PETs包括匿名回邮系统、网页浏览措施,以及戴维·乔姆的付款人匿名电子现金或电子钱币,它们采用一种盲法技术,向银行发送随机加密的数据,然后(通过使用某种数字货币)验证这些数据,并将数据返回到硬盘。只提供一个序列号,收件人不知道(也不需要知道)付款的来源,这个过程提供了更加强大的匿名性保护。在项目的电子版权管理系统（ECMS）方面，它具有相当大的潜力，比如欧洲委员会ESPIRIT①方案正在开发的传输电子文件的版权（CITED）和COPICAT等项目。人们常常需要在未经版权所有者同意或支付版税的情况下，下载和销售受版权保护作品的全文，而这些项目寻求技术解决办法，根据这些办法，用户使用这些材料可能被起诉。这种对用户的"追踪"构成了对隐私明显的威胁：用户的阅读、聆听或观看习惯可能被储存起来，为了潜在的阴险或有害的目的获取这些习惯。盲签似乎是一种相对简单的隐去用户姓名的方法。

　　匿名是一种重要的民主价值观。即使在电子时代之前，匿名也有助于个人参与政治进程，否则人们可能会放弃参政。事实上，美国最高法院已经认定，《宪法第一修正案》保护匿名言论的权利。我想用化名来隐瞒自己的身份或以其他方式实现匿名的原因有很多。在互联网上，我可能想公开身份，但使用匿名邮件转发器进行对话（可以是已知身份，也可以是匿名身份）。我甚至希望没有人知道我的电子邮件收件人的身份，我也可能不想让任何人知道我属于哪个新闻组，或者我访问过哪些网站。

　　而且，对举报人、虐待行为的受害者和那些需要各种帮助的人而言，匿名都有明显的个人和政治益处。同样（一如既往？），这种自由也可能庇护犯罪活动，尽管匿名言论的权利并不会延伸到非法言论。匿名与隐私和言论自由有着独特的关系。互联

---

　　① European Strategic Program on Research in Information Technology，欧洲信息技术研究战略计划。——译注

网提供了大量的匿名机会，我们很可能只是在这两个领域里发现其潜力。这就提出了（有些令人不安的）关于我们是谁的问题，即我们的身份问题。

为保护通信安全而使用强大的加密技术，这种做法已经遇到了阻力（尤其是在美国和法国），有的人提议完全禁止加密，有的人提议通过诸如公钥托管等手段，保留拦截信息的权力。执法者和密码学家之间的斗争可能会旷日持久，特别是因为强大的加密文化被普通计算机用户所接受的方式，即使用"热情"一词来表达也过于温顺了，考虑到菲尔·齐默尔曼的加密软件"相当好的隐私"（PGP）可在不到五分钟内生成，并且还可以在互联网上免费获得。

现代密码学的一个核心特征是"公钥"。在电信安全方面采取了闭锁和密钥的办法。锁是一个公钥，用户可以将其传送给收件人。要解锁邮件，收件人需使用个人加密代码或"私钥"。公钥加密大大增加了加密/身份的可用性，因为双密钥系统允许将加密密钥提供给潜在的通信方，同时将解密密钥保密。例如，它允许银行向若干客户提供其公钥，但不允许他们读取彼此的加密信息。

技术解决办法尤其有助于掩盖个人身份。弱形式的数字身份已被广泛用于银行账户和社会保障号码的形式。它们只提供有限的保护，因为将它们与它们所代表的人相匹配是一件简单的事情。智能卡的出现将产生虚拟身份的转变，这将促进真正的交易匿名性。"盲法"或"盲签名"和"数字签名"将极大地增强对隐私的保护。数字签名是一种独特的"密钥"，它提供了比本人书面签名更强的认证。公钥系统包括两个密钥：一个是公钥，另一个是私钥。公钥系统的优点是，如果你能够解密信息，那么你就知道它只能由发送方创建。

最重要的问题是：我的身份是否**真**的是有关行为或交易所**要求**的？这就是第五章所讨论的数据保护原则的作用。

P3P

隐私政策管理系统的一个重大发展是，具备允许用户根据其个人隐私偏好对其浏览内容做出知情选择的技术。这些协议中最广为人知的是由万维网共同体（W3C）开发的隐私偏好平台（P3P）。它允许网站能够制作其隐私政策的机读版，从而使浏览器配备了P3P阅读器的用户在与网站的隐私政策相比较后，能够自动获得其特定的隐私偏好。这将清楚地说明该网站收集了什么信息，以及它将如何处理这些信息。如果网站的政策与用户的隐私偏好不一致，用户就会收到通知。

然而，作为主要的隐私权倡导组织之一，电子隐私信息中心（EPIC）却并不买账。该组织把P3P戏谑为"相当糟糕的隐私"（Pretty Poor Privacy），并抱怨说，P3P不符合隐私保护的基本标准：

> P3P是一个复杂和令人困惑的协议，它使互联网用户更加难以保护自己的隐私。P3P也未能解决与互联网特别相关的诸多隐私问题。

该组织认为，良好的隐私标准要建立在公平的信息实践和

真正的PETs的基础上才更为妥当,从而最大限度地减少或消除个人可识别信息的收集:

收集和使用个人信息的简单、可预测的规则也将支持消费者的信任和信心。另一方面,P3P有可能会削弱公众对互联网隐私保护的信心。

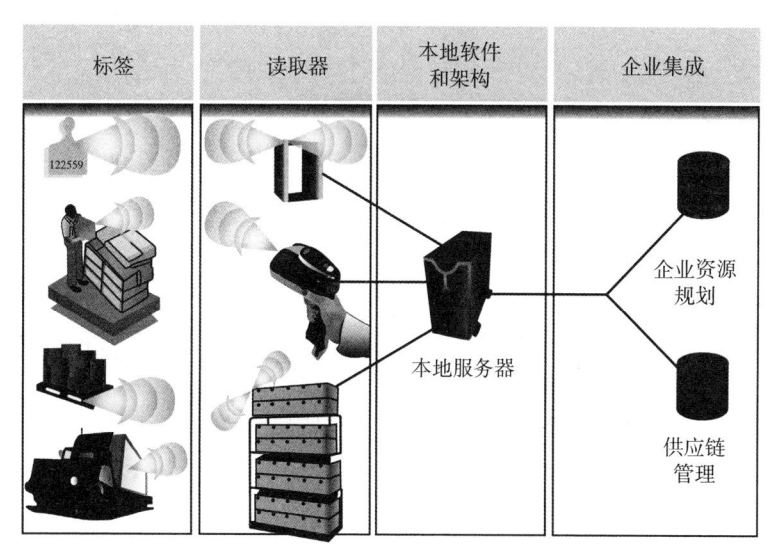

图7 RFID技术的使用不断升级,对隐私构成的威胁不胜枚举

RFID

RFID技术作为一种替代条码的库存控制手段应运而生。一个RFID系统由三部分组成:每个消费项目上的一个微型芯片(一个RFID标签),它存储了一个独特的产品标识符,一个RFID读取器,以及一个连接到读取器上的计算机系统,这个系统可以访问库存控制数据库。该数据库包含广泛的产品信息,包括产

品的内容、来源和生产制造历史。给产品贴上标签也会披露产品的位置、价格和销售地点，而对于运输公司来说，还会披露其运输行程。RFID可以应用于召回缺陷商品或危险商品、追踪被盗的财产、防止假冒，并提供审计线索以阻止腐败。

RFID的潜力是巨大的，它正被越来越多地用于"非接触式"支付卡、护照以及对行李、图书馆书籍和宠物的监控。没有理由认为人类不能像我们的狗那样被植入微型芯片，它可以帮助识别走丢的老年痴呆症患者的身份。将RFID和无线保真网络（Wi-Fi）结合起来，可以促进对无线网络（如医院）中的物体或人进行实时跟踪。对隐私方面的担忧是，接受这些善良的应用可能会引起不那么善意的用途；可能会有人呼吁给性犯罪者、囚犯、非法入境者和其他"不受欢迎的人"贴上标签。

还有一种担心是，如果RFID数据可以与其他数据（例如，储存在信用卡或积分卡中的信息）汇集在一起——将产品数据与个人信息相匹配，这样就可以对消费者的个人情况进行全面的收集。此外，在公共场所、家庭和企业中增加使用RFID可能预示着监控社会的扩大。例如，我在车子挡风玻璃上贴了一个RFID，可以自动从我的银行账户中扣除通行费，我的车子刚刚通过比萨收费站的事实记录可能对于对我的行动感兴趣的一方有用。显然，精密的PETs是有必要的。

全球定位系统（GPS）

GPS用卫星信号来定位。目前，GPS芯片在车载导航系统和移动电话中已经很普遍。通过将GPS生成的数据纳入数据库并与其他信息汇集以创建地理信息系统（GIS），是有可能的。

为了打电话或接电话，移动电话将其位置传送到基站。因此，实际上，它们每隔几分钟就发送一次用户的位置。

诸如无线信号的洛基三角定位服务，允许用户获得当地天气报告，找到附近的餐馆、电影院或商店，或者与朋友们共享他们的位置。根据该网站的介绍，"当你在旅行时，MyLoki可以通过你最喜欢的平台——Facebook、RSS Feeds、博客的徽章，甚至Twitter——自动让你的朋友知道你在哪里"。它声称不收集个人信息，以此来保护隐私。

遗传信息

探索我们基因结构的能力带来了许多隐私问题，尤其是医生有义务保护患者的私密性，而《希波克拉底誓言》中所规定的保护患者隐私的义务在多大程度上充分保护了这一敏感信息不被泄露。这也引起了一个棘手的问题，即患者的血亲，甚至伴侣和配偶对了解这些资料的兴趣远非小事。

不能低估这些和其他对隐私的侵入所带来的挑战。我们是如何来到这种局面的？下一章试图提供一种答案。

第二章

一种经久不衰的价值

当代人们对隐私的忧虑大多来自技术的作恶能力,而对私人领域的渴望,则远在电子监控和闭路电视的这些比特和字节"勇敢的新世界"之前。事实上,人类学家已经论证过,在原始社会中存在着一种近乎普遍的追求个人和群体隐私的欲望,而这一点在适当的社会规范中也得以体现。此外,并非只有人类寻求庇护,动物也需要隐私。

什么是隐私?

在最一般的层面上,隐私的概念包含想独处、自由地做自己且不受他人窥视的束缚的欲望。这种窥视的束缚涵盖了从窥探和未经请求的公之于众,到对我们所需的"空间"的侵扰,这种空间是我们做出不受政府侵扰的私密决定所必需的。因此,"隐私"常常被用来描述一个被界定为"私人"的区域,在这个区域中,例如,妇女可以选择是否愿意堕胎,个人可以自由表达他或她的性倾向。因此,有关隐私的争论往往与有争议的道德问题

（包括使用节育手段和色情制品的权利等）纠缠在一起。

　　在任何情况下，很明显，我们关心保护隐私的核心是个人与社会关系的概念。一旦我们认识到公共领域和私人领域之间的分离，我们就假定了一个共同体的存在，在这个共同体中，不仅这样的划分有意义，而且存在一种体制结构，使得这样一种解释成为可能。换句话说，假定"私人"的存在是以预设"公共"为前提的。

> **隐私和动物**
>
> 　　人类喜欢认为其对隐私的渴望是独特的人类本性，是人类独有的伦理、智力和艺术需求的一种产物。然而，对动物行为和社会组织的研究表明，人类对隐私的需求很可能是由于其祖先是动物，而且人类和动物在自己的同伴中都有一些索要隐私的基本机制……对属地的研究甚至粉碎了这样一种浪漫的观念，即知更鸟的歌唱或猴子的尖叫完全是因为"动物的生趣"。但实际上，这常常是为获得隐私而发出的桀骜不驯的呐喊……动物研究的一个基本发现是，几乎所有的动物都在寻找个体隐居或小群体亲密的时期……动物为在隐私和参与之间取得平衡所做的努力是动物生命的基本过程之一。从这种意义上来说，对隐私的追求并不局限于人类本身，而是在所有有生命的生物和社会过程中产生的。
>
> 　　艾伦·韦斯汀，《隐私和自由》，鲍利海出版公司，1967年，第8—11页。

在过去的大约一个世纪里,人们对社会公共领域的参与遭受了持续不断的削弱。我们更加以自我为中心。正如社会学家理查德·桑内特生动表明的那样,我们对执着"联络"我们自己情感的后现代心理,彻底破坏了一个真正的政治共同体的前景。矛盾的是,过度亲密的关系已经毁掉了这个政治共同体:人们走得越近,交际就越少,痛苦就越大,他们的关系就越会自相残杀。

事实上,希腊人认为,在"自己"的隐私中度过的一生,顾名思义,就是"白痴的"。同样,罗马人认为隐私仅仅是一种暂时的避难所,是为了逃避公共领域的生活。汉娜·阿伦特对此有很好的描述:

> 在古代人的感觉中,隐私这个词本身所表明的隐私的私人特质,是非常重要的;它字面上的意思是被剥夺某物的状态,甚至是被剥夺了人的最高和最人性的能力的状态。一个只过着私人生活的人,像奴隶一样不被允许进入公共领域,或者像野蛮人一样选择不建立这样的领域的人,就不是完全的人。

只有在罗马帝国晚期,人们才能察觉出隐私作为亲密区域的最初阶段。

正如人们所预料的那样,古代和原始社会的人们对隐私表现出不同的态度。在开创性的研究《隐私权:道德和法律基础》中,巴林顿·摩尔研究了一些早期社群的隐私状况,包括古雅典、《旧约》所揭示的犹太社会和古代中国。在中国的案例中,他阐明了儒家对国家（公共）和家庭（私人）不同领域的区分，以及关于恋爱、家庭和友谊的早期文献如何产生了脆弱的隐私权。在公元前4世纪的雅典，隐私权得到了更有力的保护。他的结论是，只有在一个具有强大自由传统的复杂社会里，才能实现通信隐私。

我们对公共和私人区域的现代划分是政治法律思潮双重运动的结果。在16—17世纪，民族国家和主权理论的出现产生了一个明显的公共领域的概念。另一方面，确认一个不受国家侵犯的私人领域，是对君主（在一定时候是议会）主张的不受限制的立法权的回应。换言之，现代国家的出现、对社会和经济活动的管制，以及对私人领域的承认，是这种公私分离的自然先决条件。

然而，历史证据只能说明故事的一部分。社会学模型有力地表达了体现这种转变的社会价值。一个特别有用的社会学二分法是社区（Gemeinschaft）与社会（Gesellschaft）①之间的区别。从广义上来说，前者是一个由内在化的规范和传统组成的共同体，这些规范和传统是按照地位来管理的，但通过爱、责任、共识和共同的目标来调节。另一方面，社会是自利的个体在所谓的自由市场上为个人物质利益而竞争的一种共同体。

这种区别通常表现为社区和协会之间的区别。前者几乎没有表现出公共和私人的区分，而后者的公私区别则很明显：法律正式规定了什么被认为是公共的。这种分化也阐明了政治和经济秩序。

---

① 源自德国社会学家斐迪南德·滕尼斯在1887年出版的《社区与社会》（*Gemeinschaft and Gesellschaft*）。德文"Gemeinschaft"一词也可译作"共同体"。——译注

公共和私人领域的分离也是自由主义的核心原则。事实上,"可以说,自由主义在很大程度上是关于私人领域的界限在哪里、根据什么原则来划分、干预从何而来,以及如何对干预加以审查的论争"。法律在多大程度上可以合法地侵入"私域",这是一个反复出现的主题,特别是在19世纪的自由主义学说中:"19世纪法律思想的中心目标之一就是在宪法、刑法和管制法——公法,以及私人交易法——侵权行为法、合同法、财产法和商法之间,建立明晰的分离。"而刑法在执行"私人道德"方面的界限问题,则持续困扰着法律哲学家和道德哲学家。

约翰·斯图亚特·穆勒在《论自由》一书中阐述的"伤害原则",自该书出版一百五十多年来,仍然是对大多数自由主义者关于干涉个人私生活界限的论述的一个试金石,而这也是对这一原则的一种检验。对穆勒来说:

> 人类有理由单独或集体干预他们中任何人行动自由的唯一目的是自保。对一个文明社会的任何成员,违背其意愿而正当地行使权力的唯一目的是防止对他人造成伤害。该成员自己的利益,无论是物质上的还是精神上的,都不是充分的理由。

隐私的价值

没有隐私的生活是不可思议的。但隐私实际上起到什么作用呢?除了在自由民主理论中的重要性外,隐私还为创造力、心理健康、爱的能力、建立社会关系、促进信任、亲密和友谊界定了一个领域。

艾伦·韦斯汀在他的经典作品中指出了隐私的四个功能，并将这一概念的个人维度和社会维度结合起来。第一，它产生了个人自主性；个人的民主原则与这种自主性的需要相关联——避免被他人操纵或支配的愿望。第二，它提供了情感释放的机会，隐私使我们能摘下我们的社交面具：

> 在任何一天，一个男人都可能在严厉的父亲、体贴的丈夫、搞笑的拼车人、熟练的车床操作员、工会代表、饮水机旁闲聊调情的人和美国退伍军人委员会主席等角色中转换。当他在一个特定阶段从一个场景转换到另一个场景时，他所扮演的角色在心理上是不同的……隐私……给了个人从工厂工人到总统，都有面具放到一边休息一下的机会。如果永远"戴着"面具，就会毁坏人体机能。

第三，它使我们能够进行自我评价——形成和检验有创造性的道德行为和思想的能力。第四，隐私为我们提供了一种环境，使我们能够分享秘密和亲昵的言行，并进行有限的受保护的交流。

私下的不检点

私下的言语包括相互之间直呼其名、合作决策、亵渎神灵、公开谈性、繁复的抱怨、吸烟、粗俗的非正式着装、"懒散"的坐姿和站姿、使用方言或不够标准的语言、喃喃低语和大喊大叫、顽皮地攻击和"开玩笑"，不顾及他人的行为，

> 这些行为虽微不足道,但具有潜在的象征意义、轻微的身体活动,比如打呼噜、吹口哨、咀嚼、轻咬、打嗝和胀气。
>
> 欧文·戈夫曼,《日常生活中的自我呈现》,道布尔戴出版社,1959年,第128页。

隐私的困境

然而,隐私并不是一种绝对的善,可以简要地指出其七点不足之处。第一,隐私有时被认为是一种相当古板、拘谨的维多利亚价值观,用一位作家的话来说,隐私具有"一种受了伤害的文雅气质"。第二,更严重的是,对隐私的保密可能掩盖了家庭内部的压迫,尤其是男性对女性的压迫。女权主义者认为,女性受压迫的一个重要原因是她们被降格到家庭和家人的私人领域。而且,虽然国家倾向于控制公共领域,但国家不愿意侵犯私人领域——而这常常是剥削和暴力侵害女性的场所。

> **隐私与对女性的压迫**
>
> 当隐私法限制侵入亲密关系时,它就禁止改变对亲密关系的控制……女权主义认为,妇女处于屈从地位的核心事项,正是身体这种地位、异性恋这种关系、性交和生殖这种行为,以及正是这种亲密的情感,构成了隐私原则所涵盖的核心,这很可能不是巧合。从这个角度来看,隐私的法律概念可以而且已经庇护了殴打、婚内强奸和妇女被剥削劳

> 动的场所。
>
> 凯瑟琳·麦金农,《无须修改的女性主义：关于生活与法律的论述》,哈佛大学出版社,1987年,第101页。

第三,对隐私的庇护会削弱对罪犯和恐怖分子的侦查与逮捕。当然,对安全的威胁占据了当下的中心位置。有些人担心,过分积极地保护隐私可能会妨碍当局执法者履行其职责。第四,隐私可能会妨碍信息的自由流动,影响人与人之间的透明度和坦诚。第五,隐私会妨碍商业效率,增加成本。过分关注隐私会损害关键性个人信息的收集,减缓商业决策的制定,从而降低生产率。

第六,某些社群主义批评家认为,隐私权是一种不适当的个人主义权利,不应允许它凌驾于其他权利或社群价值之上。第七,如美国法官和法学家理查德·波斯纳,提出了一个反对隐私权的强有力的例证。他们认为,从经济角度来看,隐瞒贬损的个人信息可能构成一种欺骗。这一重要的批评值得仔细研究。

在试图隐瞒或限制个人信息的传播时,特别是当信息描述了他不光彩的一面的时候,个人是否以一种欺骗的形式参与其中？波斯纳断言：

> 如果人们为了误导而隐瞒个人信息,那么从这种程度来看,对信息提供法律保护的经济理由几乎相当于允许在货物销售中进行欺诈。

但是，即使人们认可经济角度，也不能意味着人们会接受对隐瞒个人信息的经济价值的评估。个人可能愿意放弃自己在限制这种信息传播上的利益，来换取个人信息自由流动的社会利益。换句话说，波斯纳没有证明，也可能无法证明他对"相互竞争的"利益的计算必然是正确的，或者至少最有可能是正确的。

波斯纳还认为，对交易成本方面的考虑可能不利于对个人信息的法律保护。如果信息是不光彩而且准确的，就存在一种让公众普遍获得信息的社会诱因：准确的信息越发依赖于同信息有关的个人。因此，让一个社会有权获得这种信息，而不是允许个人隐瞒，是具有社会效益的。在没有不光彩信息或虚假信息的情况下，隐瞒信息对个人的价值超过了社群接触这种信息的价值。虚假的信息不会促进理性决策，因此没什么用处。

隐私权的含义

到目前为止，我一直在杂乱地使用"隐私"这个术语。我用它来描述各种各样的情况或利益——从寻求庇护到亲密的关系。这个概念根本就不是条理清楚的，这一点也不奇怪。虽然存在普遍的共识，认为我们的隐私受到了侵犯，因为私人领域受到了各种攻击——以监视、拦截我们的通信和狗仔队的活动为形式，但当众多额外的怨愤充斥于隐私的保护伞之下时，这个问题就被搅浑了。

关于这一主题的文献汗牛充栋，但并没有产生明确或前后一致的价值含义，从而为争辩妇女的权利（特别是在堕胎方面）、使用避孕药具、男女同性恋者的自由、阅读或观看淫秽材料或色情制品的权利，以及为艾滋病毒/艾滋病引发的一些私密性问题提供一个平台。在利用隐私来追求如此多完全不同的、有时是相互冲突的政治理想的过程中，已经产生了大量分析上的混乱。

图8 对名人八卦的嗜好助长了越来越多追求轰动效应的媒体

> **对隐私问题无动于衷**
>
> 　　监控技术和日常监视活动在很大程度上没有引起人们的注意。人们早就习惯了摄像机、打折卡和广告信息……尽管有时会惹恼人们，但透明的市民还是能意识到在电脑时代生活要轻松容易得多。人们毫不犹豫地放弃了不被人注意、匿名和不被人找到的做法，对少了一点个人自由没有任何感觉。人们甚至不知道自己还有什么需要被辩护的。人们太不重视自己的私人空间，以至于不想以牺牲其

> 他利益为代价来保护这种私人空间。隐私不是一种能够赢得选票的政治纲领……人们留下的痕迹比他们意识到的要多。人们再也不能脱离社会,不受纠缠地生活……个体不能偷偷地更换面具而变成别的什么人。人们既不能伪装自己,也不能暂时消失。人们的身体定期进行X光检查、人们的生命旅程被记录下来、人们的生活发生变化也被记录下来……没有什么被忽略、忽视、丢弃……当每一个粗心的行为、每一个错误、每一件稍纵即逝的小事都被记录下来时,就再也不会有什么自发的行为了。一个人所做的每一件事情都要经过评价和评判,没有什么逃得过监控。过去使现在窒息……如果数据不定期清除,人们就会被囚禁在自己历史的地牢里。然而,这种观点似乎并没有吓到任何人。
>
> 沃尔夫冈·索夫斯基,《隐私:一种宣言》,普林斯顿大学出版社,2008年,第7—8页。

隐私作为一种普遍的道德、政治或社会价值,其价值是不可否认的,但隐私的概念越被延伸,其模糊性就越大。为求清楚起见,可以说,隐私的核心是一种愿望,也可能是一种需求,即防止与我们有关的信息在未经我们同意的情况下让别人知道。但是,如上所述,还有其他问题越来越多地进入隐私领域。这在美国最为明显。最高法院表达了诸如隐私权之类的"未列举的权利",因为它在格里斯沃尔德诉康涅狄格州案和罗伊诉韦德案(他们分别支持在避孕和堕胎方面的宪法隐私权)中做出了影响深远的决定,导致隐私权被等同于个人选择的自由:从事各种活动的自由,尽管这些活动通常在私人场所进行。换言之,隐私权的概念包括控制获取和使用身体的权利。而且,由于与管制堕胎和某些性行为相关的法律对个人隐私和政府权力都有深远的影响,因此,承认这一类别的法律包含做出个人决定的权力,即所谓的"决定隐私权",可能是有益的。

对家庭、办公室或"私人空间"的入侵也催生了"位置隐私"的概念——这是一个不恰当的说法,它捕捉了个人领域受到公开或隐蔽的攻击所侵犯的隐私特征。

一个定义?

一个可接受的隐私定义仍然难以得出。韦斯汀那个似乎普遍存在且有影响力的想法把隐私理解为一种要求:"个人、团体或机构为他们自己确定何时、如何、在何种程度上把他们的信息传达给他人"。将隐私视为一种要求(或者更确切地说,视为一种权利),虽然假定了隐私的价值,但未能界定其内容。而且,它还包括使用或披露有关个人的**任何**信息。那些将隐私理解为"生活领域"或一种心理状态的观念也会受到类似的批评。

然而,韦斯汀的定义在个人对自己信息的**控制**程度方面对隐私的描述产生了更大的影响。如果将个人对信息的控制权等同于隐私,而如果个人被阻止行使这种控制,那么即使他或她不能披露个人信息,也不得不说他或她已经失去了隐私。这意味着隐私的价值是假定的。

同样,如果我明知并自愿披露个人信息,我并不会因此而失去隐私,因为我是在行使而不是放弃控制权。但是这种意义上的控制并没有充分地描述隐私,因为虽然人们可以控制是否要披露这些信息,但人们也有可能通过其他方式获得这些信息。而如果控制意味着一种更强的含义(即披露信息,即使是自愿披露,也会失去控制权,因为我不能够限制他人传播信息),这就描述了**潜在的**而非**实际的**隐私损失。

因此,我可能不会吸引他人的任何兴趣,也正因此,我的隐私将得到保护,无论我是否有此愿望!我控制自己的信息流和人们事实上对我的了解是有区别的。根据这一论点,为了确定这种控制是否确实保护了我的隐私,还必须知道,例如,信息的接收者是否受到限制性规范的约束。

此外,如果隐私权被视为广义控制权(或自主权)的一个方面,那么问题的关键就是人们选择隐私权的自由。但是,正如上面所表明的,你可以选择放弃自己的隐私。因此,基于控制的隐私定义涉及你做出哪些选择的问题,而不是你实施它们的方式。换句话说,这种定义预设了隐私的价值。

鉴于这些令人头痛的问题,答案是否在于试图描述隐私的特征?不过,也存在着相当大的分歧。一种观点认为,隐私包括"有限的可访问性"——由三个相互关联但独立的构成要素组成的集群:保密性,关于个人信息被知悉;匿名性,对个人的关注;以及独处,对个人的身体接触。

与侵犯隐私权不同的是,隐私的丧失发生于这样一种情况,即其他人获得关于个人的信息、关注或接触个人。这种方法声称的优点在于:第一,它是中立的,有助于客观地识别隐私的丧失;第二,它展示隐私作为一种价值的逻辑连贯性;第三,它表明了这一概念在法律环境中的效用(因为它确定了需要法律保护的场合);第四,它包括"典型的"侵犯隐私行为,并排除了上文提及的问题,这些问题虽然常常被认为是隐私问题,但根据其自身的性质,最好被视为道德或法律问题(如噪声、臭味、堕胎、避孕、同性恋等)。

然而,即使是这种分析也存在困难。特别是为了避免假定隐私权的价值,这种分析不接受将隐私的概念限制在被泄露的信息的特征上。因此,它摒弃这样一种观点,这种观点认为,要构成隐私的一部分,有关信息必须是"私人的",即与个人的身份有密切关系或联系。如果有关个人的任何信息(保密部分)被外人知悉,都会导致隐私的丧失,这就会严重弱化隐私的概念。

将传播有关个人信息的**每一种**情况都描述为隐私的丧失,这是一种曲解。然而,如果隐私权是关于个人信息或知识的一种功能,在这种程度上,这样的理解似乎是不可避免的。换言之,就有关个人信息的问题而言,需要有某种限制或控制因素。可以说最被认同的因素是,这些信息必须是"个人的"。

声称无论何时,只要个人被他人关注或接触,就必然会失去隐私,这再次使我们忽视对隐私含义的关注。如果有人把注意力集中在你身上,或者不请自来地闯入你的独处生活,本身就是令人反感的,但我们在这些情况下对个人隐私的关注,在他或她进行我们通常认为是私人的活动时,才是最强烈的。偷窥狂汤姆比那些在公共场合跟踪我们的人更有可能冒犯我们的"隐私"观念。

有时有人争辩说,通过保护作为隐私权基础的价值(财产权、人的尊严、防止或赔偿蒙受的精神痛苦等),可以免除关于隐私权的道德和法律论述。如果是真的,这将削弱隐私概念的独特性。并且，即使是那些否认隐私权派生性的人们，对隐私权主要概念特征的看法也很少有一致意见。

更糟糕的是，关于隐私含义的争论经常是在根本不同的前提下进行的。因此，如果隐私被描述为"权利"，那么这个问题就不会和那些认为隐私是"条件"的人认真地结合在一起。前者通常是关于隐私需求的规范性陈述（无论如何定义隐私），后者仅仅是对"隐私"进行描述性陈述。此外，关于隐私的可取性的主张往往会混淆其工具性价值和内在价值；隐私本身被一些人视为目的，而另一些人则将其视为一种手段，用以确保诸如创造性、爱或情感释放等社会目的的达成。

隐私和个人信息

是否还存在别的办法？在不损害隐私作为一项基本价值的重要性的前提下，答案是否在于将引起个人诉求的问题予以单独考虑？毫无疑问，最初隐私领域有代表性的投诉与美国法律所称的"公开披露私人事实"和"侵犯个人的隐居、独处或私事"有关。当然，最近电脑化个人资料的收集和使用，以及与电子社会有关的其他问题，已成为人们关注的主要隐私问题。

看来很明显，这些问题在本质上都有一个共同点，那就是限制关于个人的私事分别被公布、入侵或误用的程度。这并不是说，某些情况（如单身一人）或某些行为（如电话窃听）不应分别被定性为隐私或侵犯隐私。

在将隐私问题定位在个人信息层面的过程中，出现了两个明显的问题：第一，"个人"一词应理解为什么？第二，在什么情况下才算是"个人"事项？某个"个人"事项是否仅仅因为个人声称它是"个人"的，或者存在本质上是个人的事项？声称我的政治观点是个人的，必须取决于某些规范，这些规范禁止或限制对这些观点进行调查或未经授权的报道。不过，我只援引我有权保留自己的意见这条规范就足够了。

买卖隐私

你不能就个人或私人信息达成协议。法律并不授予你垄断权来换取你公布这些事实。这就是隐私的独特之处：个人应该能够控制自己的信息。我们应该通过给予他们这样做的结构和权利，热心地帮助他们保护这种信息。我们重视或渴望和平，因此，一个允许我们通过控制私人信息来实现这种和平的体制是一个符合公共价值观的体制。在这种体制下，当局应该支持……在我的体制下，没有任何东西可以让个人最终或完全控制他们可以出售的数据种类或他们可以购买的隐私种类。P3P体制原则上可以实现对隐私权的上游控制及对个人的控制……这样的体制没有理由必须保护所有类型的私人数据……你自己的一些事实可能是不许隐瞒的；更重要的是，可能会有一些关于你自己的声明是不被允许的（"我是律师"，或者"拨电话给我，我是医生"）。不应允许你从事欺诈或伤害他人的事。

劳伦斯·莱斯格，《网络空间的法典和其他法律》，基础图书出版公司，1999年，第162—163页。

这些规范显然既与文化有关，也是可变的。如上所述，人类学证据表明，原始社会对隐私的态度是有差别的。毫无疑问，在现代社会中，对"私人"的理解会出现波动。在大多数现代社会中，就私人生活的某些方面而言，肯定没有五十年前那些典型的社会那么缺乏信心。难道没有一类信息可以被合理地描述为"个人的"吗？通常有人反对说，"私密性"不是信息本身的属性；同样的信息在一种情况下可能被认为是非常私密的，而在另一种情况下就不是如此或根本就不私密。

> **反隐私时刻**
>
> 过去十年似乎产生了更多的所谓"反隐私时刻"——公众舆论中的情绪特点表现为愿意让越来越多的个人数据脱离个人控制。欧洲和北美的大规模恐怖主义的冲击是造成这种情绪的一个诱因，尽管它并不是唯一因素。过去十年似乎没有发生的事情，更多的是像水门事件或对德国过度人口普查要求的反抗——这些戏剧性事件强化了公众对侵犯隐私行为的免疫反应，并巩固了建立在这种反应基础上的制度和实践。
>
> 詹姆斯·B.鲁尔，载于J.B.鲁尔和G.格林利夫编，《全球隐私保护：第一代》，爱德华·埃尔加出版社，2008年，第272—273页。

当然，简可能更倾向于向她的分析师或密友透露私人事实，而不是向她的雇主或合伙人透露，她对报纸披露信息的反对可能更强烈。但是在所有这三种情况下，这些信息仍然是"个人的"。不同的是，她可以决定在多大程度上允许这些信息被公开或被使用。将第一种情况（向分析师透露）中的信息描述为"根本不是私人的"甚至"不是那么私人的"都是违反直觉的。我们当然要说，精神病医生正在倾听讨论中的个人事实，如果谈话被秘密记录下来，或者精神病医生被要求就其患者的同性恋关系或不忠行为出庭做证，我们应该会说，个人信息被记录下来或被披露了。情况已明显发生改变，但它影响的是，可合理预期个人在何种程度上会反对人们使用或传播其个人信息，而非信息本身的质量。

因此，"个人信息"的任何界定都必须包括两个要素，它应当既提及信息的**质量**，也提及个人**对信息使用的合理期望**。一个要素在很大程度上是另一个要素的应变量。换句话说，这里提出的"个人信息"的概念既是描述性的，也是规范性的。

个人信息包括与个人有关的事实、通信或意见，可以合理地期望这些信息被他或她认为是私密的或敏感的，因此希望隐瞒或至少限制收集、使用或传播这些信息。当然，"事实"并不局限于文本数据，而是涵盖了广泛的信息，包括图像、DNA和其他遗传与生物识别数据，如指纹、面部和虹膜识别，以及越来越多种类的与我们有关的信息，这些信息是通过技术能够被发现和利用的。

更清晰？

有人可能会立即提出反对意见，就是通过将"个人信息"的概念置于对个人期望的客观确定之上，对"个人信息"的界定实际上是纯粹的规范性定义，因此会避免有关保护"个人信息"是否可取或其他方面的问询。但是，任何将信息归类为"个人"、"敏感"或"私密"的尝试，都假定了这些信息需要被特别对待。

如果有必要参照某些客观的标准来界定信息，那么不可避免地，分类就取决于那些可以合法地被宣称是"个人的"信息。在任何试验中，只有那些希望隐瞒的信息是合理的，才有可能成为我们关注的焦点，特别是在我们想寻求有效的法律保护的情况下更是如此。例如，如果一个人认为有关他的汽车的信息是个人的，并因此想隐瞒汽车发动机大小的细节，那么他会发现很难说服任何人，他的车辆的登记文件构成了"个人信息"的泄露。对于什么是"个人的"进行客观测试，通常都会排除此类信息。

但是，如果个人的要求涉及影响其私生活的信息，这就会变得更加困难。例如，一个人希望阻止披露有关其因盗窃而受审和定罪的事实，这并非不可理喻。将建议的个人信息定义作为判断这类信息是否属于个人信息的第一顺序标准，可能意味着这种要求是合法的。但是，这种要求很可能被否决，理由是，司法行政的程序是公开的。然而，时间的推移可能会改变这类事件的性质，一度属于**公共**事务的事项可能在若干年后被合理地视为私人事务。

同样，将从旧报纸上获得的曾经公开的信息出版，若干年后可能会被认为是对个人信息的冒犯性披露。因此，这意味着客观标准并不妨碍在隐瞒个人信息的权利或要求与社会在言论自由等方面的利益冲突之间取得平衡。通过自愿披露、同意使用或传播个人信息，个人并不放弃对个人信息保留一定控制权的主张。例如，他或她可以允许将信息用于一种目的（如医疗诊断），但在用于另一种目的（如就业）时可以反对。

至于第三方表达的关于个人的意见，如果该意见的存在是个人所**知道**的（如求职申请所要求的证明材料），可以合理地期望她只允许那些与决定是否雇用她有直接关系的人获得这些材料。如果对她的评估是她**不**知道的（例如，她在信贷咨询机构的数据库中被描述为"风险很大"），或者她的通信已被截获或记录，可以合理地预知她会反对使用或披露这些信息（在秘密监控的情况下，反对实际采集的信息），特别是**在她意识到**这些信息实际上或可能是误导或不准确的情况下，更是如此。

的确，就其本身而言，一条信息可能是完全无伤大雅的，但当与另外一条同样并无恶意的数据结合在一起时，这些信息就会转化为某种真正私密的东西。因此，黄女士的地址是公开的，这本身很难构成"私人"信息。但如果把这个和她的诸如职业等信息联系起来，这种结合就会把数据转换成易受攻击的细节，对此，她有合法权利隐瞒个人信息。

个人信息的客观概念并不忽视数据产生的完整背景。在评估有关资料是否符合"个人"的最低要求时，个人所投诉的事实，显然需要"全面"研究。受害者认为，公开的数据（电话号码、地址、车牌等）是他们希望控制或限制披露或传播的信息，这是不合理的。一般来说，只有当这些数据变得敏感时，例如将它们与其他数据联系在一起时，才可以说是实现了一个合理的申诉。

合理性并不完全排除个人习性的运作，只要其影响与个案的情况有关。客观的检验方法也不会否认这些因素在决定个人将信息视为个人的是否合理方面的重要性。例如,英国人在透露其工资问题上出了名的含糊其词,而斯堪的纳维亚人远没有这样做。文化因素不可避免地会影响到人们将信息视为个人信息是否合理的判断。这在特定的社会中也同样如此。

在任何情况下,没有一项信息本身是个人的信息。一份匿名医疗档案、银行对账单或性丑闻的露骨披露本是无害的,直到其与某个人挂起钩来。只有当信息主体的身份被揭露时,它才成为个人信息。一旦这一门槛被突破,这也就是不争的事实;只有在满足客观检验的情况下,个人信息才值得保护。但这不是在概念或社会真空中发生的,必须具体情况具体分析。

尽管在隐私的含义、范围和限制方面存在分歧,但对隐私的意义和对保护隐私所面临的威胁,几乎没有什么不确定性。基本上人们都认为必须制止对这种基本价值的侵蚀。下一章考虑将隐私认定为合法权利。

第三章

一种法定权利

　　维多利亚女王和阿尔伯特亲王都是技艺高超的蚀刻师。1849年,这对皇室夫妇想要制作一些供他们私人使用的复制品,于是他们把一些蚀刻画的版面交给宫廷印刷商,其中之一就是斯特兰奇。有几版画不知怎么落到了第三方贾奇的手里,贾奇显然是通过斯特兰奇雇用的"卧底"得到的。后来,斯特兰奇从贾奇那里得到了这些画,并确信,在维多利亚和阿尔伯特的同意下,它们将被公开展示。于是,他们制作了一个画册并开始安排展览。当他得知不存在皇室的同意时,斯特兰奇退出了参展,但决定继续印刷画册。他的建议是将画册连同皇家艺术家的亲笔签名一起出售。

　　皇室夫妇对此并不开心。亲王申请禁令,以防止展览和预定展品画册的传播。不用说,禁令被批准了,法院的确厚着脸皮地承认,"本案的重要性完全来自原告的崇高地位……"。

　　虽然本案的判决主要依据的是蚀刻画版是王子的财产这一事实,但法院明确承认,这为法律提供了更广泛的基础,在此基础上,法律"保护致力于创作的作者希望不为人所周知的思想和

图9 皇室夫妇不开心

感情的隐私与隐匿性"。

美国发轫

这一判决是1890年的传奇性文章的一个重要因素,而这一决定在1890年催生了法律对隐私权本身的承认。由塞缪尔·D.沃伦和路易斯·D.布兰代斯撰写的评论,发表在颇具影响力的《哈佛法律评论》上。几年前,伊士曼·柯达发明的一种价格低廉的便携式照相机改变了世界。个人可能在家里、工作或玩耍时被抓拍,隐私寿终正寝的时刻就要到了。

当时,波士顿律师、社会名流沃伦和1916年被任命为最高法院法官的布兰代斯,对新媒体的入侵,即所谓的"黄色新闻"感到愤怒,写了一篇被广泛认为是有史以来最具影响力的法律评论文章。人们常常认为,促使他们愤怒的原因是媒体对沃伦女儿的婚礼进行了窥探。但这似乎不大可能,因为在1890年,她才六岁!他们恼火的原因更有可能是波士顿上流社会的八卦杂志发表了一系列的文章,描述了沃伦奢华的宴会。

无论如何,那篇著名的文章谴责了新闻界的厚颜无耻(也预示了柯达的新发明对隐私的威胁),并认为普通法默示并承认隐私权。他们援引英国法院关于违反保密、财产、版权和诽谤的裁决,认为这些案件不过是一般隐私权的实例和应用。他们声称,虽然形式不同,但普通法保护受到窥探记者之类的人侵犯的个人隐私。在这样做时,法律承认人的精神和智力需求的重要性。他们的声明很有名:

> 生命的强度和复杂性,伴随着文明的进步,使人们不得不躲避这个世界,而人在文化的强大影响下,对公共性变得更加敏感,以至于独处和隐私对个人来说变得更加重要;但是,现代企业和发明通过侵犯个人隐私,使人们遭受精神上

隐私

图10 后来成为美国最高法院杰出法官的路易斯·布兰代斯

的痛苦和忧虑，其程度远远超过单纯的身体伤害所造成的后果。

沃伦和布兰代斯认为，普通法已经从对自然人和有形财产的保护发展到对个人的"思想、情感和感觉"的保护。但是，由于晚近的发明和商业方法及新闻界对隐私的威胁，普通法需要进一步发展。一个人有权决定他的思想、情感和感觉在多大程度上向他人传播，这种权利已经受到法律保护，但这种法律仅适用于保护文学和艺术作品及书信的作者，他们可以禁止未经授权出版自己的作品和书信。虽然英国承认这一权利的相关案例是基于对财产的保护，但实际上它们也是对隐私的承认，是对"不可侵犯的人格"的承认。

不久，他们的论证方法就受到了考验。1902年，有原告起诉称，在未经她同意的情况下，其形象被用于为被告的商品做广告。她的形象被描绘在一袋袋面粉上，上面写着凄惨的双关语："家庭面粉"①。纽约上诉法院的多数法官没有接受沃伦和布兰代斯的论点，认为隐私权的论据"在我们的法理中还没有一个永恒的地位……如果不对既定的法律原则采取暴力，现在就不可能将隐私权纳入"。然而，少数法官很赞同J.格雷关于隐私的想法，宣称原告有权保护自己的形象免受被告为商业利益而利用，"任何其他的裁决原则……都是不符合公平原则的，理性思考起来也是令人震惊的"。

---

① "Flour"一词还有表示摔碎、粉碎之意。——译注

流言蜚语的邪恶

流言蜚语不再是游手好闲者和邪恶者的资源,而成为厚颜无耻、孜孜以求的一种交易。为了满足好色之徒的口味,两性关系的细节在日报的专栏上广为传播。为了让懒人有事可忙,一个个专栏充斥着闲言碎语,而这只能靠侵入内部圈子来获得……这种侵入所造成的伤害也不仅限于那些可能成为新闻业或其他行业调查对象的人所遭受的痛苦。

在这方面,如同在其他商业分支一样,供给创造需求。每一茬不合时宜的流言蜚语,都会变成更多流言蜚语的种子,并且与其传播成正比,从而导致社会标准和道德水平的降低。即使是表面上无害的闲言碎语,如果广泛持续地流传,也会带来强烈的恶果。它既目空一切又腐化堕落,它通过颠倒事物的相对重要性而贬低事物,从而使一个民族的思想和愿景犬儒化。当闲言碎语获得印刷品的礼遇,并挤占了社区真正感兴趣的事物的空间时,无知和轻率的人就误以为它有相对重要性,这就不足为奇了。

八卦容易理解并诉诸人性的弱点,因此我们邻居的不幸和脆弱永远不会让我们把八卦完全抛在脑后。所以任何人都不会惊讶于八卦篡夺了我们大脑中的其他兴趣点。琐碎的事情会同时摧毁思想的稳健和感情的细腻。任何热情都不能蓬勃发展,任何慷慨的冲动都不能在它的阴影下生存。

塞缪尔·D.沃伦和路易斯·D.布兰代斯,《隐私权》,1890年,《哈佛法律评论》第196卷第5期。

关于这个案件的法院裁决引起了普遍的不满。这导致纽约州颁布了一项法令，规定未经授权将个人的姓名或形象用于广告或贸易目的是非法的。但三年后，在一个涉及类似事实的案件中，佐治亚州最高法院采纳了J.格雷的理据。沃伦和布兰代斯的论点在发表十五年后占了上风。自那以后，美国大多数州都将"隐私权"纳入其法律。然而，尽管两位作者高度依赖英国法院的判决，但在英格兰或其他普通法法域没有出现类似的进展。

多年以来，美国普通法对隐私权的保护一直在稳步扩大。1960年，卓越的侵权法专家迪安·普罗瑟阐述了这样的观点，即法律现在所承认的并非一种侵权行为，而是由四种不同利益组成的复合体……它们以共同的名称联系在一起，但在其他方面没有什么共同之处。他将它们的性质阐述如下：

> 第一种侵权行为是侵扰原告的隐居、独处或私生活。过错行为是对原告的独处或隐居的故意干涉，它包括对原告住所的实际侵入和窃听（包括电子监控和影像监控、装窃听器和电话窃听），并且必须满足三项要求：（a）必须存在实际的窥探行为；（b）这种侵扰一定冒犯了通情达理的人；（c）这种侵扰必须是对私人的侵犯。

> 第二种侵权行为是公开披露有关原告的令人尴尬的私人事实。普罗瑟区分了这种侵权行为的三个要素：

> （a）必须存在公之于众的情况（向一小批人披露事实，

不足以构成公之于众);(b)所披露的事实必须是私人事实(将政府备案材料事项公之于众并不构成侵权);(c)所披露的事实必须是对具有通常敏感度的通情达理的人而言有冒犯性的。

第三,他指出了一种侵权行为,即在公众瞩目下把原告置于虚假的宣传中。这通常发生在这种情况下:一种意见或言论(诸如伪造的书籍或错误的观点)被公开认为来自原告,或者他的照片被用来说明他与之没有合理联系的书或文章。这种公开宣传必须也是"对一个通情达理的人的严重冒犯"。

最后,普罗瑟区分了被告为其自身利益盗用原告姓名或肖像的侵权行为。被告获得的好处不一定是经济上的好处,例如,如果原告在出生证上被错误地命名为父亲,就会产生这种好处。另一方面,几个州存在的法定侵权行为通常要求未经授权将原告的身份用于商业(通常是广告)目的。对这种侵权行为的承认确立了"公开权"的概念,根据这一概念,个人能够决定如何在商业上利用自己的名字或形象。在普罗瑟看来,侵犯隐私的四种形式只有在一种情况下是相互关联的,即每一种形式都构成了对"独处的权利"的干涉。

有人认为,这种对隐私权的四重区分是错误的,因为这种区分破坏了沃伦和布兰代斯的"不可侵犯的人格"的原理,忽视了隐私权的道德基础:这种道德基础作为人类尊严的一个方面而存在。尽管如此,这种分类在美国侵权法中占据了突出地位,正如一位法学家哈里·卡尔文所预测的,这种分类方法在很大程度上将概念僵化为四种类型:

鉴于法律思维追求整齐的标签和类别的弱点，并考虑到普罗瑟应有的威望，可以有把握地预测，隐私权四分论的观点将主导未来任何有关隐私权的思考。

这四种侵权行为的变迁，已经在大量的学术和通俗读物中得到了论述，这种发展也并非局限于美国。几乎每一个先进的法律体系都或多或少地寻求承认隐私权的某些方面，这些国家和地区包括奥地利、加拿大、中国大陆和中国台湾、丹麦、爱沙尼亚、法国、德国、荷兰、匈牙利、爱尔兰、印度、意大利、立陶宛、新西兰、挪威、菲律宾、俄罗斯、南非、韩国、西班牙、泰国和大多数拉丁美洲国家。

宪法赋予的权利

这四种侵权行为仍然是美国法律保护隐私的有效手段，它们或多或少也标志着宪法对隐私的保护范围。当然，沃伦和布兰代斯主要关注的是我们现在所称的媒体侵扰。然而几年后，1928年，在奥姆斯特德诉美国一案中，布兰代斯表达了强烈的异议。他宣称，《宪法》赋予人"独处的权利以对抗政府"，并补充说，"为了保护这一权利，政府对个人隐私的每一次无理侵犯，无论采取何种手段，都应视为违反了第四修正案"。最高法院在卡茨诉美国案中采纳了这一观点。自那以来，隐私权作为一种独处的权利，一再被最高法院援引。

1965年，最高法院对格里斯沃尔德诉康涅狄格州案的裁决，是最重要且最具争议的进展。它宣布康涅狄格州禁止使用避孕药具的法令违宪，因为该法令违反了婚姻隐私权，这是一项"比

《人权法案》更古老"的权利。宪法并没有提到隐私权,然而,在一系列案件中,最高法院通过《人权法案》(尤其是第一、第三、第四、第五和第九修正案),承认"结社隐私"、"政治隐私"和"律师隐私"等隐私权,还规定了对窃听和非法搜查进行防范的限度。

到目前为止,最高法院做出的最具争议性的"隐私"裁决是1973年罗伊诉韦德案。它凭借多数票认为得克萨斯州的堕胎法因为侵犯了隐私权,所以是违宪的。根据该法律,堕胎是犯罪行为,除非是为了挽救孕妇的生命。法院认为,各州可以禁止堕胎,以保护胎儿的生命,但只能禁止在妊娠的最后三个月堕胎。这一被称为"无疑是美国最高法院有史以来最著名的案件"的判决受到女权主义者的欢迎,但同时也遭到许多基督徒的强烈谴责。这个判决使得美国妇女获得了实现合法堕胎权的一线希望。似乎没有任何中间立场。法理学家罗纳德·德沃金直截了当地描述了这场冲突的激烈程度:

> 反堕胎群体和他们的反对者之间的战争是17世纪欧洲可怕的宗教内战的美国新版本。大批反对派人士在街道上游行,或挤在堕胎诊所、法院和白宫的抗议人群中,对彼此大吼大叫、唾沫横飞、深恶痛绝。堕胎问题把美国撕得四分五裂。

最高法院做出的另一项引起轩然大波的"隐私"判决,是1986年鲍尔斯诉哈德威克案,在该案中,法院以勉强的多数票认定,正当程序条款中的隐私保护并没有扩展到成年人之间私下

图 11　美国最高法院 1973 年对罗伊诉韦德案的裁决引发了一场持续至今的争论

自愿的同性恋行为："无法证明家庭、婚姻或生育与同性恋行为之间存在任何联系。"

这一判决在劳伦斯诉得克萨斯州案中被明确否定。在该案中，最高法院以六比三的票数裁定，该判决对自由利益的解释过于狭窄。多数派认为，第十四条修正案所规定的实质性正当程序包括进行私下自愿的性行为的自由。它的作用是废止全美国旨在将成年同性私下自愿的鸡奸行为定为犯罪的所有立法。

美国的经验既有影响力，又有启发意义。其他普通法法域继续努力解决隐私的定义和范围、协调隐私权与其他权利，特别是隐私权与言论自由之间的关系等棘手问题。可以公平地说，一般而言，英美法系往往是以利益为基础的，而大陆法系往往是

世界监控社会地图

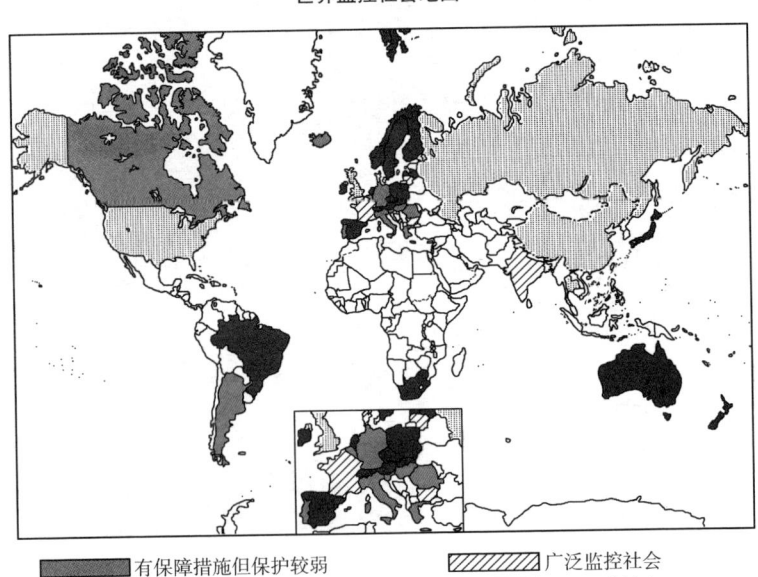

有保障措施但保护较弱
维护保障措施的系统性失灵
广泛监控社会
普遍监控社会

图12　隐私在全球范围内被赋予不同程度的保护

以权利为基础的。换言之，例如，英国法律对保护隐私权采取了务实的逐案处理的路径，而法国法律则将隐私权视为一项基本人权。然而，由于受《欧洲人权公约》和欧盟其他宣言、指令的影响，这种差异已经缩小。英国1998年通过的《人权法案》最明显地表明了这种强烈的风向，下文将清楚地说明这一点。

普通法的磨难

不仅英格兰和威尔士的法律仍然在努力解决隐私权的困境。澳大利亚、新西兰、爱尔兰、加拿大、中国香港和其他普通法法域，也都深陷优柔寡断和犹豫不决的泥潭。

尽管英国有几个委员会并试图立法，英国的法律仍然是不确定和模棱两可的。1972年，青年委员会拒绝了法律所规定的一般隐私权的理念。其结论是，一般隐私权的理念会让法院背负"具有社会和政治性质的争议性问题"。法官很可能会在平衡隐私和言论自由等相互冲突的利益之间遇到问题。委员会建议设立一项新的罪行和侵权行为，即非法监控；一项新的侵权行为，即披露或以其他方式非法获得信息；以及审议关于违反保密义务的法律（该法保护一方委托给另一方的机密信息），以此作为保护隐私权的一种可能的手段。其他普通法法域也曾提交过类似的报告。

近年来，一连串的名人诉讼为法院提供了一个机会来审查，在缺乏明确的普通法隐私保护的情况下，法院是否可以为违反保密义务的补救提供一种权宜之计。这些问题最好在第四章中探讨。它们表明了隐私权是如何无精打采地走向最高法院而诞生的。其中一个案例涉及电影明星迈克尔·道格拉斯和凯瑟

琳·泽塔—琼斯的婚礼照片被偷拍并公开,这也会在第四章讨论。霍夫曼勋爵已在上议院宣布:

> 1998年《人权法案》的生效削弱了以下论点,即需要一种一般性的侵犯隐私的侵权行为来填补现有解决办法中的空白。该法案第6条和第7条本身就填补了很大的空白;如果一个人根据公约第8条规定所应享有的权利确实受到公共当局的侵犯,那么他将有法定的补救办法。一般侵权行为的确立将……预先解决一个有争议的问题,即《欧洲人权公约》要求国家为非公共当局的个人侵犯隐私权的行为提供多大程度(如果有的话)的解决。

该法案(将《欧洲人权公约》第8条纳入英国法律)的影响无论怎样强调都不为过。它规定保护尊重家庭生活、住宅和通信隐私的权利。至少在一名高级法官看来,这项措施给予了"英国法律承认隐私权的最终推动力"。尽管他的看法不一定得到司法机构所有成员的认同,但最近一些案件中所显示的对隐私权的分析表明,《欧洲人权公约》第8条的作用至少是为本条中权利的横向适用提供可能性。的确,在最近的一些判决中可以发现一种意愿,即允许第8条阻止全面的隐私侵权行为的产生,这并非毫无理由。你几乎可以听到剑回鞘中的咣当声。

和英国一样,澳大利亚各州和联邦一级的法律改革委员会都在审议法律保护的必要性。法院也没有闲下来,在2001年一项意义重大的裁决中,澳大利亚高等法院的多数法官小心翼翼地倾向于承认隐私侵权行为。在澳大利亚广播公司诉利纳野味肉类有限公司一案中，法院承认澳大利亚法律的不足，表示它支持普通法法域内对侵犯隐私提起普通法诉讼的司法发展。在详细说明什么会构成对隐私的无理侵犯时，法院指出：

> 关于某人的某些种类的信息，例如有关健康、人际关系或财务的信息，可能很容易被认定为私人信息；同样，一个通情达理的人在适用当代道德和行为标准时，也可能会认为某些类型的活动意味着不为人所知。如果要求对有关信息或行为进行披露或监视，会对具有一般敏感度的通情达理的人造成极大的冒犯，这在许多情况下就是对"私人"的有用而可行的检验标准。

图13　尽管道格拉斯夫妇试图秘密举办婚礼，但最终还是被偷拍了照片，从而在英国引起了旷日持久而意义重大的诉讼

这项裁决虽然在核心问题上没有定论，但的确表明，如果高等法院在面对一个更值得帮助的原告时（本案是澳大利亚广播公司希望揭露一家屠宰场的残酷做法），则可能会认识到隐私侵权行为并非完全不可想象。

2005年，新西兰上诉法院在承认普通法隐私侵权方面迈出了重要一步。在霍斯金诉伦廷一案中，被告拍下了原告十八个月大的双胞胎女儿的照片，当时原告在街上用婴儿车推着她们，婴儿的父亲是一个著名的电视人物。原告夫妇申请禁制令阻止照片公之于众。审判法院认为，新西兰法律不承认基于公开披露在公共场所拍摄的照片而导致隐私诉讼的理由。然而，虽然上诉法院驳回了原告的上诉，但它（以三比二的票数）裁定，对"因公开私人和个人信息而侵犯隐私权"的行为给予补救办法。这种观点主要是基于它对英国法院对违反保密义务的解决方法的分析所做的阐明，以及符合新西兰根据《公民权利和政治权利国际公约》和《联合国儿童权利公约》规定所应承担的义务这一事实。法院还认为，他们的判决有助于调和相互冲突的价值，并使新西兰能够借鉴美国的广泛经验。

P. 高尔特和J. 布兰查德在其判决中详述了诉求成功的两点基本要求。第一，原告必须对隐私有一种合理的期望；第二，必须公开私人事实，而这些事实的公开会被认为是对一个客观的、通情达理的人的高度冒犯。

新西兰1993年的《隐私法案》规定，任何人都可以向隐私事务专员提出申诉，宣称任何行动是或似乎是"对个人隐私的干涉"。如果隐私事务专员认为申诉有实质内容，他可将申诉转交给根据1993年《人权法案》任命的诉讼专员，诉讼专员可转而向申诉审查法庭提出诉讼。法庭可发布命令,禁止指控的行动再次发生或要求纠正这种干涉。法院有权裁定损害赔偿。

虽然爱尔兰没有明确承认普通法中的一般隐私权,但法院根据《宪法》第40.3.1条制定了隐私权的宪法权利,根据这一条款,国家保证尊重、捍卫和维护公民的个人权利。例如,1974年,最高法院的大多数法官认为隐私权包括在公民的个人权利之中。之后的诸多判决表明,该条款延伸到通过拦截通信和监视侵犯隐私权的某些行为。

其他路径

大陆法系对隐私权的态度是以"人格权"的概念为基础的。在德国,这项权利受《基本法》的保障。该法第1条规定,所有国家机构都有义务尊重和保护"人的尊严";第2条第1款规定,"人人有权自由发展其人格,只要他不侵犯他人的权利或违反宪法秩序和道德准则"。这两条结合起来,就确立了一般性的个人人格权,而尊重个人私生活领域的权利正是这一人格权利的体现。

此外,法院还将隐私权作为《民法典》规定的人格权的一部分加以保护。它们还利用侵权行为法,对损害人的尊严的行为提供解决办法。例如,未经许可不得擅自公布个人私生活的私密细节,未经患者同意不得发布医疗报告,未经本人知情和同意不得对谈话进行录音,不得打开私人信函——不论信函是否已被实际阅读,未经同意不允许拍照,公正描述个人生活,个人信息不得被新闻界滥用。

德国法院承认人格的三个领域:"亲密"、"私人"和"个人"

领域。"亲密领域"包括一个人的思想和情感及其表达、医疗信息和性行为。由于这类信息具有特别的私人性质,因此享有绝对的保护。"私人领域"包括既不亲密也不保密(如关于家庭和家庭生活的事实)的信息,但这些信息仍然是私人的,因此受到适当的保护,但为了公众利益而披露可能是合理的。"个人领域"涉及个人的公共、经济和职业生活、社会和职业关系,它受到最低程度的保护。

在法国,隐私权受到积极的保护。虽然《法国宪法》没有明确提及隐私权,但宪法委员会于1995年将第66条中的"个人自由"的概念扩展到隐私权。因此,隐私权被提升为一种宪法权利。此外,《法国民法典》第9条规定,"人人享有尊重自己私生活的权利……"。法院对此的解释是,这包括一个人的身份(姓名、出生日期、宗教信仰、住址等)和有关一个人的健康、婚姻状况、家庭、性关系、性取向及其通常的生活方式等信息。通过拍照或录音故意侵犯私人场所也属于刑事犯罪,可判决违法者承担损害赔偿。

《意大利宪法》保护作为个人人格组成部分的隐私权。因此,侵犯隐私权可能引起根据《民法典》提出的索赔主张,该法规定,故意或过失地对他人造成不合理损害的行为人,有责任对受害人进行赔偿。《民法典》还宣布,如果公开一个人的肖像会导致其尊严或名誉受损,这种行为可受到限制。

《荷兰宪法》第10条保障隐私权,但这是一项需加以限定的权利。尽管最高法院认为言论自由权不能成为侵犯隐私权的借口,但它将在隐私诉讼中考虑所有情况,记者可以论证有关出版物是合理的。《民法典》第1401条规定了对他人造成不法损害的一般责任,该条款被解释为包括无正当理由公布有害的私人信息所造成的损害。刑法规定,侵入他人住宅、窃听私人谈话、擅自拍摄个人私人财产的照片及公布通过这种方式获得的照片,均应受到处罚。

虽然《加拿大宪法》及其《权利和自由宪章》都没有明确提到隐私权,但法院通过将不受无理搜查或没收的安全权(《权利和自由宪章》第8条)解释为包含个人享有对隐私权的合理期望,填补了这一空白。美国没有普通法规定保护隐私权,但下级法院表现出愿意扩大现有的诉因,如侵害或妨害,以保护受害者的隐私。通过规定侵犯隐私权的法定侵权行为,这一普通法缺陷在加拿大的一些省份已得到解决。在不列颠哥伦比亚省、马尼托巴省、纽芬兰省和萨斯喀彻温省,"侵犯隐私权"的侵权行为是可诉的,受害人无须证明损害的存在。但对侵权行为的确切表述则在各省有所不同。

魁北克作为一个大陆法系法域,通过对原《民法典》中民事责任一般规定的解释,发展了其法律程序的解决办法。不过,目前对隐私权的保护已明确纳入新的《民法典》。新的《民法典》规定,人人有权获得对自己名誉和隐私的尊重,任何人不得侵犯他人的隐私,除非得到该人或其继承人的同意,或经法律授权。规定的侵犯隐私行为的形式涵盖了相当广泛的行为。此外,魁北克《人权和自由宪章》第5条宣布,人人都有获得其私生活受尊重的权利,这项规定可在公民之间直接执行。1994年的《统一隐私法》澄清并补充了现有的省级法规。

国际层面

一种相当宽泛意义上的隐私权是一项公认的人权,在大多

数国际文件中都得到承认。举例来说,《联合国人权宣言》第12条和《公民权利和政治权利国际公约》第17条均规定:

(1)任何人的私生活、家庭、住宅或通信均不得受到任意或非法干涉,其荣誉和名誉不得受到非法攻击。
(2)人人有权得到法律保护,以免受这种干涉或攻击。

《欧洲人权公约》第8条规定:

(1)人人有权享有使自己的私人和家庭生活、家庭和通信得到尊重的权利。
(2)公共当局不得干涉这项权利的行使,除非符合法律并在民主社会中为国家安全、公共安全或国家经济福祉、防止混乱或犯罪、保护健康或道德、保护他人的权利和自由所必需。

位于斯特拉斯堡的欧洲人权法院,一直忙于对个人就据称违反第8条规定的行为寻求补救的申诉进行裁判。他们的申诉暴露了欧洲法域内若干国家国内法的不足。例如,在加斯金诉英国案中,法院认为,尊重私人和家庭生活的权利使个人有义务向公共当局提供其本人的个人信息。在利安德诉瑞典一案中,法院裁定,如果信息与国家安全有关,例如,为了审查个人的敏感职位,可以合法地拒绝向申请人提供这种信息,但条件是有一个令人满意的程序,可以对不提供信息的决定进行复查。下文将讨论法院在电话监听方面的两项主要裁决。

侵　犯

今天的间谍不再孤立无援地依靠自己的眼睛和耳朵了。正如我们在第一章中看到的，一系列的电子装置使他的任务相对简单。面对技术进步，传统的实物或法律保护手段不太可能特别有效，前者是因为有了雷达和激光束，墙壁或窗户的阻挡毫无意义；后者是因为在不侵犯个人财产的情况下，非法侵入方面的法律将不会帮助被电子监控所困扰的受害者。受保护的利益是原告的财产，而不是其隐私。

对私人场所的实际侵入引起了类似于拦截私人谈话和信件（无论是电子的方式还是其他方式）所产生的问题。没有有效搜查令（通常由法院签发），任何文明社会都不能允许未经许可擅自进入并搜查一个人的住宅。预防、侦查和起诉犯罪行为常常需要警察和其他执法当局对私人住宅进行搜查。这是一个超出隐私保护范围的更深层次的政策问题。不过，尤其是在现代工业化社会，电子监视、截取通信和电话窃听显然需要系统和相当周密的立法机制来控制，特别是在法律允许使用这些装置的情况下，以及在追捕罪犯和执行刑事司法过程中对这些装置的合法运用。

许多民主国家的法律对司法当局秘密监视的行为做了调整。通常，法院的命令规定了对行使这种权力的限制，包括时间限制，因为这种权力尤其有害，它不仅监听被监听对象所说的话，而且还涉及他或她说话的对象。大多数人很可能是完全无辜的对话者。

监控和恐怖主义

在所谓的"反恐战争"中,一个强有力的武器就是窃听器。可以预见,自2001年9月11日的恐怖袭击以来,窃听器的使用有所加强。在这一天之后的六个星期内,美国国会颁布了《美国爱国者法案》。这只是为授权一些执法官员对范围广泛的活动(包括电话、电子邮件和互联网通信)进行监视而采取的若干措施之一。在这之前的一系列法规,如《窃听法》、《电子通信隐私法》和《外国情报监控法》的规定已得到实质性修订,从而大大削弱了它们的隐私保护措施。

隐私权倡导者和公民自由论者谴责了该立法的许多内容。他们关注的一个问题是,该法通过将私人互联网通信置于最低限度的审查标准之下,减少了对电子监控的司法监督。该法还允许执法当局获得事实上的"空白逮捕令";授权"漫无目的"的情报监听令,这种监听令不需要具体说明搜查地点,也不要求只监听目标人的谈话。

该法另一个令人不安的特征是,它赋予联邦调查局(FBI)权力,使之能够利用其情报机构来逃避对宪法第四修正案中规定的"合理根据"的司法审查,因为该修正案要求搜查令要指明具体搜查的地点。它防止滥用权力,例如根据搜查他人住宅的授权对无辜者的住宅进行任意搜查。换言之,在电子监控的情况下,第四修正案的具体要求强制执法官员必须申请法院命令,指明他们希望窃听的电话。

最高法院在1967年卡茨诉美国一案的著名裁决中认为,在公用电话亭外放置监听装置构成非法搜查。政府辩称,由于窃听器实际上不在电话亭内，原告的隐私没有受到侵犯。法院驳回这一观点，并宣称"第四修正案保护的是人民，而不是地方"。尽管法院后来有所退让，但它做出的裁断，即保护应取决于个人在这种情况下是否有一种"合理的隐私权期望"，这仍然是支持应将类似保护适用于互联网通信的主张的关键。然而，就目前而言，《爱国者法案》及其最新的版本，以及相关的措施，都对诸如此类的问题置之不理。

在颁布该法之前，恐怖主义和间谍案件的调查人员在嫌疑人每次更换电话或电脑时，都必须回到法庭，并获得新的搜查令才可以继续调查。

该法案允许秘密法庭发出"流动监听"令，在无法确定特定电话或嫌疑人身份的情况下拦截嫌疑人的电话和互联网通话。换言之，当流动监听令的目标进入他人住所时，执法人员可以窃听该房主的电话。

这些对隐私的立法干预真的有必要吗？根据美国公民自由联盟的说法：

> 联邦调查局已经拥有监督电话和互联网通信的广泛权力。例如，现行法律已经规定，可以对涉及恐怖袭击的罪行进行窃听，包括破坏飞机和劫持飞机行为。《爱国者法案》对监听权的大多数修改不仅适用于对涉嫌从事恐怖活动的人的监视，而且也适用于对其他犯罪的调查。根据《外国情报监控法》（FISA），联邦调查局还有权在没有合理的犯罪根据的情况下截获通信内容，以用于"情报目的"。获取FISA监听的标准低于获取犯罪窃听的标准。

笔式记录器和跟踪装置以电子方式审查电话或互联网通信。所以，一个笔式记录器会监控从一条电话线拨打的所有号码，或者所有的互联网通信都会被记录下来。《爱国者法案》授权联邦法官或地区的治安法官签发笔式记录器或跟踪令，但该命令没有指明可适用的互联网服务供应商（ISP）的名称。实际上，它可适用于美国任何地方的ISP。法官只需签发命令，执法人员填写可以送达命令的地点，从而进一步削弱了司法职能。

核准方式

早在目前的一系列反恐措施出台之前，美国就已在联邦和州一级颁布了若干法规，规定了政府拦截通信之前必须符合的标准。在根据1986年《电子通信隐私法》（ECPA）签发搜查令之前，执法人员必须说明所调查的罪行的性质、拦截点、拟拦截的对话类型，以及可能的目标人的姓名。他需要证明合理根据，且常规的调查手段无效。法院根据该法发出命令授权进行长达三十天的监视（可以延长三十天）。必须每七至十天向法院提交一份报告。

未经法院批准，窃听或使用机器获取他人通信是一种联邦犯罪，除非其中一方事先同意。使用或披露通过非法窃听或电子窃听获得的任何信息也是一种联邦罪行。此外，立法还对防止拦截电子邮件和秘密使用电话呼叫监控的做法提供保护。这些安排包括一种程序性机制，使执法人员能够在符合宪法第四修正案规定的条件下有限地查阅私人通信和通信记录，第四修正案保障不受无理搜查和扣押的权利。并规定除非有合理根据，否则不得发出搜查令。

一种解决方案？

没有完美的制度。但是，人们可以期待民主社会至少以确保其公民合法、合理的期望得到尊重的方式，来规范这种高度侵入性的监视形式。在决定是否批准进行秘密监视的搜查令申请时，法院应确定提议的侵入具有合法目的，应确保调查手段与所指控罪行的紧迫性和严重性相称，同时兼顾监视的需要与监视活动的目标人物和可能受其影响的对象与其他人的侵扰性。必须有合理的理由怀疑目标对象参与了严重犯罪。还应确信，有可能获得与监控目的有关的信息，而且此类信息不能以侵入性较小的其他手段合理获得。

在做出裁决时，人们有权假定，司法官员将考虑到严重犯罪的紧迫性和严重性或对公共安全的威胁、侵入发生的地点、所采用的侵入方法，以及使用的任何装置的性质。

法院应在特定案件情况下考虑"合理的隐私权期望"。在窃听方面，有时会听到这样的建议：如果窃听者是个人，电话用户对隐私的合理期望可被证明是正确的，但如果窃听者是根据合法授权行事的警察，则不会得到确认。虽说这是基于对风险的接受，但很难看出如何可以合法地做出这种区分。如果我有权假设我的私人谈话不会被某个个人听到，那么当窃听者是警察的时候，为什么这个假设就不那么有理据了呢？

另一个反复出现的困难是在"未经同意的监视"而非"参与者监测"的情况下所适用的标准。前者发生在非对话当事方拦截了私人的谈话，而该人没有得到任何当事方的同意。另一方面，"参与者监测"包括谈话一方使用监听设备传递会话的情况给非当事人的第三方，或者谈话的一方未经另一方同意而将谈话录下来。人们经常争辩说，虽然未经同意的监视应当受到法律控制，但参与者监视——特别是在执法中使用——是正当的。但这忽略了对保护谈话内容的关注，也许更重要的是，忽略了谈话的方式这有其特殊利益。此外，尽管参与者监测在侦查犯罪方面是一种有用的帮助，而且可以说，相对于未经同意的监视而言，参与者检测对隐私的威胁较小，但"秘密录音的谈话方能以完全有利于其立场的方式来陈述事情，因为他控制着谈话的情境，他知道自己在录音"。

欧　洲

欧洲人权法院在隐私领域特别积极。简要地比较其两项重要裁决，是有启发性的：一项涉及德国，另一项涉及英国。克拉斯诉德意志联邦共和国案中的电话窃听符合德国法规。然而，在马龙诉英国一案中，没有一个全面的立法框架。虽然两者都涉及模拟电话，但所表达的原则足以适用于数字电话通信系统和拦截书面通信，也许也适用于其他形式的监控。

德国法律对拦截规定了严格的限制条件，包括要求书面申请、事实上有理由怀疑一个人计划犯罪、正在犯罪或已经犯下某些罪行或颠覆行为，而且监视只涉及特定嫌疑人或其拟联系人，因此不允许进行探索性或常规性监视。法律还规定，必须证明其他调查方法无效或困难得多。拦截行动由一名司法官员监督，他只能透露与调查有关的信息，其余信息他必须销毁。截获的信息本身必须在不再需要时销毁，并且不得用于任何其他目的。

法律规定，这些要求一旦结束，必须立即停止拦截，而且在不损害拦截目的的情况下，必须尽可能快的通知被拦截者。他或她随后可在行政法院质疑拦截的合法性，并且，如果损害得到证实，还可在民事法院要求损害赔偿。

此外，《德国基本法》保护邮件、信函和电信的保密性。因此，根据《欧洲人权公约》第8条第2款规定，"为了国家安全的利益……或为了防止混乱或犯罪"，"符合法律"和民主社会所必需的，法院必须裁定干涉是否有正当理由。虽然法院承认有必要通过立法来保护这些利益，但它认为，问题不在于是否需要这些条款，而在于这些条款是否包含充分的保障措施以防止滥用。

申诉人争辩说，立法违反了《欧洲人权公约》第8条，因为它没有要求在监视结束后必须"总是"通知被拦截对象。法院认为，这与第8条并无内在的矛盾，但条件是，一旦可以发出通知，就在监测措施终止后，在不危及这些措施的目的的情况下，立即通知监控对象。

在马隆诉英国一案中，原告在审理一系列和处理被盗财产有关的指控时，得知他的电话交谈被窃听，于是向警察发出了一项令状。他认为，第一，电话窃听是对其隐私、财产和私密性权利的非法侵犯；第二，电话窃听违反了《欧洲人权公约》第8条；第三，由于法律没有授予这种权力，英国政府无权拦截电话。他向欧洲人权法院申诉，并在该法院取得胜诉，这种结果并不令人惊讶。法院一致认定，电话窃听确实违反了《欧洲人权公约》。这种情况导致的结果是，英国政府承认有必要制定一项法规，于是颁布了《1985年通信截收法》。该法案建立了一个相当全面的框架，其核心条款是授权国务卿在其认为为了国家安全、防止或侦查严重犯罪或保障经济福祉所必需的情况下，可签发搜查令。

虽然窃听显然有助于逮捕罪犯、防止犯罪和恐怖主义，但是，想采用这种不分青红皂白的调查方法的人有责任表明这样做的迫切性，并证明这种调查方法可能是有效的，而且没有其他可接受的替代办法。如果无法证明这一点，就几乎不可能证明这种做法是正当的，"不是因为我们想妨碍执法，而是因为我们的某些价值观念比高效的警务工作更重要"。

审慎处理这个问题，可确保在监控材料是以极不合理的方式取得并严重损害公众对司法行政部门的信心的情况下，所获取的信息不应作为证据在法庭上被接纳。

第四章

隐私权和言论自由

　　超级名模娜奥米·坎贝尔被拍到离开戒毒互助所的一次会议，英国小报《每日镜报》刊登了她的照片和声称她正在接受戒毒治疗的文章。她曾公开否认自己是瘾君子，并起诉该报要求赔偿损失。审判法院和上诉法院对她做出了不利的判决，法院认为，由于她向媒体撒谎称自己没有吸毒，因此媒体澄清事实是正当的。但她向上议院提出的上诉获得了胜诉，并因隐私遭到侵犯而获得赔偿。

　　迈克尔·道格拉斯和凯瑟琳·泽塔—琼斯的婚礼照片被偷拍，尽管所有的宾客都收到了明确通知，禁止"在婚礼或招待会上使用摄影或录像设备"。这对夫妇与《OK！》杂志社签订了独家出版合同，但该杂志社的竞争对手《Hello！》杂志社试图刊登这些图片。于是，明星夫妻找了律师并赢得了官司。

　　欧洲人权法院多次揭露了欧洲各国国内法对隐私权保护不足的问题。有一项裁决特别有启发性。摩纳哥的卡罗琳公主抱怨说，一些德国杂志社雇用的狗仔队拍下了她在各种日常活

图14 像超级名模娜奥米·坎贝尔这样的名人很容易被狗仔队穷追不舍

动中的照片,包括在餐馆庭院里吃饭、骑马、划独木舟、与孩子玩耍、购物、滑雪、亲吻男朋友、打网球、坐在海滩上等。一家德国法院做出对她有利的判决,因为这些照片虽然是在公开场合拍摄的,但是在她"寻求隐秘"时拍摄的。

但是,尽管法院承认其中一些照片足够亲密,因此要受到保护(比如她和孩子在一起,或者和男朋友一起坐在饭馆庭院的僻静区的相片),但法院驳回了她对其他照片的诉求。她转而向欧洲法院申诉,该法院承认《欧洲人权公约》第8条适用,但力求在保护公主的私生活与《欧洲人权公约》第10条所保障的言论自由之间取得平衡。法院认定,拍摄和出版照片是对于保护个人权利和声誉具有特别重要意义的一个主题,因为它不涉及"思想"的传播,而是关于包含个人私人的,甚至是私密"信息"的形象的传播。而且,小报刊登的照片经常拍摄于一种骚扰的气氛中,这种气氛使得狗仔队的猎物产生一种强烈的侵扰感,甚至是迫害感。

法院认为,在保护私生活与言论自由之间取得平衡的关键因素是,所刊登的照片和文章对公众利益的辩论所做出的贡献。法院发现,公主的照片纯属私人性质,是在她不知情或不同意的情况下拍摄的,在某些情况下甚至是秘密拍摄的。这些照片对公众利益的争论没有做出任何贡献,因为她并没有参加任何官方活动,而且照片和文章只涉及她私生活细节。此外,虽然公众可能有权获得有关信息,包括在特殊情况下了解公众人物的私生活,但在本案中,他们没有这种权利。了解卡罗琳公主的下落或者她在私生活中的行为举止,即使是在那些不能总被描述为僻静之处,也没有任何正当利益。同样,法院认为,杂志刊登照片和文章可获得商业利益,但这些利益必须让步于申请人有效保护其私生活的权利。

出风头？

娱乐圈名人——电影明星、广播电视明星、流行音乐明星、体育明星和模特等被狗仔队视为可批评的对象。英国皇室成员，尤为引人注目且可悲的是威尔士王妃，长期以来一直受到媒体的折磨。

不断有人声称，公众人物丧失了他们的隐私权。这一论点通常基于以下的推理。首先，有人说名人喜欢在情况有利于自己的时候做宣传，但当情况不利时就会对宣传感到反感。人们认为，公众人物不可能两全其美。其次，有意见认为媒体有权"澄清事实"。因此，在娜奥米·坎贝尔的案件中，由于她隐瞒自己吸毒成瘾这一事实，上诉法院认定，媒体揭露真相是与公共利益有关的。

第一个论断被媒体提出来并不令人意外，它是一个俗语"常在河边走哪有不湿鞋"似是而非的应用。这将敲响保护大多数公众人物私生活的丧钟。不能因为名人追求宣传效应——这是

一个虚假的公共利益？

认为过公共生活就等于主动放弃私生活的论点是荒谬的。还有一种观点也是如此，据报道，"任何事情都可能与评估一个人的性格有关"，许多记者利用这种观点来确立公共利益。的确，任何事情都可能与一个人的性格有关，但并不是与一个人的性格有关的一切事情都属于公共利益。例

> 如，以公共利益为由驱逐同性恋者的恶劣做法也得到了辩护……因此并非所有外表与实际不符的人都是伪君子。一个恐同者，无论自己是否同性恋，仅仅因为他人是同性恋而对其怀有敌意，是不公正的。这是公共利益。但是，如果恐同者本身也是同性恋，那么进一步宣传这一事实，既不受外部言论自由的保护，也不受公众知情权的保护。相反，这是对恐同者隐私权的粗暴侵犯。
>
> 詹姆斯·格里芬，《论人权》，牛津大学出版社，2008年，第240—241页。

获得名望的一个不可避免的特征——就剥夺他们保护自己的隐私不受公众关注的权利。

第二个论点也不完全具有说服力。假设一个名人是HIV病毒感染者或患有癌症。他或她否认自己是这些疾病的患者的正当欲求，就会被媒体"澄清事实"的权利消灭吗？事实果真如此吗？如果是这样，隐私保护就成了脆弱的芦苇。不管事实真伪如何，都不应阻止那些生活在公众视线中的人的合理期望。

但是，有怨气的不只是富人和名人。

普通百姓

佩克先生非常沮丧。有一天晚上，他在布伦特伍德大街上散步时，试图用菜刀割破自己的手腕，他没有意识到自己已经被布伦特伍德区政府安装的监控摄像机拍到。但是，监控录像视频并未显示他实际上是在割自己的手腕，操作员只对出现持刀者的画面有所警觉。警察接到通知后赶到现场,他们没收了刀,并向佩克提供了医疗救助,然后将他送到警察局。根据《精神健康法》,警察扣押了佩克。经医生检查和治疗后,佩克无罪释放,并被警察送回家。

几个月后,区政府公布了从监控录像中获得的两张照片,并配以一篇文章,标题为:"化解危险——闭路电视和警方之间的伙伴关系防止了潜在危险局面的出现"。这篇文章描述了上述事件,然而,佩克的脸没有打上马赛克。几天后,布伦特伍德周刊在其头版刊登了这一事件的照片,为一篇报道举例说明闭路电视的使用情况和好处,佩克的脸又没有被遮挡处理。随后,当地另一家报纸刊登了两篇类似的文章,以及一张从监控录像中截取的佩克的照片,并称潜在的危险局势已经得到解决,佩克已被无罪释放。一些读者从照片上认出了佩克。

然后,监控录像的片段被收录在一个当地的电视节目中,这个节目的观众人数一般能达到三十五万。这次,应政府的口头请求,佩克的身份已被模糊处理。一两个月后,佩克从邻居那里得知他被监控摄像机拍下来了,而且录像已经公布。他没有采取任何行动,因为他仍然患有严重的抑郁症。

监控录像的片段还被提供给BBC全国电视频道的系列节目《打击犯罪》的制作人,该节目观众数量平均为九百二十万人。区政府规定了若干条件,包括在录像片段中不能识别出任何人。然而,一集节目的预告片却显示了佩克没有打上马赛克的脸部。当朋友们告诉佩克他们在预告片里看到他时,佩克向区政府投诉。区政府与制片人取得了联系,制片人确认佩克的肖像已在主要节目中被遮挡处理。但当节目播出时，尽管对佩克的脸部做了模糊处理，佩克还是被朋友和家人认出了。

佩克向英国广播标准委员会和独立电视委员会（现均被英国通信管理局取代）投诉，声称他的隐私被无理侵犯并且还投诉了其他事宜。佩克的投诉成功了。但是，他向报刊投诉委员会就已刊出的文章提出异议，则没有下文。

佩克随后请求高等法院允许就区政府披露监控录像资料一事进行司法审查，而他的申请以及向上诉法院提出上诉的进一步请求均被驳回。因此，他向欧洲法院提出申诉。欧洲法院裁定，区政府公布监控录像的片段是对佩克私生活的过度干预，违反了第8条的规定。法院认为，对该条款中所表述的"私生活"一词更宽泛的解释应包括身份权和个人发展的权利。

仅仅因为这段录像是在公共街道上拍摄的，并不能说明它是一个公共场合，因为佩克既没有参加公共活动，也不是一个公众人物，而且当时是深夜。此外，由于区政府向媒体披露了这一录像，导致其观众数量远远超过了佩克可以合理预见的范围。正是媒体的披露程度侵犯了佩克根据第8条应享有的权利。法院的结论是，区政府本可以在披露录像之前征得佩克先生的同意，并且区政府本应掩盖录像和照片中佩克的脸部。

这个案件是一个重要的依据，即并不能仅仅因为一个人在公共场所，就使其行为被公开，除非在路人亲眼看见的情况下。正是各种各样的媒体进一步的披露，侵犯了佩克根据第8条应享有的权利。

入侵和披露

媒体对信息的追求往往需要使用侵入性的方式：欺骗、变焦镜头、隐蔽装置、对电话交谈或通信的拦截，以及第一章所描述的其他形式的监听和监视。现在有一种倾向，即把窥探新闻的记者所进行的侵入性行为与由此获得的信息的公布混为一谈，而把这两者分开是很重要的。

迪特曼诉《时代》周刊公司一案的判决就理智地采纳了这种立场。在该案中，两名《生活》杂志的记者欺骗原告，使原告允许他们进入他家里，于是他们在原告家中设置了隐蔽的监视装置来监视原告。原告是一个几乎没有受过教育的水暖工，他声称自己可以诊断和治疗身体疾病。由此产生的新闻报道确实让公众了解了一个有新闻价值的话题——无证行医，但法院不得不考虑记者在秘密新闻的采访技巧方面是否享有豁免权。经上诉，法院维持了有利于原告的其隐私受到侵犯的判决。在回应被告声称《宪法第一修正案》的保护范围不仅包括信息发布，还包括调查方式时，法院评论称，该修正案"从来没有被解释为赋予新闻记者在新闻采写过程中对侵权或犯罪行为享有豁免权"。

重要的是，在评估损害赔偿时，法院不仅考虑到侵入行为的性质和程度，而且也考虑到信息发布行为。法院指出："《宪法第一修正案》没有规定保护新闻媒体精心策划的不当行为，（因此）事后发布信息的事实（可能会）导致增加对侵入行为的赔偿。"

不过，就《宪法第一修正案》而言，"收集信息的权利在逻辑上是先行的，而且实际上是行使（发布权）所必需的……除非该先行的权利得到承认，否则无法赋予出版权完整的意义"。普通法不给予媒体收集信息的一般特权。因此，法院正确地将侵入行为和披露行为这两个问题分开，根据由前者发展而来的普通法原则来评估被告新闻采写技术的合理性，并避免任何关于第一修正案的争论，因为这必然会涉及后者。

答案在于制定独立的标准，据此来评估何时可以正当地侵入个人的隐居生活。正如存在着一些标准，根据这些标准来判定何时可以为了公众利益而披露私人事实。

言论自由

我们现在都是信息发布者了。互联网为我们创造了前所未有的言论自由的机会。博客数量以每天十二万的速度增长。社交网络是社区的新形式；Facebook有大约三亿用户，MySpace约有一亿用户。然而，尽管有这些惊人的发展，核心问题仍然是不变的，即如何协调隐私权与言论自由？

电子时代仍然需要解决沃伦和布兰代斯的恳求（已在第三章中有过探讨），法律应当防止因私人信息被无偿公开发布而造成的痛苦。

在民主社会中，言论自由的正当理由是什么？这些理由往往是基于行使自由所产生的积极后果，或者是基于保护个人言论自由的权利。前者——结果论的论点通常借鉴了约翰·弥尔顿和约翰·斯图亚特·穆勒提出的言论自由的理由。后者——基于权利的论点认为，言论是个人自我实现权利的一个不可或缺的组成部分。

图15 披露个人信息通常令人难以抗拒

网络八卦

　　即使网络上的八卦从未出现在传统媒体上，但与在真实空间里相比，网络空间里的八卦能够被更广泛地传播，更容易被误读，重新唤起传统社会中令人窒息的亲密感，却没有遵守在事情发生的背景中进行评判的承诺。事实是，网络上的八卦一旦被记录下来，可以永久检索，并且可以在全球范围内获得，这增加了个人的公众形象因过去的轻率言

> 行而受到威胁的风险。在一个网络聊天小组上发表的八卦，短期内的受众不比一个小镇上邻居间的闲言碎语多多少。但是因为网络上的八卦与个人记忆不同，它永远不会消逝，并且可以在未来被人们重现，而这些人并不了解当事人，因此无法将有关信息置于更广泛的背景中。与小镇上的八卦不同，网络上的八卦很难回应，因为它的潜在受众是匿名的，而且数量无限。
>
> 杰弗里·罗森，《多余的凝视：美国隐私的毁灭》，兰登书屋，2000年，第205页。

这些原则往往会被合并，甚至被混淆。因此，以托马斯·埃默森为例，他识别出以下四种主要理由（这些理由包括上述两种主张）：个人自我实现；获得真理；确保社会成员参与社会决策（包括政治决策）；提供维持社会稳定与社会变革之间平衡的手段。

另一方面，如第二章所述，隐私权的捍卫者几乎完全依赖基于权利的论点。但是，法律在多大程度上可以合法地限制损害个人隐私的言论，常被说成两种重要权利之间的较量：言论自由权与隐私权。但这可能只是似是而非的冲突。为什么呢？因为"在大多数情况下，隐私法和维护新闻自由的法律并不相互矛盾，相反，它们是相辅相成的，因为二者都是个人权利基本制度的重要特征"。

一种更好的路径？

一旦我们把注意力集中在隐私的本质上，隐私的迷雾就会散去。当我们认识到我们的核心关注点是保护个人信息时，这场辩论的真正性质就被揭示了。令人高兴的是（尽管很少有），在浩瀚文献的黑暗深处，一束束睿智之光出现了。例如，在对公开披露侵权行为进行详细讨论之后，一位作者总结道：

> 如果隐私权法的重点是查明（最好是通过法规）哪些信息交流应在其起源地得到保护，而不是继续使用目前反复无常的责任追究办法（只有最终向广大公众传播这些信息，才追究其责任）……那么隐私权法才可能更加公正和有效。认真查明交换个人信息的特别敏感的情况，并同样认真地界定对如何使用这种信息的适当期望，可在不严重妨碍言论自由的情况下大大遏制滥用信息的行为。至少，这种可能性值得较之目前更多的考虑，因为它可以替代沃伦和布兰代斯对于侵权行为所提出的观点。

就连托马斯·埃默森也暗示，可能会有"另一种路径，在我看来更有成效"：

> 这种路径更加强调发展平衡的隐私一端。它会承认宪法第一修正案的利益，但它主要关注一系列因素，这些因素最终源于隐私的功能，以及现代社会中普遍存在的对隐私权的期望。

这些因素中，第一个因素是：

确定隐私范围时的亲密因素。因此，就（公开披露）的隐私侵权而言，隐私权的保护范围将只限于与个人生活的私密细节有关的事项：个人不与他人分享或只与最亲近的人分享的那些活动、思想或情感。这将包括性关系、身体机能的体现、家庭关系等。

因此，有一些积极的迹象表明，寻求隐私与言论自由之间难以捉摸的平衡，使人们对传统路径产生了一些怀疑，这种路径在一种逻辑不自洽的隐私概念中没落。

谁的自由？

言论自由是保护说者的利益还是听者的利益？或者，更煞有介事的问题是，言论自由的正当理由是以个人为基础还是以社群为基础？

前者是以权利为基础的，主张个人自主、尊严、自我实现，以及行使言论自由保障或促进的其他价值的利益。后者是以社群为基础的，是结果主义或功利主义的。它利用民主理论或宣扬真理来支持言论自由，以鼓励不受限制地交流思想、传播信息和扩大参与自治的其他手段。

言论自由和隐私权往往被视为个人的权利或利益——有时与整个社会的权利或利益相提并论。而且，更麻烦的是，言论自由被视为一端，而隐私则被视为另一端，从而这两者的任何"平衡"都有问题！就个人利益而言，它们通常也有着相同的关切。的确，如上文所述，隐私权的社会功能与言论自由的社会功能难以区分。将两者都视为个人权利似乎是简化这一问题的一个重要步骤。

政策和原则

旨在保护受众言论自由的理论一般都是基于这种自由对社群的重要性而提出的政策论点。另一方面，那些促进发言者利益的论点通常是原则论点，它们将个人的自我实现置于社会利益之上。法学家罗纳德·德沃金曾建议，如果言论自由被视为维护发言者的权利，并作为一种原则存在，那么它就有可能得到更有力的保护。从广义上讲，隐私也是基于权利而不是基于目标存在的。如果这是正确的话，将至少有助于促进平衡实践中更大程度的均衡。

不幸的是，这个问题更为复杂。乍看之下，这一策略提供了一个合理的基础，从而不能说损害他人利益的发表行为促进了发言者或发表者自我利益的实现。披露一个超级名模是瘾君子的行为"实现"了谁的利益？谁可以说某些言论形式是否有助于实现这一目标？

而且，这一论点"未能将智力上的自我实现与其他欲望和需求区分开来，因而未能支持一种明确的言论自由原则"。它也是以自由传播思想而非信息的原则为基础的，这就降低了其在当前情况下的效用。最令人尴尬的是，这种观点很难用来维护新闻自由，因为新闻自由似乎完全建立在社会利益的基础上，而非个体的记者、编辑或出版商的利益。

说者的动机是什么？如果说报纸编辑和经营者可能对利润有一点兴趣，这并不过分虚伪。而且，正如埃里克·巴伦特所言，"将以盈利为目的的言论排除在外，如果仔细考察这种动机，将没有什么不受监管"。观众也不一定关心；好的读物就是好的读物,不管作者是受贪婪驱动还是受教化使然。

事实真相

约翰·斯图亚特·穆勒著名的真相论证是基于这样的思想：任何对言论的压制都是一种"无错臆断"，只有通过无限制地传播思想才能揭示真相。但从逻辑上讲，这将阻止任何削弱发言权（至少是说出真相的权利）的行为。除了穆勒关于存在客观"真相"的令人怀疑的假设和他对理性支配地位的信心之外，他的理论使得关于个人信息披露（以及其他几种伤害他人的言论形式）的法律规制变得极其难以证成。这种理论认为，言论自由是一种社会善，因为它是帮助人们增进知识和发现真相的最佳过程，其逻辑起点是，通过考虑正反两方面的所有事实和论点，得出最明智和理性的判断。而且，根据埃默森的说法，这种自由的思想市场应该存在，不管新的观点看起来是多么有害或虚假，"因为没有办法在压制虚假的时候不压制真实"。

但是，从真相出发的论点真的与保护隐私有关吗？弗雷德里克·肖尔质疑真相是否真的是终极的、非工具性的，它是否并未获得诸如幸福或尊严这样的"更深层次的善"的地位？如果真相是工具性的，那么更多的真相是否会因此加强更深层次的善，这是一个事实问题，而不是从定义中得出的必然的逻辑确定性。对肖尔而言，真相的论证是一种"知识的论证"，一种其价值在于让人们相信事情实际上是真实的论证。

> **真相与谎言**
>
> 纵然所有的教义之风在地球上恣意吹动,真相也在场,我们许可和禁止怀疑她的力量,以此来伤害她。让她和谎言相争吧,谁会知道真相在自由和公开的情况中变得更糟呢?
>
> 我无法赞美逃亡的、与世隔绝的人的美德,没有经过锻炼和威胁的美德从不会出击迎面她的对手,而是在竞赛中溜走,在那里,没有风尘劳顿,就不可能追逐不朽的花环。
>
> 约翰·弥尔顿,《论出版自由》(1644),麦克米伦出版社,1915年。

民　主

言论自由在促进和维护民主自治方面发挥着非常重要的作用。正如美国政治理论家亚历山大·米克尔约翰所说的,这是从真相出发的论点的延伸:

> 言论自由原则源于自治计划的必要性。它不是抽象的自然法则或理性法则,它是从美国基本协定中推演出来的,即公共事务应该通过普选来决定。

然而,正如从真相出发的论点一样,我们必须质疑,揭露诸如一个人的性倾向等私密性事实,是如何促进或提升自治的?真是"言论"吗?

在某些情况下，这类信息可能与自治有关：例如，如果通过民选政府行事的人认为某一行动具有足够的反社会性质，构成刑事犯罪，那么逮捕和惩罚罪犯就符合自治利益。同样，如果一个人担任公职，并因此实际上代表人民行事，代表并执行人民的政治观点，那么与他或她适合履行这一职能直接相关的任何活动，都是社会正当的关注点。可悲的是，有太多的政客鼓吹"家庭价值观"，其本人却被曝光为通奸者或更坏的人。在这些例子中，公共利益的检验能够支持言论自由。从民主出发的论点不应该被用来证明隐私领域的言论自由是不受限制的。

新闻自由

从民主出发的论争在这里正如火如荼。对弥尔顿和布莱克斯通来说，言论自由最险恶的威胁来自事先对新闻界的限制。18世纪的法学家威廉·布莱克斯通爵士宣称：

> 新闻自由的确对自由国家的性质至关重要；但这包括不对出版物预先设置任何限制，也包括在出版时免受刑事问题的责难。每个自由人都有在公众面前表达自己想法的无可置疑的权利，禁止这样做，就是破坏新闻自由。但是，如果他发表了不适当、恶意或非法的言论，他就必须承担自己的鲁莽行为所造成的后果。

然而，无论新闻界的概念还是新闻自由的界限，在今天来说，都要宽泛得多。因此，"新闻界"通常不限于报纸和期刊，而包括范围更广的出版媒体：电视、广播和互联网。新闻自由的范围也不限于禁止"事先限制"。

对言论自由的政治辩护是从真相出发的论点的适用。我们应该记得穆勒的第二个假设是"无错臆断",它为我们有信心相信我们所认为的真实的东西实际上是真实的指明了条件。这个论点认为,实现这一目标的最安全的方法是给予个人想法交锋的自由:让这些想法面临矛盾和驳斥。对这种自由的干涉会降低我们获得理性信念的能力。

这是一个强有力的想法,即使它似乎是基于一个理想化的政治进程模式,在这个模式中,民众积极参与政府的政治进程。新闻自由确实有可能使民众产生这种意识并促进其行使。

诉诸真相的民主的论点,为言论自由确立了独立的基础,而基于说者利益的论点则没有。但新闻界发表的很多东西,即使是最慷慨的想象,也与这些崇高的追求毫不相干。这是否表明他们没有资格享受特殊待遇?支持对新闻界给予特殊待遇的论据,往往没有司法依据。显然,如果与《每日镜报》在娜奥米·坎贝尔一案中的情况不同,新闻界冒犯了礼仪,而不是违反了法律,则可以提出更有力的理由。因此,可以用这一论点来说明发表某一特定报告的政治进程的重要性。可以说,关于政府部长、官员、政治家,甚至是皇室成员的私生活的报告,都值得特别对待。在这方面,引起关注的焦点是信息的性质,而不是其传播的媒介。这种方式并不区分是在新闻界还是在酒馆里行使自由。它还有一个好处,就是避免了界定"新闻界"的问题。

《宪法第一修正案》

在美国,言论自由的问题是在《宪法第一修正案》禁令的背景下进行辩论的,该禁令规定:"国会不得制定任何法律……限制言论自由或新闻自由。"美国法院和评论者提出了一些关于言论自由的理论,这些理论既有以权利为基础的,也有结果论的,这些理论试图说明以各种形式行使表达自由的情况。不过,尽管将努力调和隐私权和言论自由所遇到的问题视为一个单独的问题是人为的,但美国的法律似乎确实形成了隐私权/言论自由理论的框架。

特别是,存在着一种对《宪法第一修正案》进行有目的解释的倾向。这就提出了这样的问题:什么样的言论或出版形式由于其对政治民主的运行有贡献而应当受到保护?这种思路被用于将公众人物和普通个人加以区分的若干裁决,其后果各有不同。实际上,最高法院将著名诽谤案《纽约时报》诉沙利文案中采用的原则用于时代公司诉希尔的隐私权案(见下文)。在前一案的判决中,法院明确表达了自己的观点:

> 国家对以下原则做出了深刻的承诺:关于公共问题的辩论应当不受限制、强劲有力和广泛地公开。这些辩论很可能包括对政府和政府官员的激烈、刻薄,有时甚至是令人不快的猛烈抨击。我们就是在这种背景下考虑该案的。

在这种方式中,《宪法第一修正案》的主要目的是保护所有公民了解政治问题的权利,以使他们能够有效地参与民主政府的运作。这一方案为受到无正当理由曝光的个人采取行动提供了相当大的余地。然而,在实践中,往往是那些经常出现在公众视线中的人——正是出于这个原因——吸引了小报的注意。因此，这种理论需要回答的难题是，这些公众人物在多大程度上有权得到涉及其个人生活各个方面的保护。而这反过来又涉及一个微妙的调查，即在推动政治辩论的过程中，公众人物生活中的哪些特征可以被合法地曝光。他的性生活？她的健康状况？他们的财务状况？

尽管这一理论试图区分自愿和非自愿的公众人物，但它的应用，除了作为言论自由本身存在的一般依据外，对涉及不必要曝光的个案中各自的权利和义务，未能提供确定的指导。如果不试图清楚界定各种信息，而这些信息是所有人表面上可能期望得到保护的（即使这种保护随后被公共利益的考量所压倒），那么承认个人对限制信息传播享有利益的核心目的之一——信任、坦诚和信心——就被削弱了。

平衡利益冲突

是否有可能提出一种合乎逻辑的言论自由理论，这种理论既足够广泛，能够反映行使自由的复杂性，又足够明确，能够解释其各种应用？从民主出发的论点得到了比穆勒或以自治为基础的理论更多的支持，但所有这些理论充其量只能在媒体对公开披露个人信息进行合法管制方面提供最一般性的指导。

以利益为基础的理论具体规定了信息披露所涉当事人的特殊利益，这种理论引起了许多困难（与以利益为基础的隐私论述并无不同）。此外，尽管对诸如公布私人事实所涉及的"人格"利益与受到诽谤性出版物影响的"名誉"利益或受到违反保密义务影响的"商业"利益进行区分，是有用的，但这种方式未能解释在面对各种相互冲突的言论自由的要求时，哪些信息种类需要得到保护。

美国最高法院在调解这两种利益时，采用了一种"平衡"程序，将言论自由的利益与诸如国家安全、公共秩序等其他利益进行权衡。如果这些利益被认为是"令人信服的"或"实质性的"，或有明显的现实的危险，即该言论会对公共利益造成重大损害，法院便会支持对言论自由进行限制。

限制的动力

埃默森用这个短语来描述这样一个主张，即言论自由中的公共利益必须符合一种"更全面的社会价值观和社会目标方案"。到目前为止，我已经谈到了某些言论自由的理由是不具有适用性的；我允许隐私权毫发无损地逃脱。如果这两种价值之间存在真正的冲突，如何保护隐私？或者换句话说，为什么言论自由要服从个人信息的保护呢？

在什么情况下，对言论自由的绝对保护可能会受到限制？埃默森提出三种情况。第一种情况是，损害对个人而言是直接和特定的，而不是与他人共同遭受损害。第二种情况是，当利益是私密的和私人的利益时：这种利益包括一个隐私领域，国家和其他个人都应被排除在该领域之外。第三种情况是，社会是否将保护个人利益的责任留给个人，例如承认个人有法律上的诉因。

在前两种情况下，损害可能是直接的且不可补救的。此外，如果个人有责任证明自己的案由，那么国家的资源就不太可能被整合成一个限制言论自由的连贯机制。埃默森认为："只要隐私的利益是真实的，追偿的条件是清楚界定的，救济办法是留待个人诉讼的,则极不可能过分偏重于限制言论。"

即使在《宪法第一修正案》的背景下,埃默森的方法也是有说服力的。而在保障言论自由方面,英国法律在宪法中的沉默也是如此。一位高级法官这样说:

> 除了既有的例外情况,或议会根据《保护人权与基本自由公约》规定的义务可能实施的任何新的例外情况之外,不存在言论自由与其他利益之间的平衡问题,这一点再怎么强调也不过分。言论自由是一张王牌,永远是赢家。

然而,法院承认,"隐私权可能是言论自由的一个合法例外"。其他法官也承认,在一些特殊情况下,打算出版的报刊显然是非法的,会对无辜的人造成严重伤害,或严重妨碍司法公正。另一位法官则宣称,"布莱克斯通非常担心政府干预媒体。布莱克斯通的时代与默多克先生的时代无关"。

公共利益

什么时候才是符合公共利益的?法院一直在努力制定合理的标准,以此来做出这一有争议的判决。似乎与之相关的考虑事项如下:向谁提供信息?受害者是公众人物吗?他或她是在公共场所吗?这些信息是否属于公共领域?受害人是否同意发布信息?这些信息是如何获得的?揭露受害者的身份是否必要?这种侵犯行为严重吗?出版商披露这些信息的动机是什么?

在美国,出版商只需提出基于公共利益或新闻价值的辩护意见，就可以推翻针对媒体无理公布私人事实的防范措施。因此，在席德斯案①中，法院宣称："在某一时刻，公众对获得信息的兴趣将凌驾于个人对隐私的渴望之上。"《第二次侵权法重述》将这种特权定义为扩大到"公众合法关注"的信息，这一结论是通过权衡公众知情权与个人私密事实不受公众关注的权利之间相互冲突的利益而得出的。这可以由法官在法律上或更多情况下由陪审团作为事实问题来决定。《第二次侵权法重述》中的检验内容如下：

> 在确定什么是合法的公共利益问题时，必须考虑到社会的习俗和惯例；归根结底，何为适当的问题变成社区习俗的问题。当媒体不再提供公众有权得到的信息，而变成了为自己的利益而对私人生活进行病态和耸人听闻的窥探时，就会被划清界限。一个通情达理的公众，只要有正派的标准，就会说他不关注他人的私生活。

随着法院越来越意识到审查准确报道所涉及的言论自由问题，具有新闻价值的信息种类也在稳步增加。性事——可以理解——占据了主导地位。两个加利福尼亚的案例就说明了这一点。第一个案例中，一位前海军陆战队队员挫败了暗杀福特总统的企图，从而引起了媒体对他的极大兴趣。《旧金山纪事报》

---

① 该案原告威廉·詹姆斯·席德斯曾是1920年代美国家喻户晓的神童，但青年后沦为平庸，甚至行事古怪。《纽约客》杂志记者采访中年席德斯之后，发表了"伤仲永"题材的文章。席德斯向法院诉称自己多年来保持低调以求回避关注，个人生活不应再受曝光。但法院认为，席德斯既然年少成名，社会基于对儿童教育问题的关心而对其发展轨迹有兴趣，因此席德斯必须继续容忍媒体对他的报道。——译注

透露，西普勒是同性恋社群的一位杰出成员，这的确是事实，对此，他却以公开披露私人事实为由提起侵权诉讼，因为他声称自己一直对自己的亲属隐瞒其同性恋事实。法院以两个理由驳回了他的诉讼。第一，信息已经属于公共领域；第二，法院认为，所披露的事实是有新闻价值的，因为这一揭露行为是希望反对把同性恋者说成是"胆小、软弱和怯懦"的思维陈规，并讨论总统的潜在偏见（有一份报纸指出，总统在感谢西普勒时沉默是因为西普勒是同性恋）。

在另一起案件中，报纸上的一篇文章透露，加利福尼亚州一所大学的第一位女性的学生会主席迪亚斯是变性人。法院认为，其变性是一个私人事实，而且，尽管她卷入了一场公开的争议（因为她指控学校滥用学生资金），但新闻披露的事实与这一问题无关，因此不具有报道价值。法院强调，第一修正案保护的目的是，"让公众知情，以便他们能够就对自治的民众来说至关重要的事项做出明智的决策。" 法院进一步解释说："她是变性人这一事实并不影响其诚实和判断力。她是学生会的第一位女主席，这一事实本身也不能保证她的整个私生活都要接受公众的监察。"

如何调和这两个判决？答案可能就在迪亚斯文章的主旨中。该报认为，该报道旨在描述"妇女在社会中不断变化的角色"，但从文章的语气来看，作者的目的很显然止于"赤裸裸的曝光"。这两个判决的一个重要特点是，这些文章旨在描述不同的生活方式。因此，可以说，如果关于迪亚斯的文章试图认真地描述妇女在社会中的角色不断变化，法院可能就会抵制要求对其进行审查的呼声。

名　人

我们的星球是追星的星球。哪怕是一个名人的最微不足道的流言蜚语似乎也能激起人们极大的兴趣和迷恋。报摊上摆满了各种杂志，不断提供这些转瞬即逝、通常是空洞无物的事实。明星的身份会消灭隐私吗？尽管《美国法律重述》评论说，"可能会有一些生活中私密的细节，比如性关系，这些私密的细节即使是女演员也有权不公开"，但安—马格瑞特诉上流社会杂志公司一案的裁决表明，法院还没有接受这种慎重的态度。在该案中，这位女演员因自己的裸照曝光而寻求法律救济，但被法院驳回。部分原因是这张照片是"一个被许多电影观众幻想的女人"，因此"许多人对这张照片非常感兴趣"。

人们常常声称，法院只是接受新闻界关于什么是有新闻价值的判断。一位作者认为，"遵从新闻界的判断实际上可能是对调查新闻价值的适当而有原则的回应"，但这忽略了主题存在争议的原因。她评述道，出版商和广播公司的生存取决于它们能否提供公众将购买的产品。她还认为，"大部分人希望了解些东西以应对他们生活的社会"，而市场竞争会导致报纸产生出"对这一点的反应"。

公共利益的概念很容易掩盖新闻界的商业动机。更糟糕的是，它伪装成消费者选择的民主实践：我们得到了我们应得的轰动效应。这两种形式的见利忘义的小报忽视了那些碰巧成为公众人物的人所面临的后果，因为他们非常不幸地被抛入了公众视线。

一种道德观的测试

要评估什么是"高度冒犯性",美国法院已经发展出所谓的"道德观测试"。因此,在梅尔文诉里德案中,一部名为《红色和服》的电影揭露了原告过去做过妓女并在一起耸人听闻的谋杀案审判中是被告的事实,这部电影就是以这些事件为基础的。在她被宣告无罪后的八年里,她被"体面的社会"所接纳,并且结婚,加入了新的朋友圈,这些朋友对她的过去一无所知。她因被告的真实披露行为导致其隐私受到侵犯而提起了诉讼,并得到了加利福尼亚法院的支持(该法院之前还未承认过侵犯隐私权的诉讼)。

另一方面,在席德斯诉F.-R.出版公司一案中,原告之前是一名神童,十一岁时在哈佛大学教授数学,后来成为一名隐士,并致力于研究奥卡马克米塞特印第安人和收集有轨电车换乘票。《纽约客》杂志发了一篇文章:"他们现在在哪里?愚人节玩笑",该文由詹姆斯·瑟伯用笔名发表。关于席德斯的身体特征和习惯的细节,他住在哪间单人房,以及他目前的活动都被披露了。该杂志的文章承认,席德斯曾告诉追踪采访他的记者,他生活在曝光的恐惧中,并且一旦他的雇主或同事得知他的过去,他就会换工作。纽约地方法院驳回了他的侵犯隐私权的诉讼,理由是法院认为,"对于报纸或杂志发表正确描述一个人的生活或行为的文章",它找不到"支持侵犯了'隐私权'的裁决……除非是在反常的情况下,这种情况不存在于正在审讯中的本案"。在上诉中,第二巡回法院维持了驳回隐私权诉讼的判决,但似乎是基于对该篇报道的冒犯性与原告的公私特点的平衡而做出的决定。

然而,梅尔文和席德斯都没有适当地试图考虑所披露的信息在多大程度上是"私人的"。"社区习俗"、"新闻价值"和出版物的"冒犯性"等含糊不清的概念,使这些和其他许多关于"公开披露"的裁决在一个具有相当重要的宪法意义的领域毫无帮助。最高法院在涉及影响原告隐私权的出版物方面划定《宪法第一修正案》的界限,也是如此。例如,在时代公司诉希尔案中,法院认为,原告侵犯隐私权的诉讼败诉,因为他(和他的家人)是一份基本上虚假报告的主角。被告发表了一篇文章,描述了一部改编自小说的新剧本,小说虚构了原告及其家人在家中被一群越狱囚犯挟持为人质时所遭受的苦难。

最高法院采用了它对诽谤所适用的检验标准,并以多数票认为,除非有实际恶意的证据(即被告明知故犯地发表了不真实的报道),否则诉讼就会败诉。如果出版物有新闻价值,仅凭虚假并不能剥夺被告受《宪法第一修正案》保护的权利。而且,由于"与实际事件相关的新剧本的开演是一个公共利益问题",原告因为无法表明恶意而败诉。然而,这个裁决似乎并不真正涉及公开披露私人信息问题——不管这是不是一场真正的诽谤诉讼!

未　来

世上没有金羊毛存在。如果明天在任何一个地方颁布一项全面的隐私法令,都会给司法机构带来新的问题,即在司法上对受害者的权利进行司法解释,使其免受不请自来的对其私生活的侵扰。如果法院采取普通法的个案审查的保护路径,这些困难也不会减少。新闻界将继续每天接受考验——或许更集中思考关于报道是否符合"公共利益"的问题。

对公正平衡的追求永远不会结束。关键的问题是，像通常情况那样，个人利益是否要在人为的公共利益的祭坛上被牺牲？对不想要的公开披露进行法定甚至进行非法检查的反对者，喜欢把对受害者的关注描述为过时或大惊小怪。这与新闻界对真相的强烈追求是有区别的。当然，在许多情况下，报纸和所有商业机构一样，受其股东利益的影响，股东对报纸所刊载的内容可能没有对其资产负债表上所显示的内容那么关心。由于新闻界经常承认它应该抵制迟钝地披露私人事实的做法，因此它几乎不可能把这种担心说成是伪善的或吹毛求疵的。

隐私权的拥护者很可能包括言论自由的敌人，但是，与认为主张言论自由的人包括贪得无厌的报纸经营者的论点比起来，这并不是一个更合理的反对理由。然而，永远不能低估新闻界游说团体的力量。有多少职业生涯岌岌可危的政客，希望通过限制报道所谓的"桃色新闻"而招致小报的敌意呢？媒体总爱谴责以公共利益的名义公开私生活，但这同时不可避免地关闭了反对立法的队伍。不幸的是，当大多数小报宣扬家庭价值观时，他们往往很少关心或尊重受害者的家人。

第五章

数据保护

信息不再仅仅是权力，它还是大买卖。近年来，国际贸易中增长最快的组成部分就是服务部门，它占世界贸易的三分之一以上，而且份额还在继续扩大。作为现代工业化社会的一个核心特征，其对信息存储的依赖是司空见惯的事。当然，使用计算机可以大大提高收集、储存、使用、检索和传递信息的效率与速度。

政府和私人机构的日常职能要求其不断地收集有关我们的数据流，以便有效管理作为当代生活重要组成部分的无数的服务。提供保健服务、社会保障、信贷、保险，以及预防和侦查犯罪都需要有大量的个人数据，因此，个人必须愿意提供这些数据。这些通常高度敏感的信息的计算机化加剧了其被滥用的风险。

或者确实是粗心造成的损失。例如，英国最近发生了一些安全丑闻。2008年，载有数千名罪犯信息的电脑记忆棒丢失了；有关巴基斯坦基地组织和伊拉克安全局势的文件被内阁办公室情报官员落在了火车上；2007年，财政大臣承认，载有两千五百万人的个人信息和七百二十万个家庭的私人信息的电脑磁盘不见了。

发　　端

1960年代信息技术兴起，人们对不受控制地收集、储存和使用个人数据所带来的威胁感到日益焦虑。对"老大哥"的恐惧引起了一些国家要求对这些具有潜在侵扰性的活动进行管制的呼声。第一部数据保护法于1970年在德国黑森州颁布。接着是瑞典（1973年）、美国（1974年）、德国（1977年）和法国（1978年）的国内立法。

在这个初期阶段，产生了两项关键的国际文件：欧洲理事会1981年《关于在个人数据自动处理方面保护个人的公约》和经济合作与发展组织（OECD）1980年《关于保护个人数据隐私和跨界数据流动的指导原则》。这些文件制定了管制整个电子数据管理过程的明确规则。自经合组织的指导原则颁布以来，数据保护立法的核心是，在没有真正的目的和有关个人同意的情况下，不应该收集与可识别个人有关的数据。

在稍高一点的抽象层面上，它概括了德国宪法法院所谓的"信息自决"原则——表达基本民主理想的原则。

> **经合组织的原则**
>
> **收集限制原则**
>
> 　　收集个人数据应受限制，任何这类数据应以合法和公平的手段获取，并在适当情况下，应在数据主体知情或同意

的情况下获取。

数据质量原则

个人数据应与其使用目的相关,并在这些目的所需的程度上应准确、完整并保持不断更新。

目的明确原则

收集个人数据的目的,应在不迟于收集数据时明确下来,随后所收集的个人数据只用于实现这些目的或不违反这些目的的其他目的,并在每次目的变更时应进行说明。

使用限制原则

除下列情况外,不得披露、提供或以其他方式将个人数据用于第九段所指明用途以外的用途:

(a)经数据主体同意;

(b)法律授权。

安全保障原则

个人数据应受到合理的安全保障措施的保护,以防丢失或未经授权获取、销毁、使用、修改或披露数据等风险。

开放性原则

在个人数据的发展、实践和政策方面,应有一个开放的总体政策。应有办法方便获得确定个人数据的存在和性质、其使用的主要目的,以及数据控制员的身份和惯常住所。

个人参与原则

个人应享有以下权利:

(a)从数据控制员处获取个人数据,或以其他方式确认数据控制员是否有与他相关的数据；

（b）向他人提供与他有关的数据；

（i）在合理时间内；

（ii）如果有任何费用,该费用并不过分；

（iii）以一种合理的方式；

（iv）以一种他容易明白的方式；

（c）如果根据（a）项和（b）项提出的请求被拒绝,应说明理由,并能质疑这种拒绝；

（d）质疑与他有关的数据,如果质疑成功,数据将被删除、纠正、补齐或修订。

问责原则

数据控制员应负责遵守为落实上述原则而采取的措施。

OECD,《关于保护个人数据隐私和跨界数据流动的指导原则》（第二部分）,1980年9月23日通过。

遵守或更确切地说,执行这一目标（以及相关的获取和纠正的权利）的情况已经融入了制定数据保护立法的约四十个法域中。这些法规大多以上述两项国际文件为基础。欧洲理事会《关于在个人数据自动处理方面保护个人的公约》第1条规定,其目的是在每一缔约国境内,确保每个人,不论其国籍或住所,在自动处理与其有关的个人数据方面,尊重其权利和基本自由,特别是其隐私权（"数据保护"）。

这些原则的重要性再怎么强调也不过分。特别是使用限制和目的明确原则,是公平信息实践的重要准则,加上以公平、合法方式收集个人数据的原则,这些原则提供了一个用以保障使用和披露这类数据的框架,并(在公平收集原则中)限制诸如截取电子邮件信息等侵入性活动。除非数据主体同意,使用或披露个人数据只能用于收集数据的目的或一些直接相关的目的。这一关键原则对管制互联网上个人数据的滥用有很大帮助。但这些原则要求,在已存在的地方更有效率,在部分实施的地方抓紧采用(最明显的是在美国)。

数据保护立法的制定,仅在一定程度上是由利他主义推动的。新的信息技术瓦解了国家边界;个人数据的国际流通是商业生活的一个常态特征。在数字世界中,如果B国没有对个人数据的使用进行控制,那么在B国计算机上检索个人数据,就会使得A国对个人数据提供的保护毫无意义。因此,有数据保护法的国家经常禁止向缺乏数据保护的国家转让数据。事实上,欧盟已在其一项指令中明确要求消灭这些"数据天堂"。如果没有数据保护法,各国就有可能被快速扩展的信息商业拒之门外。

有关处理个人数据的《欧洲联盟指令》

第3条

　　1. 本指令应适用于全部或部分以自动方式处理个人数据,以及以非自动方式处理构成文件系统一部分,或旨在构成文件系统一部分的个人数据以外的其他方式的处理;

　　2. 本指令不适用于下述情况的个人数据处理:不属于

共同体法律范围的活动,在该活动中的数据处理……在任何情况下,都不适用于处理涉及公共安全、国防、国家安全(包括涉及国家安全事务时国家的经济利益)的行动及国家在刑法领域的活动;也不适用于纯粹的个人或家庭活动过程中自然人进行的活动。

第6条

　　1. 成员国应规定,个人数据必须:

　　(a) 公正、合法地处理;

　　(b) 为特定、明确和合法的目的而收集,并且不以不符合这些目的的方式加以进一步处理。为历史、统计或科学目的进一步处理数据不应被视为不相容,但成员国应提供适当的保障措施;

　　(c) 充分、相关和不过分,与所收集和/或进一步处理的目的相关联;

　　(d) 准确,并在必要时不断更新;必须采取一切合理步骤,确保在考虑到收集数据或进一步处理数据的目的的情况下,删除或纠正不准确或不完整的数据;

　　(e) 以一种允许识别数据主体身份的形式保存,其保存时间不超过收集或进一步处理数据以达到目的所必需的时间。成员国应制定适当的保障措施,将长期储存的个人数据用于历史、统计或科学用途。

1995年10月24日的欧洲议会和欧洲理事会指令

数据保护的要点

任何数据保护法的核心,都是"在个案的情况下,以合法及公平"的原则收集个人数据,此处引用1995年中国香港的《个人资料(隐私)条例》的用语,作为这方面的范例。在此类数据的使用和披露方面,未经数据主体的同意,只可将其用于收集数据或某些直接相关的目的。

这些规定得到了六项"数据保护原则"的支持,而这六项原则实际上是立法机制的主干。简言之,第一项原则禁止收集数据,除非这些数据是为与数据使用者的职能或活动直接相关的合法目的而收集的,而且这些数据较之该目的而言是充分而不过分的。个人数据只能以合法和公平的方式收集。这就要求数据使用者向数据主体通报使用数据的目的、可向其传输数据的各类人员、数据主体提供数据是自愿的还是强制的、未能提供数据的后果,以及数据主体有权请求访问和更正个人数据。

第二项原则要求,数据使用者确保所持有的数据是准确和最新的。如果有疑问,数据使用者应该立即停止使用该数据。数据保存时间不应超过为达到数据收集目的所需的时间。第三项原则规定,在未经数据主体同意的情况下,个人数据不得用于收集数据时所通报的使用目的以外的任何其他目的。

第四项原则要求,数据使用者有义务采取适当的安全措施来保护个人数据。他们必须确保个人数据得到充分的保护,不受未经授权或意外的访问、处理、删除或被无权限的其他人使用。第五项原则是关于数据使用者须就所持有的个人数据的种类及其处理个人数据的政策和做法,向公众公布有关信息。这通常通过"隐私政策声明"来实现,该声明包括数据的准确性、保存期、安全性和使用的细节,以及在数据访问和数据更正请求方面采取的措施。

最后一项原则涉及数据主体有权获取关于其本人的个人数据,并要求提供该数据使用者所持有的此种个人数据的副本。如果发现数据不准确,则数据主体有权要求数据使用者更正记录。

受到侵扰或披露的受害人,可向个人数据隐私专员投诉违反这些原则的行为。他(她)有权发出"执行通知",以强制侵权人遵守相关法律,如果侵权人不遵守这种通知,即为犯罪,可处以罚金和两年监禁。法律还规定了赔偿,包括对感情伤害的赔偿。

数据保护法的一个重要元素是隐私专员有权批准实务守则,为数据使用者及数据主体提供"实践指引"。隐私专员迄今颁布的都是实质性文件,是与有关各方进行详细和长时间磋商的结果。此外,虽然法律规定,数据使用者不遵守守则的任何部分,不应导致民事或刑事诉讼,但在这类诉讼中,数据使用者未能遵守守则的指控可作为证据予以采纳。

什么是"个人数据"?

任何数据保护法的出发点都是"个人数据"的概念,或者,在某些法规中,是"个人信息"的概念。在本书中,这个术语已经使用过无数次了,但它具体包括什么呢?尽管各国国内法规之间存在着差异,但它们都对这一用语有着相当宽泛的定义。《欧洲联盟指令》第2条(a)款对"个人数据"采用了以下表述:

与已识别或可被识别的自然人("数据主体")有关的任何信息；可被识别的自然人是指可以直接或间接地被识别的个人，特别是通过身份证号码或与其身体、生理、心理、经济、文化或社会身份特征相关的一个或多个因素予以识别。

但是，通过嵌入在产品或服装中的信息记录程序或RFID标签生成的数据又如何呢？它们不一定是指向个人，但由于它们便于对一个人做出决定，因此应在个人数据的标题下得到保护。

虽然现行立法对个人数据的定义明显包括获取或披露可被适当地称为侵犯隐私权的信息，但其范围之广博，忽略了这些问题。我个人认为，主要是一些私密或机密的信息，应以隐私的名义获得保护。但是，尽管该指令和国内数据保护立法忽视了这种类型的信息，但正如我们将看到的那样，立法并没有完全忽视这种信息。

尽管事实上任何数据保护制度对信息的保护远远超出了基本上属于私人性质的信息，而且其是（也许是不可避免的）程序性而非实质性的性质，但它们为更有效地应对挑战，特别是解决电子隐私问题提供了有用的路标。

《欧洲联盟指令》第25条规定，任何正在处理或待处理的个人数据的转让，必须受到其所送达法域的充分保护。保护是否充分，要参照数据的性质、拟处理的目的和期限、来源国和最终目的国、有关法域内的一般或部门条例，以及安全措施的性质和范围来评估。这立即危及世界上最大的市场——美国的商业前景。我将在下文再回到这个难题。

敏感数据

某些个人信息在本质上比其他信息更敏感,因此需要更有力的保护。这些类型的信息可能是什么?《欧洲联盟指令》第8条要求,成员国禁止处理"披露种族或族裔出身、政治观点、宗教或哲学信仰、工会成员身份,以及涉及健康状况或性生活"的个人数据。但是,这一限制有若干例外情况,其中包括除非国内立法另有明确规定,数据主体明确同意这种处理。在必要时,也允许在就业法领域中保护控制者的权利和义务,或保护数据主体的"重要利益"。

其他欧洲法域的立法也有类似的规定。英国1998年的《数据保护法》将下列数据归类为"敏感"信息:数据主体的种族或族裔出身、政治观点、宗教或类似信仰、工会成员身份、身心健康、性生活、实施或被指控实施的任何犯罪行为,或与实施或被控实施任何犯罪行为有关的任何诉讼程序。

诸如此类的任何清单显然都需要解释。你留在医院的扭伤脚踝的数据明显不如你HIV阳性状态的数据敏感。但是,一定程度的常识应该能够确保这样的区别得以划分出来。

鉴于其高度敏感性,保护病历隐私尤为重要。一个日益严重的问题是,有大量的非医务人员能够获得患者的数据。他们并不总是遵守严格的保密义务。

最近,欧洲人权法院对芬兰政府进行了惩罚,因芬兰政府未能保护医院保存的患者数据不受非法访问。这项判决确立了人权法规定的隐私权与保护个人信息之间的联系。法院认为,《欧洲联盟指令》第8条包含了确保个人数据安全的积极义务。该医院的病历档案系统泄露患者数据违反了芬兰本国的法律，即要求医院保护个人数据，防止未经授权的访问。上诉人是正在接受艾滋病治疗的医院护士，她怀疑她的同事通过阅读她的保密病历，发现她是艾滋病病毒感染者。虽然医院规定禁止查阅这些档案，但为了治疗的目的，实际上医院的所有工作人员都可以查阅患者的病历。

法院认为，医院没有安全的病历系统这一事实本身就足以使其对该名护士的私人医疗数据的泄露承担责任，因为其他原因都无法解释为什么会发生泄露。

同样令人不安的是，存储在磁盘或内存棒上的敏感数据会被粗心大意地丢失。例如，2008年底，伦敦北部一家医院丢失了存有近一万八千名国民保健服务的个人信息的磁盘。医院承认，磁盘是在邮寄时丢失的！

艾滋病患者或艾滋病病毒感染者的病例特别敏感。然而，有人已经提出了一些论据来证明违反这些患者的医疗私密性的正当性。特别是医生需向公共卫生当局报告病例，以遏制疾病的蔓延。事实上，在一些法域，艾滋病是一种需要报告的疾病，因此产生了医生向当局通报艾滋病出现的法律义务。如果要有效地研究艾滋病的起因和扩散，就必须提供准确的信息，这一点显然非常重要。但没有令人信服的理由说明这些数据为什么不能匿名。鉴于这类信息的披露可能产生痛苦的后果，卫生部门有责任证明披露数据的好处大于保护患者的私密性权利。

事实上，如果不能充分保护这些数据，很可能适得其反，许多人可能就不会接受病毒检测。这将使信息来源枯竭，同时也会间接导致疾病的进一步传播。

在医疗数据安全方面的其他一些低级失误使人们对数据保护法的正确执行没有多少信心。伦敦一家顶级医院的两名医生最近进行的一项调查显示，四分之三的医生携带着带有机密数据的不安全的记忆棒。医生经常携带含有姓名、诊断、X光片和治疗细节的记忆棒。在这家医院的105名医生中，有92人持有记忆棒，其中79人的记忆棒存有机密信息，这里面只有5个人的记忆棒有密码保护。

数字数据

计算机和计算机网络的普及实现了几乎可以即时地存储、检索和传输数据——这与手工归档系统的世界相比真是天壤之别。更引人注目的是，控制互联网及其运作或内容的努力，都明显地失败了。事实上，它的无政府状态和对监管的抵制被广泛吹嘘为互联网的力量和吸引力。除了人们有理由认为自己的谈话是私密的问题之外，互联网上的交流性质也会产生不同的问题和期望，因此，需要不同的解决办法。

虽然对数字电话系统的监控（见第一章）看起来与电子邮件的发送和接收类似，但互联网的使用对监管提出了棘手的挑战。例如，虽然监听我的电话或拦截我的信件很简单，但互联网文化鼓励了多种行为，对这些行为的观察为那些希望监管或控制私密数据和敏感数据的人提供了不可抗拒的机会。

数据保护和隐私

但是，你有权问，数据保护与隐私有什么关系？两者之间的关系并非一开始就显而易见。它们显然是重叠的；实际上，后者通常被当作是激发前者的利益。但是，即使在信息社会，个人隐私并不总是被收集、使用、储存或转让个人数据所侵犯。这不仅是因为"个人数据"在数据保护法规中被广泛定义为包括有关"个人"的信息，而"个人"不必然是"私人"的。简单的答案是，在试图保护个人数据时，真正私人性质的信息也会无可奈何地落入保护网中。事实上，认为我们在定义隐私方面遇到的一些问题，在数据保护的框架下可能会得到更实际的解决，也并非完全不可能。

图16 收集和使用个人数据容易且常被不诚实地证明符合公共利益

想想第四章中讨论的派克和卡罗琳公主的案例。欧洲人权法院根据《欧洲人权公约》第8条关于隐私权的条款对它们进行了审议,核心问题是在公共场所秘密摄影的合法性。数据保护法并不是为了全面保护个人隐私而制定的,但它们通常规定,必须以合法和公平的方式收集个人数据。因此,这种立法为隐私权提供了附带保护。

美国之谜

或者也许正是由于其信息市场的规模,美国一直在抵制按照欧洲的方式采取数据保护立法——至少在私营部门是如此。美国的自我管制方法与欧盟模式的全面方法形成了鲜明的对比。这在一定程度上归因于一种回避强有力的监管机构的政治文化——在2008年次贷危机的背景下,这太过明显了。很难想象,独立的联邦隐私专员的任命会获得批准。

为了避免与欧洲的贸易战,美国创建了试探性的"安全港"框架。该计划旨在让欧盟确信,支持该计划的美国公司将提供欧盟数据保护指令所定义的充分的隐私保护。欧盟于2000年批准了这一折中方案。

令人失望的是,该计划只吸引了少数美国公司,因为美国公司不喜欢该计划给它们带来的可察觉的负担。欧盟委员会注意到,一些美国公司并没有遵守这一要求,却在它们可公开获得的隐私政策中声明,它们遵守了这七项原则。此外,这些隐私声明通常并不包含所有的原则,或者声明中存在翻译上的错误。

安全港原则

1. 通告：一个组织必须向个人通报该组织收集其有关信息的目的、如何与该组织联系以进行任何查询或投诉、该组织向其披露信息的第三方的类型，以及个人提出的限制该组织使用和披露信息的选择与手段。

2. 选择：一个组织必须使个人有机会选择（避免）他们提供的个人信息是否且如何被用于或向第三方披露（如果这种使用不符合最初收集信息的目的或与向个人通报的任何其他目的不相符）。

3. 在前转让：一个组织只可向第三方披露与通告原则和选择原则一致的个人信息。

4. 安全：创建、维持、使用或传播个人信息的组织必须采取合理措施，确保其预期用途的可靠性，并采取合理的预防措施，保护个人信息免受丢失、滥用、擅自获取、披露、修改和销毁。

5. 数据完整性：根据这些原则，一个组织只能处理与其收集目的有关的个人信息。在实现这些目的所需的范围内，该组织应采取合理步骤，确保数据准确、完整和及时。

6. 获取方式：个人必须能够合理地获取一个组织所持有的关于自己的个人信息，并能够在信息不准确时更正或修正该信息。

7. 执行：有效的隐私保护必须包括确保遵守安全港原则的机制、因与数据相关的个人不遵守上述原则而受到影响时的追索权，以及不遵守这些原则对组织造成的后果。

> **安全港不安全？**
>
> 　　也许因为它的强制力非常弱，安全港在今天被视为一纸空文。大多数将个人数据输入美国的组织似乎完全无视这一措施。一位就隐私问题向公司客户提供咨询的顾问告诉我，他建议他们就这样做，因为他认为，执法如此松懈，不遵守规定不可能受到任何制裁。
>
> 　　詹姆斯·B.鲁尔，《处于危险中的隐私》，牛津大学出版社，2007年，第138页。

　　实施"安全港"政策的一个重大缺陷是，采用该制度的公司没有一个执行投诉的机制。

网上个人数据保护

　　未来就在此处。我们所创建的数字世界不久将出现光纤网络，以数字码传送几乎无穷的电视频道、家庭购物和银行业务、交互式娱乐和视频游戏、计算机数据库和商业交易。这个宽带通信网络将把家庭、企业和学校与过多的信息资源连接起来。当个人信息以比特的形式呈现时，其易被滥用的情况，特别是在互联网上，是不言而喻的。

　　我们已建立了一个多功能的电信网络，将以前独立的所有网络连接起来。而且，过去功能单一、固定和大型硬件现在变成了多功能、便携式和小型化的，我的iPhone可供我收发电子邮件、做买卖、看电视、读报等。

计算机的容量以惊人的速度增长；根据所谓的"摩尔定律"，计算机的容量每十八个月翻一番，而其价格却不受影响。换言之，经过十五年的时间，计算机的处理和储存能力增强了一千倍。

匿名和身份

如第一章所讨论的那样，匿名是一种重要的价值。但这不一定是我所追求的绝对匿名。相反，对某个人而言，我的信息具有计算机与法律研究中心主任伊夫·普莱所说的"功能的不可识别性"。因此，匿名的概念也许应该被"化名"或"不可识别性"所取代。当然，这项权利不能是绝对的。必须兼顾国家安全、国防，以及侦查和起诉犯罪的要求。这可以通过使用由专业服务提供商向个人提供的"化名身份"来实现，在法律规定的情况下，专业服务提供商会被要求披露用户的实际身份。

传统账户忽略了匿名作为"新隐私"特征的价值和重要性，这是可以理解的。主体的不稳定性是后现代主义的一个中心主题。互联网似乎是一种活生生的证据，证明了一种普遍的、统一的真理的缺失，以及诸如雅克·拉康等后现代主义偶像作品中所出现的自我的偶然性和多样性的思想。

互联网上身份的流动性是其主要吸引力之一，但确定发送者身份的难度可能越来越大，特别是出于商业目的。随着越来越多的业务在网上进行，数字认证可能会变得越来越重要。

数据保护的未来

上面描述的当前数据保护的制度并非灵丹妙药。这一制度不够完善，因此互联网和 RFID、GPS、移动电话等技术的进步给保护隐私权带来了无数难以应付的挑战。普莱很好地描述了这些发展，并提出了一套新的原则来管理这些经常令人惴惴不安的发展。

电子通信服务环境的普遍性和多功能性，以及它们的交互性，网络、服务和设备生产商的国际性，终端和网络功能的不透明性，都威胁到网上隐私。因此，普莱提出了一系列21世纪的原则，包括加密和可逆匿名原则。这对于保护我们的通信内容不被获取，起到了至关重要的作用。普通计算机用户已负担得起加密软件。

另一项原则是鼓励采取符合或改善受法律保护人员处境的技术办法。这可能涉及要求软件和硬件都提供必要的工具，以遵守数据保护规则。它们应该包括最大限度的保护功能，并以此作为标准。

这项义务也适用于处理个人数据的人选择最适当的技术来尽量减少对隐私的威胁。应对第一章所述的促进隐私保护技术的开发给予鼓励和补贴，建立自愿认证和认证制度，并以合理的价格提供促进隐私保护技术。

硬件操作应该透明；用户应该对发送和接收的数据有完全的控制权。例如，他们应该能够很容易地确定在他们的计算机上聊天的程度、收到了哪些文件、其用途是什么，以及发送者和接收者是谁。任何试图阻止弹出窗口的人都会知道这个过程是多么的困难，令人十分沮丧。若没有激活信息记录程序抑制器，就不能被理解为全权同意对其进行安装。

我们的网上生活所需要的保护相当于我们在物质世界中作为消费者所享有的法律保护。为什么网上冲浪者应该容忍资料收集、垃圾邮件、差异化服务访问等？网上消费者保护立法可为一系列服务敞开大门，包括规定互联网服务供应商的职责、搜索引擎、数据库，以及防止不公平竞争和商业做法的措施。此外，正如普莱所主张的那样，为什么硬件和软件的产品责任不应超出人身和财产损害的范围，而应当包括数据保护规范的侵权责任？

Web2.0的出现使社交网络大规模爆发，Facebook和MySpace等社交网站、YouTube和Flickr等视频分享网站（这些网站均可用于共享照片），以及用户自己编写的在线百科全书维基百科的出现，明显有牺牲隐私的代价。社交网络的成员可能对广泛传播其个人信息的后果一无所知。当然，网络供应商应该告诉他们如何限制这些数据被访问。他们应该为一般的个人数据提供选择退出渠道，为敏感数据提供选择进入渠道。用户需要知道，他们的个人数据几乎没有或根本没有受到任何可以防止被复制的保护，无论这些数据是否与自己或他人有关。

除此之外，还存在其他的隐私风险。例如，Facebook允许用户在自己的简介中添加小工具，并在不离开Facebook网站的情况下使用第三方应用程序。但这引起了一些隐私问题。当用户安装Facebook应用程序时，该应用程序可以看到用户能看到的任何内容。因此，应用程序可以获得关于用户、用户的朋友，以及同一个网络的其他成员的信息。没有任何东西可以阻止应用程序的所有者收集、查看和滥用这些个人信息。Facebook的使用协定条款敦促应用程序开发者不能这样做，但Facebook没有办法发现或阻止他们从事这些活动。虽然在加拿大隐私专员的压力下，Facebook最近修改了其隐私政策，从而使得应用程序在没有得到每个朋友明确许可的情况下无法访问用户的好友信

隐私

图17 英国政府关于推行指纹和其他个人数据中央数据库的提议引起了相当大的异议

息。用户通常把他们在社交网站上的个人简介视为一种自我表达的形式,但这些信息对营销公司、相互竞争的网站和身份盗用者而言具有商业价值。数据挖掘具有严重的隐私问题：它暴露了在其他情况下可能被隐藏的信息。这是一个从不同角度分析数据,并将其归纳为可用于增加收入、降低成本或两者兼而有之的信息的过程。数据挖掘软件允许用户从多个角度分析数据、对数据进行分类,并评估已识别的关系。换言之,它可以在大型关系数据库中搜索众多字段之间的相关性或模式。

尽管数据挖掘在商业、医学或科学领域中非常有价值,但它确实会对隐私造成风险。在没有模式的情况下,原始数据片段基本上是毫无价值的。但是,当挖掘数据时,如果挖掘出的数据揭露出原本无害的行为模式,隐私威胁就会迅速地显现出来。

第六章

隐私的消亡？

"隐私已死。忘掉它吧。"太阳微系统公司的首席执行官斯科特·麦克尼利这样说。他并不孤单；越来越多的悲观主义者和预言家已经宣告了隐私的消亡。然而，演奏隐私的安魂曲尚为时过早。入侵者已在城门口，但是城堡中的人不会不战而降。

重要的迹象

然而，对许多隐私倡导者来说，隐私仍然是有呼吸的生命体，只是需要紧急恢复。隐私国际、电子前沿基金会（EFF）、电子隐私信息中心（EPIC）和其他几个团体继续发起一场艰苦的战争，反对"老大哥"似乎势不可挡的征服。自2001年"9·11"事件以来，这场战争变得特别具有挑战性。

这方面的例子比比皆是。2009年初，英国政府宣布，为了保障2012年伦敦奥运会的安全，英国政府任命一家国防公司EADS开发一个名为DYVINE的系统，该系统让中央警察控制室可以远程接入伦敦的任何闭路电视网络，并将信息绘制在一张详细的3D地图上。这引起了人们对闭路电视二十四小时全面监控的担忧。该系统将包括车辆号牌识别摄像头，以及诸如在购物中心和停车场运作的私人网络。这将有助于在全市范围内追踪嫌疑犯。先进的计算机情报系统将帮助官员们过滤掉进入控制室的无关信息，只留下最相关的闭路电视信息，从而缩短了以往从一台摄像头到下一台摄像头所花的时间。

诸如此类的系统所引发的焦虑集中在第一章讨论过的各种形式（包括电子和其他形式）的监测和侵入对隐私构成的危险。但是，在第四章中讨论的追求耸人听闻的流言蜚语的过程中，媒体也在持续地进行着同样令人不安的攻击。这两方面的问题都值得在此做一番简短的总结。

> **记忆由比特（bits）[①]构成**
>
> 摩尔定律和万维网已经改变了一切。这个世界与冷战时期的世界非常不同。麦克卢汉[②]的地球村终于到来，我们的事就是大家的事。技术的变革与意识形态的变化和对权威的不尊重意味着透明度的急剧增加，我们在可预见的将来将无法回到不透明状态。如果人们意识到他们所做事情的后果，如果他们牢记对某一行为的记忆会比此刻的记忆更长久，而且故事的受众比听众或即时的读者群体要广泛

---

① 此处语带双关。"bit"既有碎片、片段之意，也表示比特（计算机的最小信息量单位）。——译注

② 马歇尔·麦克卢汉，加拿大著名哲学家和媒介理论家。——译注

> 得多，那么他们就能够做到人们擅长的事情——根据不同的语境协商出一套细致入微的策略来披露信息。但他们需要充分意识到，线上的语境与线下的世界有些不同，特别是数字"记忆"会持续到遥远的未来。
>
> K. 奥哈拉和N. 夏伯特，《咖啡机里的监控》，Oneworld，2008年，第230页。

技术与安宁

技术创新的步伐将继续加快。与此相伴的是，我们的私生活将受到新的、更加隐蔽的侵犯。但是，隐私作为一种民主价值观实在是太重要了，不经过斗争，就不可能被击败。确实，尤其是在面对真实的或感知到的威胁时，许多人为了换取安全或安全保障而不惜牺牲自己的隐私——即使有证据表明，例如，闭路电视摄像机的扩散在遏制犯罪方面只取得了有限的成功。

因此，对隐私的侵蚀往往产生于静止的聚积：通过冷漠、漠不关心或对包装成必不可少的或看似无害的措施的默认支持。我们不应该假装在我们的数字世界里，对侵犯隐私行为的监管是毫无问题的，事实远非如此。网上隐私必然会继续受到广泛的攻击。然而，网络空间容易受到一定程度的控制，不一定是法律控制，而是通过其基本构成，即网络空间的软件和硬件。莱斯格认为，这样的代码要么产生一个自由的处所，要么产生一个压迫性控制的处所。实际上，商业上的考量日益使网络空间显然更容易受到管制；网络空间已成为一种处所，在那里，行为受到的控制比现实空间更严格。最后，他坚持认为，这个问题由我们自己来决定，如何选择是如何架构的问题：应该由什么样的代码来管理网络空间，又由谁来控制代码。在这方面，代码是核心的法律问题。我们需要选择激活代码的价值观和原则。

我们反对掠夺的辩护，还需有制定并积极执行适当的法规和行为守则的政治意愿。现有的数据保护法需要不断修订和更新，如果没有这种法律，则应立即颁布。隐私办公室或信息事务专员需要足够的资金，以便有效监管立法和其他对隐私的威胁，并适当管理和提供咨询、信息。一个拥有适当资金、获得适当支持和称职的隐私专员可以作为我们个人数据的保卫者发挥不可或缺的作用。

软件和硬件制造商、服务供应商和计算机用户的合作，以及关于如何最好地保护个人信息的咨询和信息，是任何隐私保护策略的关键组成部分。

第一章中所描述的促进隐私保护技术对于打击侵犯隐私技术的重要性，再怎么强调也不过分。人类创造了科技。因此，科技既会侵害我们的隐私，也会改善我们的隐私保护状况。防火墙、反黑客机制和其他手段是第一道防线。例如，通过P3P（见第一章）表达个人的隐私偏好，是保护我们正在消失的隐私的另一个重要方式。它是如何工作的？例如，"隐私鸟"的隐私首选项设置面板允许你设定个人隐私偏好。当它遇到不符合你的隐私首选项的网站时，浏览器标题栏会显示一个红色的警告图标。有三种预先设定的设置：低级、中级和高级。当你选择一个设置时，在该设置下触发警告的特定项旁边将出现一个√的标记。

低级设置仅在可能使用健康或医疗信息的网站上生成警告，或者帮助你拦截无法删除的营销消息或邮件。中级设置还包括一些额外的警告，当网站可共享你的个人识别信息，或者网站不允许你建立他们持有的关于你的数据时，也会触发警告。高级设置触发的警告数量最大，包括大多数商业网站。

促进这种首选项偏好设置的技术方法正在出现，与之同时出现的还有数据收集者可借此了解其责任的工具。

各类压力团体、非政府组织、说客和隐私倡导者在提高人们对隐私受到无情侵犯的意识方面发挥着至关重要的作用。

虽然数据库和网络在收集、储存、传输、监测、链接和匹配大量个人信息方面的超常能力，显然带来了相当大的风险，但技术同时也是我们的对手和盟友。

追逐狗仔队

飞短流长的欲望不太可能减弱。人们将继续通过未经授权披露个人信息的方式——线下和线上——来满足这种欲望。媒体以印刷品和数字形式、博客、社交网站和私人事实的其他在线传播者，无论是自愿的还是未经请求的，都对任何形式的监管或控制构成了难以应对的挑战。

狗仔队的力量几乎没有减弱的迹象。虽然它们的侵扰行为往往与其公布的成果混为一谈，但人们普遍承认一点，即法律在这两方面都有不足之处。

人们至少提出了四种可能的解决办法。第一个方法试图将侵犯隐私的记者和摄影师的行为入罪。例如，加利福尼亚州（其宪法明确保护隐私）颁布了一项《反狗仔队法》，对通过拍照、录

图18 这些摄影师在追逐戴安娜王妃的汽车（戴安娜王妃死于那辆车里）后被捕

像或记录某人从事"个人或家庭活动"，从而"现实的"和"建设性的"侵犯隐私的行为规定了侵权责任。

第二条反击的路线试图劝诱或迫使媒体采取各种形式的自我管制。特别是在英国，为在这一点上达成妥协从而避免立法控制，做出了长期努力，但成效甚微。

第三种做法是按照美国侵权法的思路，对故意侵犯原告的隐居或独处权，或干涉其私人事务的行为立法。这种责任不同于公开披露因侵入而获得的信息可能引起的责任。

第四个创新策略是打击狗仔队的软肋——他们的钱袋子。通过拒绝承认他们对其图片享有版权，遏制他们窥探和发表的冲动——因为这些图片将不会归他们出售。因此，如果一家小报可以重新刊发一张由狗仔队秘密获取的流行明星的照片，而不必支付大量的费用，那么这些图片的市场就会大幅下跌。狗仔队就会被击倒。

在普通法域已经存在一种薄弱但相当少见的权威范围，它拒绝给予不道德的、欺骗性的、亵渎性的或诽谤性的材料以版权，但在今天，这种做法不大可能被援引。这一提议将扩大道德沦丧行为的范围，这些行为可能导致法院拒绝对其提供保护。但是这个想法是人为的、不切实际的，并且在概念上是有问题的。如果要将隐私纳入版权范畴，那么在大多数情况下，法律所要保护的与其说是隐私权，不如说是原告的公开权，即控制在何种情况下可以买卖自己的肖像的权利。这种对狗仔队问题适当处理的吸引力是可以理解的；事实上，财产利益在隐私权的法律观念诞生时就已经存在了。如第三章所述，承认普通法保护隐私的美国第一项判决就涉及侵犯姓名或肖像权：被告为商业利益而使用——通常是为了广告目的而使用原告的身份。

但隐私本身就应该受到保护；偷偷摸摸的补救办法最终会适得其反。如何保护隐私？理想的答案是明确的、认真起草的立法，规定对严重冒犯、蓄意或鲁莽地侵犯个人的独处或隐居，以及未经授权公布个人信息的行为实施民事和刑事制裁。当然，正如在第四章中所讨论的那样，隐私总是要与言论自由相平衡。

无论是在工作中还是在家里，我们都无权认定我们的网上应用程序是安全的。我们必须同时依靠技术和法律所提供的庇护。人们常说，技术既会引起弊病，也会产生一部分解决方法。虽然法律很少能成为对付蓄意侵入者的有力武器，但保护性软件的进步、《欧洲联盟指令》所采用的公平信息做法，以及若干法域的法律，为个人数据的收集、使用和转让提供了合理和健全的规范性框架。它对个人信息的实际使用情况、收集方式，以及个人的合法期望进行了务实的分析。这些问题将在我们不确定的将来中长期主导有关隐私的讨论。我们如何处理这些问题，可能会决定我们以后能否过上秘密的生活。

附　录

《非政府组织关于建立全球隐私权标准的宣言》
西班牙马德里,2009年11月3日

非政府组织申明隐私权是一项被《世界人权宣言》、《国际公民及政治权利公约》和其他人权文件及国家宪法所规定的基本人权。

非政府组织提请欧盟成员国履行1995年《数据保护指令》和2002年《电子通信指令》所规定的义务。

非政府组织提请其他经济合作和发展组织的成员国遵循1980年经合组织《隐私权指导意见》所规定的原则。

非政府组织提请所有国家根据其本国宪法、法律及国际人权法的有关规定维护本国国民的公民权利。

非政府组织期待强化保护隐私权和个人数据的法律条款在欧盟生效。

非政府组织注意到急剧扩张的秘密和不负责任的监控措施、不断增长的政府与建立新型社会控制的监控技术的提供者之间合作的警示作用。

非政府组织注意到调查著作权侵权和其他非法内容的新型

策略对通信秘密、创作自由、正当程序造成了实质性的威胁。

非政府组织注意到基于互联网的服务在不断整合及某些公司正在没有独立监督的情况下获取大量的个人数据。

非政府组织警惕隐私权法和隐私权机构不能及时监管行为倾向调查、脱氧核糖核酸数据库和其他生物识别技术等新的监控措施、数据在公共和私人机构之间的融合,以及对儿童、移民和少数民族等弱势群体的特殊威胁。

非政府组织警惕由于隐私权保护的疏漏对言论、结社、获取信息、反歧视等相关自由及最终对宪政民主的稳定性的危害。

因此,非政府组织借第三十一届国际隐私权和个人数据保护专员会议之机,提出如下宣言:

(1)重申对建立公平信息做法的全球框架的支持,即收集和处理个人信息的一方应当承担义务,而个人信息的主体应当享有权利;

(2)重申支持建立独立数据保护政府机构,以在法律框架内透明地、不受商业利益和政治影响干预地做出决定;

(3)重申支持真正的隐私权强化技术,以保证对个人识别信息收集的最小化或者简化,以及与隐私权标准一致的有意义的隐私权影响评估;

(4)呼吁仍然没有批准欧洲理事会一零八公约及2001议定书的国家尽早采取行动;

(5)呼吁还没有建立广泛的隐私权保护体系和独立数据保护机构的国家尽早采取行动;

(6)呼吁已经建立隐私权保护法律体系的国家保证有关规定的有效实施和执行,并参与国际和地区的有关合作;

（7）呼吁所有国家保证个人信息以与收集目的不同的方式被不适当地公开和使用的个人及时得到通知；

（8）建议充分研究"非识别化"数据的技术是否满足需要，以便决定是否这些方法在实践中保护了隐私权和匿名性；

（9）呼吁在发展和实施面孔识别、全身影像、生物识别符号、埋置性无线频谱认证标签等新的大型监控系统之前建立延迟期，以便由独立的官方机构充分与透明的研发和民主的辩论；

（10）呼吁建立有非政府组织充分参与的、基于法治的、尊重基本人权的和支持民主制度的新的国际隐私权保护体系。

索 引

（条目后的数字为原书页码，见本书边码）

A

abortion 堕胎 30, 39—40, 61
AIDS/HIV, persons with 艾滋病患者/艾滋病毒感染者 120—121
Albert, Prince 阿尔伯特亲王 51—52
animals 动物 30, 31
anonymity 匿名 23—25, 43, 127—128
anti-privacy moments 反隐私时刻 46
appropriation of name or likeness, tort of 盗用姓名或肖像的侵权行为 58, 139
associational privacy 结社隐私 59
Australia 澳大利亚 64—66
autonomy 自主 4, 34—35, 42, 101

B

Barendt, Eric 巴伦特，埃里克 95
behaviour, adaption of 行为的调整 4
Bentham, Jeremy 边沁，杰里米 3
biometrics 生物识别技术 7, 9, 10—12
biotechnology 生物技术 9
Blackstone, William 布莱克斯通，威廉 97—98, 103
bots 机器人程序 13
Brandeis, Louis D. 布兰代斯，路易斯·D. 1, 54—60, 90, 92
breaches of confidence 违反保密义务 29, 63—64, 101, 120—122
bugs (computers) 漏洞（电脑）13
bugs (electronic listening devices) 窃听器（电子监听装置）2, 4—7, 71—80
buying and selling privacy 买卖隐私 45

C

Campbell, Naomi 坎贝尔，娜奥米 81—82, 99
Canadian Charter of Rights and Freedoms《加拿大权利和自由宪章》69—70
Caroline of Monaco, Princess 摩纳哥的卡罗琳公主 83—84
CCTV 闭路电视 1, 2, 4, 8—10, 86—87, 133—135
celebrities 名人 38, 63—64, 66, 81—85, 94—95, 98—100, 103, 105—108
China 中国 32
civil law jurisdictions 大陆法系法域 67—70
cloning 克隆 17
codes of practice 实务守则 117—118
cookies 信息记录程序 1, 14—15, 129
common law 普通法 54, 56, 58, 63—67, 69—70
computers 计算机 9, 15—18, 22; 参见 Internet
confidentiality 私密性 20, 29, 39, 79, 121
consequentialism 结果论 90—91, 93, 99
constitutional right to privacy 宪法

隐私

中的隐私权 60—63, 67—69
contraception, use of 节育措施的使用 40, 59
control of information 信息控制 42—43, 46, 49, 72
copyright 版权 23—24, 138—139
counsel, privacy of 律师隐私 59
crackers 解密高手 13
credit cards 信用卡 18
crime 犯罪 36, 64, 69
 anonymity 匿名 128
 biometrics 生物识别技术 12
 cyber crimes 网络犯罪 9, 17—18
 displacement 转移 8
 DNA 脱氧核糖核酸 9, 21—22
 entry and search, unauthorized 未经许可擅自进入和搜查 72
 fingerprints 指纹 10—11, 21, 131
 identity theft 身份盗用 17—18
 paparazzi 狗仔队 138
 private morality 私人道德 34
 surveillance 监控 8—9, 72, 135
culture 文化 44—45, 50

D

damages 损害赔偿 89
data mining 数据挖掘 130—131
data protection 数据保护 110—132
 AIDS/HIV, persons with 艾滋病患者／艾滋病毒感染者 120—121
 anonymity 匿名 127—129
 CCTV 闭路电视 10
 codes of practice 实务守则 117—118

confidentiality 机密 121—122
Council of Europe Convention 1981《1981 年欧洲理事会公约》 111, 113—114
Data Protection Directive《数据保护指令》114—116, 118—119, 123, 139
data protection principles 数据保护原则 116, 124—125
encryption 加密 129
identity and anonymity 身份与匿名 127—128
identity cards 身份证 20
Internet 互联网 114, 122, 126—131, 139
lawful and fair means, collection by 通过合法和公平的方式收集 114—116
medical records 病历 120—121
OECD principles OECD 原则 111—112
personal data 个人数据 110, 114, 116—119, 122—124
privacy commissioners 隐私专员 117—118, 135—136
privacy-enhancing technologies (PETs) 增进隐私保护技术 129
private and family right, right to respect for 个人和家庭权利获得尊重的权利 120, 124
Safe Harbor framework 安全港框架 124—126
security 安全 117, 119, 121
sensitive data 敏感数据 110, 119—122

140

telecommunications network 电信网络 126—127

telephone tapping 电话窃听 2, 4—7

transfer of data 数据传输 114, 124—126, 130

United States 美国 124—126

databases 数据库 10, 18—22, 131

deception 欺诈 37

decisional privacy 决策隐私 1, 40

definition of privacy 隐私的定义 38—45

democracy 民主 24, 96—101

Denial of Service (DoS) attacks 拒绝服务攻击 13

Diana, Princess of Wales 戴安娜，威尔士王妃 84

Digicash 电子钱币 23

digital signatures 数字签名 25

disclosure 披露 42—45, 47—50, 58—59, 65—66, 68, 92

discrimination 歧视 22

DNA 脱氧核糖核酸 9, 10, 11, 21—22, 48

doctor-patient confidentiality 医患保密 120—121

domestic oppression 家庭内部的压迫 35—36

Douglas, Michael 道格拉斯，迈克尔 65, 81

Dworkin, Ronald 德沃金，罗纳德 60, 94

E

e-cash 电子现金 23

economic value of privacy 隐私的经济价值 36—38

electronic copyright management systems (ECMS) 电子版权管理系统 23—24

electronic listening devices 电子监听装置 2, 4—7, 71—80

Emerson, Thomas 埃默森，托马斯 91, 93, 96, 101—103

encryption 加密 24—26, 129

entry and search, unauthorized 未经许可擅自进入和搜查 72

EU law 欧盟法 14, 114—116, 118—119, 123, 139

European Convention on Human Rights《欧洲人权公约》

DNA 脱氧核糖核酸 21

freedom of expression 言论自由 83

Germany 德国 77—79

Human Rights Act 1998《1998年人权法案》62

photographs of celebrities 名人的照片 81—83

private and family right, right to respect for 个人和家庭权利获得尊重的权利 64, 71, 78—79, 83—84, 87—88, 120, 124

surveillance 监控 78—79

exploits 利用 13

expression, freedom of 言论自由；见 freedom of expression

F

false light, placing person in 把某人

隐私

置于虚假的宣传中 57—58

female oppression 对女性的压迫 36

fingerprints 指纹 10—11, 21, 131

France 法国 10, 62, 68—69

fraud 欺诈 17—18

freedom of expression 言论自由 49, 69, 89—109, 139

 anonymity 匿名 24

 celebrities, media and 媒体和名人 100, 103, 105—107

 common law 普通法 63

 democracy 民主 96—101

 European Convention on Human Rights《欧洲人权公约》83

 individual or community-based, as 以个人或社群为基础的 93

 Internet 互联网 89—91

 limitation, dynamics of 限制的动力 101—103

 media 媒体 95, 97—109

 mores test 道德观测试 106—108

 policy and principle 政策和原则 94—95

 press freedom 新闻自由 95, 97—99, 101—102

 private and family right, right to respect for 个人和家庭权利获得尊重的权利 83—84

 public interest 公共利益 97, 103—106, 108—109

 truth 真相 95—96

 United States 美国 24, 99—101, 102—108

freedom of the press 新闻自由 95, 97—99, 101—102

G

Gemeinschaft and Gesellschaft, distinction between 社区与社会之间的区别 33

genetic information 基因信息 21, 29

geographic information systems (GIS) 地理信息系统 29

Germany 德国 10, 67—68, 77—79, 111

global positioning system (GPS) 全球定位系统 28—29

gossip 流言蜚语 38, 57, 91, 105—106, 134, 137

Greeks 希腊人 32

H

hacking 黑客 15—17

harm 伤害 34, 69, 102

harassment 骚扰 83

homosexuality 同性恋 40, 60—62

Hong Kong 香港 18—20, 116

human rights 人权 66—67, 69—70; 参见 European Convention on Human Rights

I

identity 身份

 anonymity 匿名 127—128

 cards 证件 9, 18—20

 compulsory cards 强制性身份证 18

identity theft 身份盗用 17—18, 20
smart cards 智能卡 19—20
images, use of 肖像的使用 56, 58, 59, 69
individuality 个性 34—36
interception of communications 拦截通信；见 surveillance
intermediary services 中介服务 23
Internet 互联网 134—137
  anonymity 匿名 23, 24
  data mining 数据挖掘 130—131
  data protection 数据保护 114, 122, 126—131, 139
  freedom of expression 言论自由 89—91
  malware 恶意软件 12—13
  P3P (Platform for Privacy Preferences) 隐私偏好平台 26—27, 136
  police, remote searches by 警察远程搜查 14
  service providers 服务供应商 75, 130
  social networking sites 社交网站 130
  surveillance 监控 8, 73—75
  terrorism 恐怖主义 73—75
International Covenant on Civil and Political Rights (ICCPR)《公民权利和政治权利国际公约》66, 70
inviolate personality axiom 不可侵犯的人格原理 56
Ireland 爱尔兰 67
Italy 意大利 68—69

K

Kalven, Harry 卡尔文,哈里 58

L

legal right to privacy 法定的隐私权 52—80, 92
  Canadian Charter of Rights and Freedoms《加拿大权利和自由宪章》69—70
  civil law 大陆法 67—70
  common law 普通法 54, 56, 58, 63—67, 69—70
  France 法国 68—69
  Germany 德国 67—68
  international dimension 国际层面 70—71
  Italy 意大利 69
  Netherlands 荷兰 69
  personality rights 人格权 67—69
  publicity, right of 公开权 59
  Quebec Charter of Human Rights《魁北克人权宪章》70
  tort 侵权 58—60, 92
  United States 美国 53—60
Lessig, Lawrence 莱斯格,劳伦斯 45, 134
let alone, right to be 独处的权利 1, 59, 60
likeness or name, appropriation of 盗用肖像或姓名 59, 139
locational privacy 位置隐私 1, 41
Loki global positioning system (GPS) 洛基全球定位系统 29

London Olympics 伦敦奥运会 133—134

loss of privacy 隐私的丧失 42—44

M

Madrid declaration on privacy 马德里隐私宣言 139

malware 恶意软件 12—13

media 媒体 47, 49, 54, 56—57, 59, 81—87
    celebrities 名人 94—95, 99—100, 103, 105—107
    damages 损害赔偿 89
    freedom of expression 言论自由 95, 97—109
    freedom of the press 新闻自由 95, 97—99, 101—102
    gossip 流言蜚语 105—106, 134
    harassment 侵扰 83
    Netherlands 荷兰 69
    news gathering 新闻采集 88—89
    newsworthiness 新闻价值 106—108
    ordinary people 普通人 86—88
    paparazzi 狗仔队 81—83, 137—139
    personal information 个人信息 101
    photographs 相片 81—83, 137—139
    prior constraints 事先的限制 98
    private and family right, right to respect for 个人和家庭权利获得尊重的权利 87—88
    publicity, right of 公开权 139
    self-regulation 自我管制 138
    surveillance 监控 86—89
    United States 美国 88—89, 138—139

medical records 病历 120—121

Meiklejohn, Alexander 米克尔约翰, 亚历山大 97

microchips 微芯片 11—12, 19, 27—28

Microsoft 微软 13

Mill, John Stuart 穆勒, 约翰·斯图亚特 34, 91, 95, 98, 101

Milton, John 弥尔顿, 约翰 91, 96, 97

minuscule micro-electromechanical sensors(MEMS) 微小型无线微机电传感器 7—8

mobile phones 移动电话 5, 7, 29

morality 道德 1, 30—31, 34—35

mores test 道德观测试 106—108

motes 尘埃 8

N

name or likeness, appropriation of 盗用肖像或姓名 59, 139

national security 国家安全 71

Netherlands 荷兰 69

New Zealand 新西兰 66—67

newspapers 报纸; 见 media

O

offensiveness 冒犯性 59, 65—66

ordinary people, media and 媒体和普通人 86—88

P

P3P (Platform for Privacy

Preferences) 隐私偏好平台 26—27, 136

Panopticon 圆形监狱 3

paparazzi 狗仔队 81—83, 137—139

participant monitoring 参与者监测 77

Patriot Act (United States)《爱国者法案》(美国) 73—75

personal information 个人信息 44, 45—51, 66, 101, 110, 114, 116—119, 122—124

personality rights 人格权 67—69, 101

PGP (Pretty Good Privacy) 相当好的隐私 25

phishing 网络钓鱼 13

photographs 相片 54, 81—84, 137—139

police 警察 14, 72

political privacy 政治隐私 61

Posner, Richard 波斯纳,理查德 37

privacy commissioners 隐私专员 67, 117—118, 135—136

privacy-enhancing technologies (PETs) 增进隐私保护技术 23—26, 28, 129, 136

privacy-invading technologies (PITs) 侵犯隐私技术 136

private and family right, right to respect for 个人和家庭权利获得尊重的权利 64, 71, 78—79, 83—84, 87—88, 120, 124

private and public domains, separation of 公共和私人领域的分离 31—34

private facts, disclosure of 披露私人事实 58—59

Prosser, Dean 普罗瑟,迪安 57—58

pseudonymization tools 化名工具 23

public figures 公众人物 38, 65, 66, 81—85, 94—95, 98—100, 103, 105—108

public key system 公钥系统 25—26

public interest 公共利益 83—85, 97, 103—106, 108—109

publicity 公开 57—58, 66, 84—86, 139

Q

quality of information 信息的质量 42, 47—48

Quebec Charter of Human Rights 《魁北克人权宪章》70

R

reasonable expectation of privacy 对隐私的合理期望 47—51, 66, 69—70, 74, 76—77, 85

repressive governments 专制政府 8—9, 11—12

RFID (radio frequency identification) systems 无线射频识别系统 19, 27—28

Romans 罗马人 31

S

Safe Harbor for data transfer 数据传输的安全港 124—126

satellite monitoring 卫星监测 7,

28—29

Schauer, Frederick 肖尔，弗雷德里克 96

searches 搜索 7, 14, 72—74, 76

secrecy 保密 43

self-determination 自决 111

self-governance 自治 96—97

self-regulation 自我管制 138

sensitive data 敏感数据 110, 119—122

Sennett, Richard 桑内特，理查德 32

service providers 服务供应商 75, 130

sense-enhanced searches 感官增强搜索 7

sex 性 30, 40, 41, 57, 68, 97, 104

smart identity cards 智能身份证 19—20

'smart dust' devices "智能尘埃"装置 7

隐私

social networking sites 社交网站 130

solitude 独处 43, 44, 45, 56, 57—58

South Africa, apartheid in 南非，种族隔离 4

speech, freedom of 言论自由；见 freedom of expression

spyware 间谍软件 13

surveillance 监控 1, 2—10, 40, 50, 58
　approval 核准 75—76
　behaviour, adaption of 行为的调整 4
　CCTV 闭路电视 1, 2, 4, 8—10, 133—135
　constitutional rights 宪法权利 59
　control 控制 72

crime 犯罪 8—9, 72, 135
Internet 互联网 8, 73—75
Ireland 爱尔兰 67
London Olympics 伦敦奥运会 133—134
map of surveillance societies 监控社会地图 63
media 媒体 88—89
participant monitoring 参与者监测 77
private and family right, right to respect for 个人和家庭权利获得尊重的权利 78—79
RFID (radio frequency identification) systems 无线射频识别系统 28
telephone tapping 电话窃听 2, 4—7, 71—79
terrorism 恐怖主义 72—75
United States 美国 72—77, 88—89
wiretapping 窃听 2, 4—7, 71—80
workplace 工作场所 4—5

T

tagging people 给人贴上标签 28
telecommunications 电信 126—127
telephone tapping 电话窃听 2, 4—7, 71—80
terrorism 恐怖主义 10—11, 12, 36, 46, 72—75
Textronic's textropolymer 特克斯簇尼克的"特克斯簇聚合物" 22
third parties, opinions of 第三方的

观点 49—50
tort 侵权 57—60, 63—66, 70, 92, 139
totalitarianism 极权主义 8—9
transparency 透明度 36, 40, 134
trespass 非法侵入 71
Trojan horses 特洛伊木马 12
truth 真相 95—96

U

United States 美国 18, 22, 24, 45, 76
　abortion 堕胎 39, 40, 61
　constitutional right to privacy 宪法中的隐私权 59—62
　contraception 节育 40, 60—61
　data protection 数据保护 124—126
　First Amendment《宪法第一修正案》24, 99—100, 102—105, 107—108
　freedom of expression 言论自由 24, 99—101, 103—108
　homosexual acts 同性性行为 60, 62
　legal right to privacy 法定的隐私权 51—60
　media 媒体 88—89
　mores test 道德观测试 106—88
　paparazzi 狗仔队 138—139
　Patriot Act《爱国者法案》72—75
　public interest 公共利益 103—104
　surveillance 监控 72—76, 88—89
　terrorism 恐怖主义 72—75

V

value of privacy 隐私的价值 33—38, 42, 43—46, 50
VeriSign 威瑞信 15, 17
Victoria, Queen 维多利亚女王 51—52
viruses 病毒 1, 12

W

Warren, Samuel D. 沃伦,塞缪尔·D. 1, 54—60, 90, 92
washable computing 可水洗计算 22
websites 网站；见 Internet
Westin, Alan 韦斯汀,艾伦 34, 40
wiretapping 窃听 2, 4—7, 71—80
women, oppression of 对女性的压迫 35—36
workplace, surveillance in the 工作场所中的监控 4—5
worms 蠕虫 12

Y

Younger Committee 青年委员会 63

Z

Zeta-Jones, Catherine 泽塔—琼斯,凯瑟琳 63, 65, 81
zombies 僵尸 13

Raymond Wacks

PRIVACY
A Very Short Introduction

Contents

Preface i

List of illustrations vii

1 The assault 1

2 An enduring value 30

3 A legal right 51

4 Privacy and free speech 81

5 Data protection 110

6 The death of privacy? 132

Annex 139

References 141

Further reading 147

Preface

Scarcely a day passes without reports of yet another onslaught on our privacy. Almost exactly thirty years ago I published another small book on this contentious subject. Reading *The Protection of Privacy* now, one is inescapably struck by the tectonic shifts wrought by advances in technology. Most conspicuous, of course, is the fragility of personal information online. Other threats generated by the digital world abound: innovations in biometrics, CCTV surveillance, Radio Frequency Identification (RFID) systems, smart identity cards, and the manifold anti-terrorist measures all pose threats to this fundamental value – even in democratic societies. At the same time, however, the disconcerting explosion of private data through the growth of blogs, social networking sites, such as MySpace, Facebook, YouTube, Twitter, and other contrivances of the Information Age render simple generalities about the significance of privacy problematic. The advent of Web 2.0 has enlarged the Internet from an information provider to a community creator. And the insatiable hunger for gossip continues to fuel sensationalist media that frequently degrade the notion of a private domain to which we legitimately lay claim. Celebrity is indefensibly deemed a licence to intrude.

The manner in which information is collected, stored, exchanged, and used has changed forever – and with it, the character of the threats to individual privacy. But while the electronic revolution touches almost every part of our lives, it is not, of course, technology itself that is the villain, but the uses to which it is put. Only this week I learned of a proposal in the Philippines to employ RFID chips, widely used for tracking goods and patients' medical data, to protect school pupils against kidnapping. Inserting a chip below the skin (like my dog has) would plainly have several positive advantages in tracing missing individuals, including those afflicted with dementia. But is the price too high? Do we remain a free society when we surrender our right to be unobserved – even when the ends are beneficial?

Notwithstanding these extraordinary technical developments, many of the problems I considered in 1980 have not fundamentally altered. Indeed, it is mildly reassuring to discover that I can find little to disagree with in my analysis of the central questions of privacy in that book and other writings over the last three decades! I could, of course, be wrong. But, despite the passage of more than thirty years, I still think that the generous extension of privacy to 'decisional' matters (abortion, contraception, sexual preference), and the (understandable) conflation with freedom and autonomy that it engenders, is a mistake. And I draw some comfort from the fact that in the ever-increasing dystopian prognoses of privacy's decline, rarely is mention made of these and other 'decisional' matters that often infiltrate into the province of privacy. Privacy advocates seldom agonize about these questions, important though they are, when they warn of the countless dangers posed by our information society. Is this a tacit acknowledgment that the true meaning of privacy corresponds with our intuitive understanding and use of the concept? Is privacy not primarily an interest in protecting sensitive information? When we lament its demise, do we not mourn the loss of control over intimate facts about ourselves? And the essence of that control is the explicit exercise of autonomy in respect of our most intimate particulars, whether they be pried upon or gratuitously published.

But perhaps this approach is misguided? Why should disparate privacy rights be unable to co-exist as different, but related, dimensions of the same fundamental idea? Why not allow 'informational privacy' to live in peace with 'decisional privacy'? Ironically, I think the lop-sided neglect of the former, and constitutional acceleration of the latter by the United States Supreme Court may now have come full circle, and that there are small signs of a belated recognition of the urgent need legally to protect personal information along European lines, as described in the pages that follow. It is important to clarify that my resistance to the equation of privacy and autonomy springs not from a denial of the importance of rights or even their formulation in broad terms which facilitate their legal recognition. It rests instead on the belief that by addressing the problem as the protection of personal information, the pervasive difficulties that are generally forced into the straitjacket of privacy might more readily be resolved. The concept of privacy has become too vague and unwieldy a concept to perform useful analytical work. This ambiguity has actually undermined the importance of this value and encumbered its effective protection.

My association with privacy and data protection has largely been from a legal perspective. But, although the law is an indispensable instrument in the protection of privacy, the subject obviously teems with a number of other dimensions – social, cultural, political, psychological, and philosophical, and I attempt here to consider these – and several other – forces that shape our understanding of this challenging concept.

My privacy journey began many moons ago as a research student in Oxford. Both the literature (predominantly American) and the legislation (principally Scandinavian) were thin on the ground. The first generation of data protection laws were still embryonic. Since those innocent days the position has, of course, changed beyond recognition. To describe this phenomenon as an explosion is no hyperbole. My foray into the field originated as an academic endeavour to elucidate the elusive notion of privacy. But the practical dimensions of this increasingly vulnerable right were never far away. Nor could they be; the Information Age was looming. The binary universe and its manifold digital incarnations along with new, sophisticated electronic surveillance devices and an audaciously invasive press rendered any complacency about the security of personal information ingenuous. I have, moreover, been fortunate to serve on a number of law reform and other committees dedicated to illuminating the protean nature of privacy, and formulating measures by which it might be protected. The experience gained from these opportunities has exerted a powerful influence on my understanding of and judgment about privacy and data protection. I am grateful to members of the Law Reform Commission of Hong Kong privacy sub-committee from whom I have learned so much.

The campaign to defend and preserve our privacy is indefatigably waged by several public interest research and advocacy groups around the world. This precarious frontline is patrolled by various remarkable individuals to whom a considerable debt is owed. Not only do these organizations, notably the Electronic Privacy Information Center (EPIC) in the United States, and Privacy International in Britain, champion the cause of privacy, but they undertake scrupulous research into, and provide regular intelligence on, almost every conceivable aspect of the subject, including the – often parlous – state of privacy in many jurisdictions. I salute, in particular, David Banisar, Roger Clarke, Simon Davies, Gus Hosein, and Marc Rotenberg. Among the numerous fruits of the labour of these and other individuals and groups is an important recent declaration on the future of privacy signed in Madrid in November 2009 by more than a hundred non-governmental organizations and privacy experts from over 40 countries. Though it was finalized only after this book was in press, it has been possible to include the text as an annex.

A distinguished group of colleagues, privacy commissioners, and other boffins have, over the years, provided encouragement, advice, and assistance in countless ways. Thanks are due to John Bacon-Shone, Eric Barendt, Colin Bennett, Mark Berthold, Jon Bing, the late Peter Birks, Michael Bryan, Ann Cavoukian, David Flaherty, Graham Greenleaf, Godfrey Kan, Michael Kirby, Stephen Lau, Charles Raab, Megan Richardson, Stefano Rodotà, Jamie Smith, and Nigel Waters. None should be indicted as a co-defendant for the transgressions I have committed here and elsewhere.

As always, members of Oxford University Press have been congenial collaborators in this project. I am especially grateful to Andrea Keegan, Emma Marchant, Keira Dickinson, Kerstin Demata, and Deborah Protheroe. Not for the first time, Kartiga Ramalingam and her team at SPI have done a superb job of transforming my text and images into this handsome volume.

Since putting the finishing touches to the manuscript – and even while reading the proofs – accounts of innumerable invasions relentlessly proliferated. Reader, be warned: the topic of the book in your hands is highly volatile. Fresh challenges to personal privacy lie in wait. The quest to protect and preserve this indispensable democratic ideal demands vigilance and resolve.

Raymond Wacks

List of Illustrations

1 Jeremy Bentham's Panopticon **3**
   © 2002 TopFoto

2 Wiretapping **6**
   © 2003 HowStuffWorks, Inc.

3 Privacy cartoons: covert surveillance **9**
   © Grea Korting/www.sangrea.net

4 Privacy cartoons: surfing the web **12**
   Reproduced with permission; please visit www.SecurityCartoon.com for more material

5 Human genome cartoon **15**
   Comic made on Bitstrips.com

6 DNA **21**
   © Andrew Brookes/Corbis

7 RFID technology **27**

8 Paparazzi **38**
   © Getty Images

9 Victoria and Albert **52**
   © Hulton Archive/Getty Images

10 Louis Brandeis **54**
   Courtesy of the Library of Congress

11 *Roe v Wade* **61**
   © Susan Steinkamp/Corbis

12 State of privacy map **62**
   © Privacy International (adapted)

13 Catherine Zeta-Jones and Michael Douglas **65**
   © Nicolas Khayat/ABACA USA/ Empics Entertainment

14 Naomi Campbell **82**
   © Getty Images

15 Cartoon: revealing personal information is hard to resist **90**
   © 2008 Geek Culture

16 Cartoon: the use of personal data is justified as being in the public interest **123**
© Sidney Harris/CartoonStock.com

17 Privacy International poster **130**
© Privacy International

18 Princess Diana paparazzi **136**
© Handout/Getty Images

Chapter 1
The assault

Once upon a time, passengers boarded an aircraft without a search. Hacking described a cough – probably caused by a virus; and cookies were to be eaten rather than feared.

You are being watched. The ubiquity of Big Brother no longer shocks. 'Low-tech' collection of transactional data in both the public and private sector has become commonplace. In addition to the routine surveillance by CCTV in public places, the monitoring of mobile telephones, the workplace, vehicles, electronic communications, and online activity has swiftly become widespread in most advanced societies.

Privacy in its broadest sense extends beyond these sorts of intrusions whose principal pursuit is personal information. It would include a multiplicity of incursions into the private domain – especially by the government – captured in Warren and Brandeis's phrase 'the right to be let alone'. This comprehensive notion, redolent of the celebrated 17th-century declaration by Sir Edward Coke that 'a man's house is his castle', embraces a wide range of invasions that encroach not only upon 'spatial' and 'locational' privacy, but also interfere with 'decisional' matters often of a moral character such as abortion, contraception, and sexual preference.

In the case of surveillance, a moment's reflection will reveal some of its many ironies – and difficulties. Its nature – and our reaction to it – is neither straightforward nor obvious. Is 'Big Brother is Watching You' a threat, a statement of fact, or merely mendacious intimidation? Does it make any difference? Is it the knowledge that I am being observed by, say, a CCTV camera, that violates my privacy? What if the camera is a (now widely available) imitation that credibly simulates the action of the genuine article: flashing light, probing lens, menacing swing? Nothing is recorded, but I am unaware of its innocence. What is my objection? Or suppose the camera is real, but faulty – and no images are made, stored, or used? My actions have not been monitored, yet subjectively my equanimity has been disturbed. The mere presence of a device that appears to be observing and recording my behaviour is surely tantamount to the reality of my unease.

In other words, it is the *belief* that I am being watched that is my grievance. It is immaterial whether I am in fact the subject of surveillance. My objection is therefore not that I am being observed – for I am not – but the possibility that I may be.

In this respect, being watched by a visible CCTV camera differs from that other indispensable instrument of the spy: the electronic listening device. When my room or office is bugged, or my telephone is tapped, I am – by definition – usually oblivious to this infringement of my privacy. Yet my ignorance does not, of course, render the practice inoffensive. Unlike the case of the fake or non-functioning camera, however, I *have* been subjected to surveillance: my private conversations have been recorded or intercepted, albeit unconsciously. The same would be true of the surreptitious interception of my correspondence: email or snail mail.

In the former case, no personal information has been captured; in the latter, it has, but I may never know. Both practices are subsumed in the category of 'intrusion', yet each exhibits a distinctive apprehension. Indeed, the more one examines this

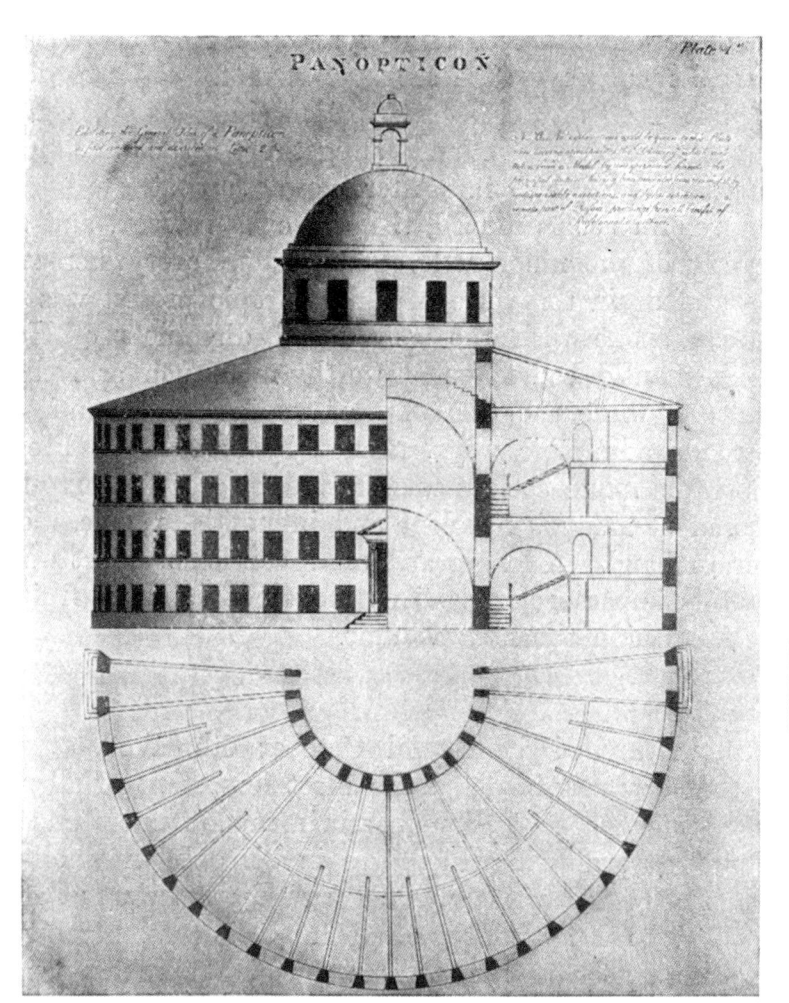

1. The English Utilitarian Jeremy Bentham designed a prison that facilitates the surreptitious observation of inmates. The term 'panopticon' is used metaphorically in a pejorative sense to describe the monitoring of individuals' personal information, especially online

(neglected) problem, the less cohesive the subject of 'intrusion' becomes. Each activity requires a separate analysis; each entails a discrete set of concerns, though they are united in a general anxiety that one's society may be approaching, or already displays features of, the Orwellian horror of relentless scrutiny.

The question is fundamentally one of perception and its consequences. Although my conviction that I am being monitored by CCTV is based on palpable evidence, and my ignorance of the interception of my correspondence or conversations is plainly not, the discomfort is similar. In both cases, it is the distasteful recognition that one needs to adjust one's behaviour – on the assumption that one's words or deeds are being monitored. During the darkest years of repression in apartheid South Africa, for example, the telephones of anti-government activists were routinely tapped by the security services. One's conversations were therefore conducted with circumspection and trepidation. This inevitably rendered dialogue stilted and unnatural. It is this requirement to adapt or adjust one's behaviour in public (in the case of CCTV) or in private (on the telephone, in one's home, or online) that is the disquieting result of a state that fails properly to regulate the exercise of surveillance.

The increasing use of such surveillance in the workplace, for instance, is changing not only the character of that environment, but also the very nature of what we do and how we do it. The knowledge that our activities are, or even may be, monitored undermines our psychological and emotional autonomy:

> Free conversation is often characterized by exaggeration, obscenity, agreeable falsehoods, and the expression of antisocial desires or views not intended to be taken seriously. The unedited quality of conversation is essential if it is to preserve its intimate, personal and informal character.

Indeed, the slide towards electronic supervision may fundamentally alter our relationships and our identity. In such a world, employees are arguably less likely to execute their duties effectively. If that occurs, the snooping employer will, in the end, secure the precise opposite of what he hopes to achieve.

Wiretapping

Both landlines and mobile phones are easy prey to the eavesdropper. In the case of the former, the connection is simply a long circuit comprising a pair of copper wires that form a loop. The circuit carrying your conversation flows out of your home through numerous switching stations between you and the instrument on the other end. At any point a snoop can attach a new load to the circuit board, much in the way one plugs in an additional appliance into an extension cord. In the case of wiretapping, that load is a mechanism that converts the electrical circuit back into the sound of your conversation. The chief shortcoming of this primitive form of interception is that the spy needs to know when the subject is going to use the phone. He needs to be at his post to listen in.

A less inconvenient and more sophisticated method is to install a recording device on the line. Like an answering machine, it picks ups the electrical signal from the telephone line and encodes it as magnetic pulses on audiotape. The disadvantage of this method is that the intruder needs to keep the recorder running continuously in order to monitor any conversations. Few cassettes are large enough. Hence a voice-activated recorder provides a more practical alternative. But here too the tape is unlikely to endure long enough to capture the subject's conversations.

The obvious answer is a bug that receives audio information and broadcasts it using radio waves. Bugs normally have diminutive microphones that pick up sound waves directly. The current is sent to a radio transmitter that conveys a signal that varies with the current. The spy sets up a radio receiver in the vicinity that picks up

How Wiretapping Works Basic Wiretapping Techniques

Outside lines can be tapped directly with a hardwired tap.

Bugs can be installed in the wall socket, the handset or anywhere along the phone line.

With the right equipment, bugs and wireless communications can be monitored from a distance.

A simple recording device can be attached to a phone line, but it can be easily detected.

Privacy

©2006 Howstuffworks

2. Tapping a telephone is a fairly simple operation

this signal and transmits it to a speaker or encodes it on a tape. A bug with a microphone is especially valuable since it will hear any conversation in the room, regardless of whether the subject is on the phone. A conventional wiretapping bug, however, can operate without its own microphone, since the telephone has one. All the wiretapper needs to do is to connect the bug anywhere along the phone line, since it receives the electrical current directly. Normally, the spy will connect the bug to the wires inside the telephone.

This is the classic approach. It obviates the need for the spy to revisit the site; his recording equipment may be concealed in a van that typically is parked outside the victim's home or office.

Tapping mobile phones requires the interception of radio signals carried from and to the handsets, and converting them back into sound. The analogue mobile phones of the 1990s were susceptible to easy interception, but their contemporary digital counterparts are much less vulnerable. To read the signals, the digital computer bits need to be converted into sound – a fairly complex and expensive operation. But mobile phone calls may be intercepted at the mobile operator's servers, or on a fixed-line section that carries encrypted voice data for wireless communication.

When you call someone on your mobile phone, your voice is digitized and sent to the nearest base station. It transmits it to another base station adjacent to the recipient's via the mobile carrier's switch operators. Between the base stations, transmission of voice data is effected on landlines, as occurs in the case of fixed-line phone calls. It seems that if an eavesdropper listens to such calls over the landline connection segment, mobile phones are not dissimilar to conventional phones – and as vulnerable.

The privacy prognosis

The future of surveillance seems daunting. It promises more sophisticated and alarming intrusions into our private lives, including the greater use of biometrics, and sense-enhanced searches such as satellite monitoring, penetrating walls and clothing, and 'smart dust' devices – minuscule wireless micro-electromechanical sensors (MEMS) that can detect everything from light to vibrations. These so-called 'motes' – as tiny as a grain of sand – would collect data that could be sent via two-way band radio between motes up to 1,000 feet away.

As cyberspace becomes an increasingly perilous domain, we learn daily of new, disquieting assaults on its citizens. This slide towards pervasive surveillance coincides with the mounting fears, expressed well before 11 September 2001, about the disconcerting capacity of the new technology to undermine our liberty. Reports of the fragility of privacy have been sounded for at least a century. But in the last decade they have assumed a more urgent form. And here lies a paradox. On the one hand, recent advances in the power of computers have been decried as the nemesis of whatever vestiges of our privacy still survive. On the other, the Internet is acclaimed as a Utopia. When clichés contend, it is imprudent to expect sensible resolutions of the problems they embody, but between these two exaggerated claims, something resembling the truth probably resides. In respect of the future of privacy at least, there can be little doubt that the questions are changing before our eyes. And if, in the flat-footed domain of atoms, we have achieved only limited success in protecting individuals against the depredations of surveillance, how much better the prospects in our brave new binary world?

When our security is under siege, so – inevitably – is our liberty. A world in which our every movement is observed erodes the very freedom this snooping is often calculated to protect. Naturally, we need to ensure that the social costs of the means employed to enhance security do not outweigh the benefits. Thus, one unsurprising consequence of the installation of CCTV in car parks, shopping centres, airports, and other public places is the displacement of crime; offenders simply go somewhere else. And, apart from the doors this intrusion opens to totalitarianism, a surveillance society can easily generate a climate of mistrust and suspicion, a reduction in the respect for law and those who enforce it, and an intensification of prosecution of offences that are susceptible to easy detection and proof.

Other developments have comprehensively altered basic features of the legal landscape. The law has been profoundly affected and challenged by countless other advances in technology. Computer fraud, identity theft, and other 'cyber crimes' are touched on below.

Developments in biotechnology such as cloning, stem cell research, and genetic engineering provoke thorny ethical questions and confront traditional legal concepts. Proposals to introduce identity cards and biometrics have attracted strong objections in several jurisdictions. The nature of criminal trials has been transformed by the use of both DNA and CCTV evidence.

Orwellian supervision already appears to be alive and well in several countries. Britain, for example, boasts more than 4 million CCTV

HEY BOSS ... I'M NOT SURE OUR COVERT SURVEILLANCE IS REAL COVERT ANY MORE.

3. The ubiquity of CCTV cameras may diminish their efficacy

cameras in public places: roughly one for every 14 inhabitants. It also possesses the world's largest DNA database, comprising some 5.3 million DNA samples. The temptation to install CCTV cameras by both the public and private sector is not easy to resist. Data-protection law (discussed in Chapter 5) ostensibly controls its use, but such regulation has not proved especially effective. A radical solution, adopted in Denmark, is to prohibit their use, subject to certain exceptions such as in petrol stations. The law in Sweden, France, and Holland is more stringent than in the United Kingdom. These countries adopt a licensing system, and the law requires that warning signs be placed on the periphery of the zone monitored. German law has a similar requirement.

Biometrics

We are all unique. Your fingerprint is a 'biometric': the measurement of biological information. Fingerprints have long been used as a means of linking an individual to a crime, but they provide also a practical method of privacy protection: instead of logging into your computer with a (not always safe) password, increasing use is being made of fingerprint readers as a considerably more secure entry point. We are likely to see greater use of fingerprint readers at supermarket checkouts and ATMs.

There is no perfect biometric, but the ideal is to find a unique personal attribute that is immutable or, at least, unlikely to change over time. A measurement of this characteristic is then employed as a means of identifying the individual in question. Typically, several samples of the biometric are provided by the subject; they are digitized and stored on a database. The biometric may then be used either to identify the subject by matching his or her data against that of a number of other individuals' biometrics, or to validate the identity of a single subject.

In order to counter the threat of terrorism, the future will unquestionably witness an increased use of biometrics. This includes a number of measures of human physiography as well as DNA. Among the following examples of characteristics on which biometric technologies can be based are one's appearance (supported by still images), e.g., descriptions used in passports, such as height, weight, colour of skin, hair, and eyes, visible physical markings, gender, race, facial hair, wearing of glasses; natural physiography, e.g., skull measurements, teeth and skeletal injuries, thumbprint, fingerprint sets, handprints, iris and retinal scans, earlobe capillary patterns, hand geometry; biodynamics, e.g., the manner in which one's signature is written, statistically analysed voice characteristics, keystroke dynamics, particularly login-ID and password; social behaviour (supported by video-film), e.g., habituated body signals, general voice characteristics, style of speech, visible handicaps; imposed physical characteristics, e.g., dog-tags, collars, bracelets and anklets, bar-codes, embedded microchips, and transponders.

The fear is that in authoritarian countries, biometrics may be imposed on the public. Biometrics providers will thrive by selling their technology to repressive governments, and establish a foothold in relatively free countries by seeking soft targets; they

The limits of biometrics

One identification option often mentioned is to implant microchips into people to store and broadcast identity, but we cannot rule out the possibility that the chip could be surgically removed and replaced, or that the information could be changed via remote access. Even if we take a DNA sample from a baby when it is still attached to its mother, there is still the possibility of substituting another sample on its journey to the lab for analysis. There is no absolutely foolproof method of securing the identity of a person, even via the most accurate of biometrics.

K. O'Hara and N. Shadbolt, *The Spy in the Coffee Machine* (Oneworld, 2008), pp. 68–9 may start with animals or with captive populations such as the frail, the poor, the old, prisoners, employees, and so on. A less gloomy scenario is that societies will recognize the gravity of the threat and enforce constraints on technologies and their use. This would require public support and the courage of elected representatives who will need to resist pressure both from large corporations and the national security and law enforcement authorities that invoke the bogeymen of terrorism, illegal immigration, and domestic 'law and order' to justify the implementation of this technology.

The Internet

Online activity is especially vulnerable to attack. The artillery of malicious software (or 'malware') includes viruses, worms, Trojan horses, spyware, 'phishing', 'bots', 'zombies', bugs, and exploits.

A virus is a block of code that introduces copies of itself into other programs. It normally carries a payload, which may have only nuisance value, though in many cases the consequences are serious. In order to evade early detection, viruses may delay the performance of functions other than replication. A worm generates copies of itself over networks without infecting other programs. A Trojan horse is a program that appears to carry out a positive task (and sometimes does so), but is often nasty, for instance, keystroke recorders embedded in utilities.

4. Surfing is beset with hazards

Spyware is software – often hidden within an email attachment – that secretly harvests data within a device about its user, or applications made by the device. These are passed on to another party. The data may include the user's browsing history, log individual keystrokes (to obtain passwords), monitor user behaviour for consumer marketing purposes (so-called 'adware'), or observe the use of copyrighted works. 'Phishing' normally takes the form of an email message that appears to emanate from a trusted institution such as a bank. It seeks to entice the addressee into divulging sensitive data such as a password or credit card details. The messages are normally highly implausible – replete with spelling mistakes and other obvious defects – yet this manifest deceit manages to dupe an extraordinarily high number of recipients.

Some malware filches personal data or transforms your computer into a 'bot' – one which is remotely controlled by a third party. A 'bot' may be employed to collect email addresses, send spam, or mount attacks on corporate websites. Another form of attack is 'Denial of Service' (DoS), which uses a swarm of 'bots' or 'zombies' to inundate company websites with bogus data requests. A 'zombie' creates numerous processors dotted around the Internet under central or timed control (hence 'zombies'). An attack will pursue a website until it has been taken offline. This may endure for several days, incurring considerable costs to the victim company. They are typically accompanied by demands for money.

Bugs are errors in software – particularly Microsoft Windows – that may render the user's system vulnerable to attack by so-called 'crackers'. Microsoft normally responds by issuing a patch for downloading – until the next bug materializes. An 'exploit' is an attack on a particular vulnerability. Standard techniques are supported by established guidelines and programming code that circulate on the Internet.

It was reported in early 2009 that police in the European Union have been encouraged to expand the implementation of a rarely used power of intrusion – without warrant. This will permit police across Europe to hack into private computers when an officer believes that such a 'remote search' is proportionate and necessary to prevent or detect serious crime (one which attracts a prison sentence of more than three years). This could be achieved in a number of ways, including the attachment of a virus to an email message which, if opened, would covertly activate the remote search facility.

Cookies

These are data that the website servers transmit to the visitor's browser and are stored on his or her computer. They enable the website to recognize the visitor's computer as one with which it has previously interacted, and to remember details of the earlier transaction, including search words, and the amount of time spent reading certain pages. In other words, cookie technology enables a website – by default – furtively to put its own identifier into my PC permanently in order track my online conduct.

And cookies can endure; they may show an extensive list of each website visited during a particular period. Moreover, the text of the cookie file may reveal personal data previously provided. Websites such as Amazon.com justify this practice by claiming that it assists and improves the shopping experience by informing customers of books which, on the basis of their browsing behaviour, they might otherwise neglect to buy. But this gives rise to the obvious danger that my identity may be misrepresented by a concentration on tangential segments of my surfing or, on the other hand, personal data harvested from a variety of sources may be assembled to create a comprehensive lifestyle profile.

> SIR, THEY HAVE DISCOVERED THE HUMAN GENOME CODE
>
> DAMN HACKERS...!!
> I'M GOING TO CHANGE THE PASSWORD

5. No one, it would seem, is immune to hacking

Hacking

Hackers were once regarded as innocuous 'cyber-snoops' who adhered to a slightly self-indulgent, but quasi-ethical, code dictating that one ought not to purloin data, but merely report holes in the victim's system (see box). They were, as Lessig puts it, 'a bit more invasive than a security guard, who checks office doors to make sure they are locked... (He) not only checked the locks but let himself in, took a quick peek around, and left a cute (or sarcastic) note saying, in effect, "Hey, stupid, you left your door open."'

While this laid-back culture eventually attracted the interest of law-enforcement authorities – who secured legislation against it – the practice continues to produce headaches. According to Simon Church of VeriSign, the online auction sites that criminals use to sell user details, are merely the beginning. He anticipates that

The (dubious) joy of hacking

Being a hacker is lots of fun, but it's a kind of fun that takes lots of effort. The effort takes motivation. Successful athletes get their motivation from a kind of physical delight in making their bodies perform, in pushing themselves past their own physical limits. Similarly, to be a hacker you have to get a basic thrill from solving problems, sharpening your skills, and exercising your intelligence. If you aren't the kind of person that feels this way naturally, you'll need to become one in order to make it as a hacker. Otherwise you'll find your hacking energy is sapped by distractions like sex, money, and social approval... To behave like a hacker, you have to believe that the thinking time of other hackers is precious – so much so that it's almost a moral duty for you to share information, solve problems and then give the solutions away just so other hackers can solve *new* problems instead of having to perpetually re-address old ones
... Hackers (and creative people in general) should never be bored or have to drudge at stupid repetitive work, because when this happens it means they aren't doing what only they can do – solve new problems. This wastefulness hurts everybody. Therefore boredom and drudgery are not just unpleasant but actually evil
... Hackers are naturally anti-authoritarian. Anyone who can give you orders can stop you from solving whatever problem you're being fascinated by – and, given the way authoritarian minds work, will generally find some appallingly stupid reason to do so. So the authoritarian attitude has to be fought wherever you find it, lest it smother you and other hackers... To be a hacker, you have to develop some of these attitudes. But copping an attitude alone won't make you a hacker, any more than it will make you a champion athlete or a rock star. Becoming a hacker will take intelligence, practice, dedication, and hard work... If you revere competence, you'll enjoy developing it in yourself – the hard work and dedication will become a kind of intense play rather than drudgery. That attitude is vital to becoming a hacker.

Eric Steven Raymond, *How to Become a Hacker,* http://www.catb.org/~esr/faqs/hacker-howto.html

'mashup' sites that combine different databases could be converted to criminal use. 'Imagine if a hacker put together information he'd harvested from a travel company's database with Google Maps. He could provide a tech-savvy burglar with the driving directions of how to get to your empty house the minute you go on holiday.'

Identity theft

The appropriation of an individual's personal information to commit fraud or to impersonate him or her is an escalating problem, costing billions of dollars a year. In 2007, a survey by the United States Federal Trade Commission found that in 2005, a total of 3.7% of survey participants indicated that they had been victims of identity theft. This result suggests that approximately 8.3 million American suffered some form of identity theft in that year, and 10% of all victims reported out-of-pocket expenses of $1,200 or more. The same percentage spent at least 55 hours resolving their problems. The top 5% of victims spent at least 130 hours. The estimate of total losses from identity theft in the 2006 survey amounted to $15.6 billion.

The practice normally involves at least three persons: the victim, the impostor, and a credit institution that establishes a new account for the impostor in the victim's name. This may include a credit card, utilities service, or even a mortgage.

Identity theft assumes a number of forms. Potentially the most harmful comprise credit card fraud (in which an account number is stolen in order to make unauthorized charges), new account fraud (where the impostor initiates an account or 'tradeline' in the victim's name; the offence may be undiscovered until the victim applies for credit), identity cloning (where the impostor masquerades as the victim), and criminal identity theft (in which the impostor, masquerading as the victim, is arrested for some offence, or is fined for a violation of the law).

Part of the responsibility must be laid at the door of the financial services industry itself. Their lax security methods in granting credit and facilitating electronic payment subordinates security to convenience.

Identity cards

At first blush, a compulsory ID card that contains the holder's key personal information would appear to be a panacea for the multiple problems of identity theft, tax and welfare fraud, illegal immigration, and, of course, terrorism. Yet, quite apart from their actual efficacy in curbing harmful activities, their establishment inevitably invokes fervent hostility, especially from privacy advocates, and particularly in common law jurisdictions such as the United Kingdom, Australia, Canada, the United States, Ireland, and New Zealand where attempts to introduce them have so far been unsuccessful. Resistance has been intense also in Scandinavian countries. Cultural forces clearly operate against the notion that an individual is required to carry 'papers'. In Britain, for example, there is a deep-seated objection to any compulsion to prove one's democratic right to exist!

Compulsory ID cards do, however, exist in various forms in about 100 countries, and there is considerably less opposition to the use of various types of mandatory ID cards in Europe and Asia. Eleven European Union members, including France, Germany, Spain, Portugal, Belgium, Greece, and Luxembourg, use them. In Asia, the Hong Kong experience is instructive. ID cards have been used since 1945 – principally (or, at least, ostensibly) to control the influx of illegal immigrants from mainland China. And it is undoubtedly the case that the vast majority of Hong Kong residents are perfectly insouciant about both the requirement to carry the card at all times and the personal data that it holds. Indeed, it has become a highly convenient means by which to substantiate one's identity for purposes of buying theatre tickets, booking a restaurant, and the like.

Recently the Hong Kong government 'upgraded' the cards into what are now styled 'identity smart cards' with a chip containing, *inter alia*, the holder's particulars of birth, nationality, address, marital status, occupation, and details of any spouse or children. To obtain the card, the law requires residents to be photographed and fingerprinted. The government claims that there are a number of benefits that accrue from the use of the smart card, including greater security (data engraved into different layers of the card and held in the chip can prevent lost or stolen identity cards from being altered or used by others); convenience (with the capacity of multi-applications, such as e-certificate and library card functions, the holder may use one card for various functions); 'quality service' (card holders will enjoy various kinds of public services online); and more convenient travel (the thumbprint templates stored in the chip facilitate speedy immigration clearance via the Automated Passenger Clearance System and the Automated Vehicle Clearance System).

To allay fears of the misuse of the data, the government maintains that only minimal data are stored in the RFID (radio frequency identification) chip. More sensitive personal information is kept at back-end computer systems. Data for different applications are segregated. All the non-immigration applications are voluntary. The collection, storage, use, and release of data must comply with, amongst other legislation, the Personal Data (Privacy) Ordinance. Only authorized departments have access to the relevant database; there is no sharing of databases among government departments. Cardholders may view data on the card through smart identity card readers installed at immigration self-service kiosks after their identities have been authenticated. Privacy Impact Assessments (PIA) are conducted at different stages of the Smart Identity Card

> **Twelve arguments against ID cards**
>
> 1. They won't stop crime.
> 2. They won't stop welfare fraud.
> 3. They will not stop illegal immigration.
> 4. They will facilitate discrimination.
> 5. They will create an unwarranted increase in police powers.
> 6. They will become an internal passport.
> 7. A 'voluntary' card will become compulsory.
> 8. The cost will be unacceptable.
> 9. The loss of a card will cause great distress and inconvenience.
> 10. A card will imperil the privacy of personal information.
> 11. The card will entrench criminality and institutionalize false identity.
> 12. They will compromise national identity and personal integrity.
>
> Simon Davies, *Big Brother* (Pan Books, 1996), pp. 139-51

Project. Legislative amendments have been enacted to enhance data privacy protection.

This sounds reassuring, and the attractions of greater efficiency, equity, and convenience are not to be lightly dismissed. But, as with the proposed ID card in Britain, these virtues must be balanced against the very real prospect of 'function creep', error, confidentiality, and identity theft. The temptation of any government bureaucracy to use the data for a variety of purposes, to share information between departments, and to merge databases may be irresistible. Nor is it obvious that the fraudster or terrorist will be thwarted by even the most sophisticated ID card.

6. The various uses to which DNA is put pose considerable risks to personal privacy

DNA databases

The growing use of DNA evidence in the detection of crime has generated a need for a database of samples to determine whether an individual's profile matches that of a suspect. The DNA database in England and Wales (with its 5.3 million profiles, representing 9% of the population) may be the largest anywhere. It includes DNA samples and fingerprints of almost a million suspects who are never prosecuted or who are subsequently acquitted. It is hardly surprising that innocent persons should feel aggrieved by the retention of their genetic information; the potential for misuse is not a trivial matter. This dismal prospect led two such individuals to request that their profiles be expunged following their walking free. Unable to convince the English courts, they appealed to the European Court of Human Rights, which, at the end of 2008, unanimously decided that their right to privacy had been violated.

> ### The spy in your bed
>
> Computers are getting smaller and smaller and can be made of, or fitted into, many new and interesting materials. The possibilities are endless, but so are the dangers. For instance, the field of electronic textiles or 'washable computing' provides all sorts of fascinating futures. Fabrics that can monitor vital signs, generate heat or act as switches suggest limitless possibilities, from the ridiculous – clothes that change colour constantly – to the useful – a jacket that recharges your mobile phone. Textronic's 'textropolymer' is made of fibres that change their resistance as they are deformed, stretched, and so can detect pressure. Very handy – but imagine a bedsheet that was able to detect, and broadcast, the number of people lying on it.
>
> K. O'Hara and N. Shadbolt, *The Spy in the Coffee Machine* (Oneworld, 2008), p. 9

Other jurisdictions tend to destroy a DNA profile when a suspect is acquitted. In Norway and Germany, for example, a sample may be kept permanently only with the approval of a court. In Sweden, only the profiles of convicted offenders who have served custodial sentences of more than two years may be retained. The United States permits the FBI to take DNA samples on arrest, but they can be destroyed on request should no charges be laid or if the suspect is acquitted. Among the 40 or so states that have DNA databases, only California permits permanent storage of profiles of individuals charged but then cleared.

It has been suggested that, to avoid discrimination against certain sectors of the population (such as black males), everybody's DNA should be collected and held in the database. This drastic proposal is unlikely to attract general support. What is clear, however, is that to maintain the integrity of the system and protect privacy, the vulnerability of such sensitive genetic data requires stringent regulation.

Repelling the attacks

Privacy-enhancing technologies (PETs) seek to protect privacy by eliminating or reducing personal data or by preventing unnecessary or undesired processing of personal data without compromising the operation of the data system. Originally they took the form of 'pseudonymization tools': software that allows individuals to withhold their true identity from operating electronic systems, and only reveal it when absolutely essential. These technologies help to reduce the amount of data collected about an individual. Their efficacy, however, depends largely on the integrity of those who have the power to revoke or nullify the shield of the pseudonym. Unhappily, governments cannot always be trusted.

Instead of pseudonymity, stronger PETs afford the tougher armour of anonymity that denies the ability of governments and corporations to link data with an identified individual. This is normally achieved by a succession of intermediary-operated services. Each intermediary knows the identities of the intermediaries next to it in the chain, but has insufficient information to facilitate the identification of the previous and succeeding intermediaries. It cannot trace the communication to the originator, or forward it to the eventual recipient.

These PETs include anonymous re-mailers, web-surfing measures, and David Chaum's payer-anonymous electronic cash (e-cash) or *Digicash* which employs a blinding technique that sends randomly encrypted data to my bank which then validates them (through the use of some sort of digital money) and returns the data to my hard disk. Only a serial number is provided: the recipient does not know (and does not need to know) the source of the payment. This process affords an even more powerful safeguard of anonymity. It has considerable potential in electronic copyright management systems (ECMS) with projects such as CITED (Copyright in Transmitted Electronic Documents) and COPICAT, being developed by the European Commission ESPIRIT programme. Full texts of copyrighted works are being downloaded and marketed without the owner's consent or royalty being paid. These projects seek technological solutions by which users could be charged for their use of such material. This 'tracking' of users poses an obvious privacy danger: my reading, listening, or viewing habits may be stored, and access to them obtained, for potentially sinister or harmful purposes. Blind signatures seem to be a relatively simple means by which to anonymize users.

Anonymity is an important democratic value. Even in a pre-electronic age, it facilitates participation in the political process which an individual may otherwise wish to spurn. Indeed, the United States Supreme Court has held that the First Amendment protects the right to anonymous speech. There are numerous reasons why I may wish to conceal my identity behind a pseudonym or achieve anonymity in some other way. On the Internet, I may want to be openly anonymous but conduct a conversation (with either known or anonymous identities) using an anonymous remailer. I may even wish no one to know the identity of the recipient of my email. And I may not want anyone to know to which newsgroups I belong or which websites I have visited.

There are, moreover, obvious personal and political benefits of anonymity for whistleblowers, victims of abuse, and those requiring help of various kinds. Equally, (as always?), such liberties may also shield criminal activities, though the right to anonymous speech would not extend to unlawful speech. Anonymity enjoys a unique relationship with both privacy and free speech. The opportunities for anonymity afforded by the Internet are substantial; we are probably only on the brink of discovering its potential in both spheres. It raises (somewhat disquieting) questions about the very question of who we are: our identity.

The use of strong encryption to protect the security of communications has been met by resistance (notably in the United

States and France) and by proposals either to prohibit encryption altogether, or, through means such as public key escrow, to preserve the power to intercept messages. The battle has been joined between law enforcers and cryptographers; it is likely to be protracted, especially since enthusiastic would be too meek a word to describe the manner in which the culture of strong encryption has been embraced by ordinary computer users – given that Phil Zimmerman's encryption software, PGP ('Pretty Good Privacy'), may be generated in less than five minutes, and is freely available on the Internet.

A central feature of modern cryptography is that of the 'public key'. A lock-and-key approach is adopted in respect of telecommunications security. The lock is a public key which a user may transmit to recipients. To unlock the message, the recipient uses a personal encryption code or 'private key'. Public key encryption significantly increases the availability of encryption/identification, for the dual key system allows the encryption key to be made available to potential communicants while keeping the decryption key secret. It permits, for instance, a bank to make its public key available to several customers, without their being able to read each others' encrypted messages.

Technological solutions are especially useful in concealing the identity of the individual. Weak forms of digital identities are already widely used in the form of bank account and social security numbers. They provide only limited protection, for it is a simple matter to match them with the person they represent. The advent of smart cards that generate changing pseudo-identities will facilitate genuine transactional anonymity. 'Blinding' or 'blind signatures' and 'digital signatures' will significantly enhance the protection of privacy. A digital signature is a unique 'key' which provides, if anything, stronger authentication than my written signature. A public key system involves two keys, one public and the other private. The advantage of a public key system is that if you are able to decrypt the message, you know that it could only have been created by the sender.

The paramount question is: is my identity *genuinely required* for the act or transaction concerned? It is here that data-protection principles, discussed in Chapter 5, come into play.

P3P

A significant development in privacy policy management systems are technologies that permit a user to make informed choices about their browsing based on his or her personal privacy preferences. The best known of these protocols is the Platform for Privacy Preferences (P3P) developed by the World Wide Web Consortium (W3C). It allows websites to make machine-readable versions of their privacy policies, thereby enabling users whose browsers are equipped with P3P readers to have their specified privacy preferences automatically compared to the website's privacy policy. This will state clearly what information the site collects and what it will do with it. Users are then notified if the website policy does not match their preferences.

One of the leading privacy advocate organizations, the Electronic Privacy Information Center (EPIC) is, however, unconvinced. Dubbing it 'Pretty Poor Privacy', it complains that P3P fails to comply with baseline standards for privacy protection:

> It is a complex and confusing protocol that will make it more difficult for Internet users to protect their privacy. P3P also fails to address many of the privacy problems specifically associated with the Internet.

EPIC contends that good privacy standards are better built on fair information practices and genuine PETs that minimize or eliminate the collection of personally identifiable information:

Simple, predictable rules for the collection and use of personal information will also support consumer trust and confidence. P3P, on the other hand, is likely to undermine public confidence in Internet privacy.

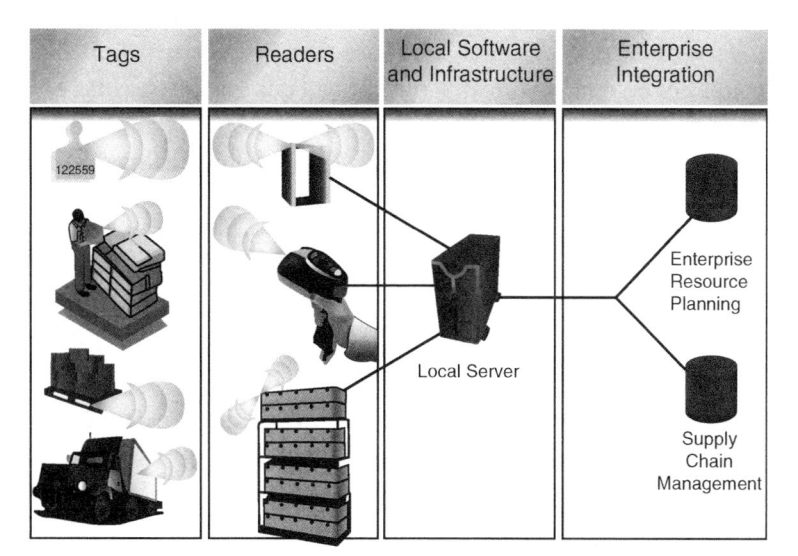

7. **The escalating use of RFID technology poses numerous threats to privacy**

RFID

The technology of radio frequency identification emerged as a means of inventory control to replace barcodes. An RFID system consists of three elements: a minuscule chip on each consumer item (an RFID tag) that stores a unique product identifier; an RFID reader; and a computer system attached to the reader having access to an inventory control database. The database contains extensive product information, including the contents, origin, and manufacturing history of the product. Assigning a tag to a product also discloses its location, rate and place of sale, and, in the case of transport companies, its progress. It has applications in recalling faulty or dangerous merchandise, tracing stolen property, preventing counterfeit, and providing an audit trail to thwart corruption.

The potential of RFID is huge, and it is increasingly being used for 'contactless' payment cards, passports, and the monitoring of luggage, library books, and pets. There is no reason why humans could not be microchipped – like our dogs. It could assist the identification of Alzheimer's patients who go astray. Combining RFID and wireless fidelity networks (Wi-Fi) could facilitate realtime tracking of objects or people inside a wireless network, such as a hospital. The privacy concern is that the acceptance of these benign applications may initiate less benevolent uses; there are likely to be calls for sex offenders, prisoners, illegal immigrants, and other 'undesirables' to be tagged.

There is also the fear that if RFID data may be aggregated with other data (for example, information stored in credit or loyalty cards) – to match product data with personal information – this could allow comprehensive personal profiles of consumers to be assembled. Moreover, an increase in the use of RFID in public places, and homes and businesses, could portend an enlargement of the surveillance society. For example, my car has an RFID affixed to the windscreen that automatically deducts the toll from my bank account. The fact that it has just passed through the toll station at Pisa may be useful to a party interested in my movements. There is plainly a need for sophisticated PETs here.

Global positioning system

Satellite signals are used by GPS to establish location. GPS chips are now common in vehicle navigation systems and mobile phones. It is possible to augment the data generated from GPS by their assimilation into databases and aggregation with other information to create geographic information systems (GIS). In order to make or receive calls, mobile phones communicate their location to a base station. In effect, therefore, they broadcast the user's location every few minutes.

Services such as Loki triangulate position using wireless signals, allowing the user to obtain local weather reports, find nearby restaurants, cinemas, or shops, or share their location with friends. According to its website, 'as you travel around, MyLoki can automatically let your friends know where you are using your favourite platform – Facebook, RSS Feeds, or badges for your blog or even Twitter'. It claims to protect privacy by refraining from the collection of personal information.

Genetic information

The ability to explore our genetic structure poses a number of privacy problems, not least the extent to which a doctor's duty to preserve patient confidentiality, enshrined in the Hippocratic Oath, adequately safeguards this sensitive information against disclosure. It raises too the intractable problem of the subject's blood relatives – and even partners and spouses – whose interest in learning of the data is far from trivial.

The challenges posed by these – and other – intrusions cannot be underestimated. How have we arrived at this situation? The next chapter attempts to provide an answer.

Chapter 2
An enduring value

While much of our contemporary disquiet about privacy tends to spring from the malevolent capacity of technology, the yearning for a private realm long precedes the Brave New World of bits and bytes, of electronic surveillance, and CCTV. Indeed, anthropologists have demonstrated that there is a near-universal desire for individual and group privacy in primitive societies, and that this is reflected in appropriate social norms. Moreover, we are not alone in seeking refuge from the crowd. Animals too need privacy.

What is privacy?

At the most general level, the idea of privacy embraces the desire to be left alone, free to be ourselves – uninhibited and unconstrained by the prying of others. This extends beyond snooping and unsolicited publicity to intrusions upon the 'space' we need to make intimate, personal decisions without the intrusion of the state. Thus 'privacy' is frequently employed to describe a zone demarcated as 'private' in which, for example, a woman exercises a choice as to whether she wishes to have an abortion, or an individual is free to express his or her sexuality. Debates about privacy are therefore often entangled with contentious moral

> **Privacy and animals**
>
> Man likes to think that his desire for privacy is distinctively human, a function of his unique ethical, intellectual, and artistic needs. Yet studies of animal behaviour and social organization suggest that man's need for privacy may well be rooted in his animal origins, and that men and animals share several basic mechanisms for claiming privacy among their own fellows... Studies of territoriality have even shattered the romantic notion that when robins sing or monkeys shriek, it is solely for the 'animal joy of life'. Actually, it is often a defiant cry for privacy... One basic finding of animal studies is that virtually all animals seek periods of individual seclusion or small-group intimacy... (T)he animal's struggle to achieve a balance between privacy and participation provides one of the basic processes of animal life. In this sense, the quest for privacy is not restricted to man alone, but arises in the biological and social processes of all life.
>
> Alan Westin, *Privacy and Freedom* (The Bodley Head, 1967), pp. 8–11

questions, including the use of contraception and the right to pornography.

In any event, it is clear that at the core of our concern to protect privacy lies a conception of the individual's relationship with society. Once we acknowledge a separation between the public and the private domain, we assume a community in which not only does such a division make sense, but also an institutional structure that makes possible an account of this sort. In other words, to postulate the 'private' presupposes the 'public'.

Over the last century or so, participation in the public realm – in society – has undergone steady erosion. We are more self-centred. Our postmodern psychological preoccupation with 'being in touch with' our feelings, as the sociologist Richard Sennett vividly demonstrates, devastated the prospect of a genuine political community. Paradoxically, excessive intimacy has destroyed it: 'The closer people come, the less social, the more painful, the more fratricidal their relations.'

In fact, the Greeks regarded a life spent in the privacy of 'one's own' (*idion*) as, by definition, 'idiotic'. Similarly, the Romans perceived privacy as merely a temporary refuge from the life of the *res publica*. This is well described by Hannah Arendt:

> In ancient feeling the private trait of privacy, indicated in the word itself, was all-important; it meant literally a state of being deprived of something, and even of the highest and most human of man's capacities. A man who lived only a private life, who like the slave was not permitted to enter the public realm, or like the barbarian had chosen not to establish such a realm, was not fully human.

Only in the late Roman Empire can one discern the initial stages of the recognition of privacy as a zone of intimacy.

As one might expect, ancient and primitive societies display diverse attitudes to privacy. In his seminal study *Privacy Rights: Moral and Legal Foundations*, Barrington Moore examined the state of privacy in a number of early communities, including classical Athens, Jewish society as revealed in the Old Testament, and ancient China. In the case of China, he illustrates how the Confucian distinction between the separate realms of the state (public) and the family (private), as well as early texts on courtship, the family, and friendship, generated weak rights to privacy. In 4th-century BCE Athens, on the other hand, privacy rights were accorded stronger protection. His conclusion was that privacy of communication was attainable only in a complex society with strong liberal traditions.

Our modern demarcation of public and private zones occurred as a result of a twin movement in political and legal thought. The emergence of the nation-state and theories of sovereignty in the 16th and 17th centuries generated the concept of a distinctly public realm. On the other hand, the identification of a private domain free from the encroachment of the state emerged as a response to the claims of monarchs, and, in due course, parliaments, to an untrammelled power to make law. In other words, the appearance of the modern state, the regulation of social and economic activities, and the recognition of a private realm, are natural prerequisites to this separation.

Historical evidence, however, tells only part of the story. Sociological models powerfully express the social values that capture this transformation. A particularly useful sociological dichotomy is the distinction between *Gemeinschaft* and *Gesellschaft*. The former, broadly speaking, is a community of internalized norms and traditions regulated according to status but mediated by love, duty, and a shared understanding and purpose. *Gesellschaft*, on the other hand, is a society in which self-interested individuals compete for personal material advantage in a so-called free market.

This distinction is often expressed as the difference between community and association. The former exhibits almost no division between the public and the private, while in the latter the separation is stark: the law formally regulates that which is conceived to be public. This differentiation illuminates also the political and economic order.

The segregation of public and private spheres is also a central tenet of liberalism. Indeed, 'liberalism may be said largely to have been an argument about where the boundaries of [the] private sphere lie, according to what principles they are to be drawn, whence interference derives and how it is to be checked'. The extent to which the law might legitimately intrude upon the 'private' is a recurring theme, especially in 19th-century liberal doctrine: 'One of the central goals of nineteenth-century legal thought was to create a clear separation between constitutional, criminal, and regulatory law—public law—and the law of private transactions—torts, contracts, property, and commercial law.' And the question of the limits of the criminal law in enforcing 'private morality' continues to perplex legal and moral philosophers.

More than 150 years since its publication, John Stuart Mill's 'harm principle', expounded in *On Liberty*, still provides a litmus test for most libertarian accounts of the limits of interference in the private lives of individuals. For Mill:

> the sole end for which mankind are warranted, individually or collectively in interfering with the liberty of action of any of their number, is self-protection. That the only purpose for which power can be rightfully exercised over any member of a civilized community, against his will, is to prevent harm to others. His own good, either physical or moral, is not a sufficient warrant.

The value of privacy

A life without privacy is inconceivable. But what purposes does privacy actually serve? In addition to its significance in liberal democratic theory, privacy stakes out a sphere for creativity, psychological wellbeing, our ability to love, forge social relationships, promote trust, intimacy, and friendship.

In his classic work, Alan Westin identifies four functions of privacy that combine the concept's individual and social dimensions. First, it engenders personal autonomy; the democratic principle of individuality is associated with the need for such autonomy – the desire to avoid manipulation or domination by others. Second, it provides the opportunity for emotional release. Privacy allows us to remove our social mask:

On any given day a man may move through the roles of stern father, loving husband, car-pool comedian, skilled lathe operator, union steward, water-cooler flirt, and American Legion committee chairman – all psychologically different roles that he adopts as he moves from scene to scene on the individual stage... Privacy... gives individuals, from factory workers to Presidents, a chance to lay their masks aside for rest. To be always 'on' would destroy the human organism.

Third, it allows us to engage in self-evaluation – the ability to formulate and test creative and moral activities and ideas. And, fourth, privacy offers us the environment in which we can share confidences and intimacies, and engage in limited and protected communication.

> **Private peccadilloes**
>
> The backstage language consists of reciprocal first-naming, co-operative decision-making, profanity, open sexual remarks, elaborate griping, smoking, rough informal dress, 'sloppy' sitting and standing posture, use of dialect or sub-standard speech, mumbling and shouting, playful aggression and 'kidding', inconsiderateness for the other in minor but potentially symbolic acts, minor physical self-involvements such as humming, whistling, chewing, nibbling, belching and flatulence.
>
> Erving Goffman, *The Presentation of Self in Everyday Life* (Doubleday Anchor, 1959), p. 128

The dilemma of privacy

Yet privacy is not an unqualified good. Seven shortcomings may briefly be identified. First, privacy is sometimes perceived as a rather quaint, prudish Victorian value; it has, in the words of one writer, 'an air of injured gentility'. Second, and more seriously, the shroud of privacy may conceal domestic oppression, especially of

> ### Privacy and female oppression
>
> [W]hen the law of privacy restricts intrusions into intimacy, it bars change in control over that intimacy... It is probably not coincidence that the very things feminism regards as central to the subjection of women – the very place, the body; the very relations, heterosexual; the very activities, intercourse and reproduction; and the very feelings, intimate – form the core of what is covered by privacy doctrine. From this perspective, the legal concept of privacy can and has shielded the place of battery, marital rape, and women's exploited labor.
>
> Catharine MacKinnon, *Feminism Unmodified: Discourses on Life and Law* (Harvard University Press, 1987), p. 101

women by men. Feminists claim that a significant cause of women's subjugation is their relegation to the private realm of the home and family. Moreover, while the state is disposed to control the public sphere, there is a reluctance to encroach into the private realm – frequently the site of the exploitation of and violence against women.

Third, the sanctuary of privacy may weaken the detection and apprehension of criminals and terrorists. Today, of course, threats to security occupy centre-stage. Some fear that an excessively zealous defence of privacy may hinder law-enforcement authorities in the execution of their responsibilities. Fourth, it may hamper the free flow of information, impeding transparency and candour. Fifth, privacy may obstruct business efficiency and increase costs. An undue preoccupation with privacy can undermine the collection of crucial personal information, and slow down the making of commercial decisions, thereby reducing productivity.

Sixth, certain communitarian critics regard privacy as an unduly individualistic right that should not be permitted to trump other rights or community values. Finally, a powerful case is made against privacy by those, like the American judge and jurist Richard Posner, who argue – from an economic standpoint – that withholding unflattering personal information may constitute a form of deception. This important critique warrants closer examination.

In seeking to withhold or limit the circulation of personal information, is the individual engaged in a form of deception, especially when the information depicts him in an unfavourable light? Posner asserts:

> To the extent that people conceal personal information in order to mislead, the economic case for according legal protection to such information is no better than that for permitting fraud in the sale of goods.

But even if one were to recognize the economic perspective, it does not follow that one would accept the assessment of the economic value of withholding personal information. Individuals may be willing to trade their interest in restricting the circulation of such information against their societal interest in its free flow. In other words, Posner has not shown, and may be unable to show, that his calculation of 'competing' interests is necessarily the correct, or even the most likely, one.

Posner also argues that transaction-cost considerations may militate against the legal protection of personal information. Where the information is discrediting and accurate, there is a social incentive to make it generally available: accurate information facilitates reliance on the individual to whom the information relates. It is therefore socially efficient to allow a society a right of access to such information rather than to permit the individual to conceal it. In the case of non-discrediting or false information, the value to the individual of concealment exceeds the value of access to it by the community. Information which is false does not advance rational decision-making and is therefore of little use.

The meaning of privacy

So far, I have employed the term 'privacy' promiscuously. I have used it to describe a variety of conditions or interests – from seeking refuge to the intimacy of close relations. It is hardly surprising that the notion is anything but coherent. While there is general consensus that our privacy is violated by onslaughts on the private domain – in the shape of surveillance, the interception of our communications, and the activities of the paparazzi, the waters grow ever murkier when a multitude of additional grievances are crowded under the privacy umbrella.

The gargantuan literature on the subject has not produced a lucid or consistent meaning of a value that provides a forum for contesting, amongst other things, the rights of women (especially

8. **The appetite for celebrity gossip fuels an increasingly sensationalist media**

in respect of abortion), the use of contraceptives, the freedom of homosexuals and lesbians, the right to read or view obscene material or pornography, and some of the problems of confidentiality generated by HIV/AIDS. Harnessing privacy in the pursuit of so many disparate, sometimes competing, political ideals has generated a good deal of analytical confusion.

Privacy apathy

Surveillance technology and the business of daily spying go on largely unnoticed. People have long since gotten used to video cameras, discount cards, and advertising messages... Although it occasionally annoys him, the transparent citizen appreciates how much easier life is in the computer age. He unhesitatingly forgoes being unobserved, anonymous, unavailable. He has no sense of having less personal freedom. He does not even see that there is something to be defended. He attaches too little importance to his private sphere to want to protect it at the expense of other advantages. Privacy is not a political program that can win votes... People leave more traces behind than they realize. No longer is one allowed to withdraw from society and live without being pestered... The individual cannot secretly change masks and become someone else. He can neither disguise himself nor temporarily disappear. His body is regularly X-rayed, his journey through life recorded, and his life changes documented... Nothing is overlooked, ignored, thrown away... When every careless act, every error, every fleeting trifle is recorded, there can no longer be any spontaneous action. Everything one does is evaluated and judged. Nothing escapes surveillance. The past suffocates the present... If data were not erased at regular intervals, people would be imprisoned in the dungeons of their own history. However, this outlook seems to frighten hardly anyone.

Wolfgang Sofsky, *Privacy: A Manifesto* (Princeton University Press, 2008), pp. 7–8

The value of privacy as a general moral, political, or social value is undeniable, but the more the notion is stretched, the greater its ambiguity. In pursuit of clarity, it is arguable that at its heart lies a desire, probably a need, to prevent information about us being known to others without our consent. But, as mentioned above, there are other issues that have increasingly entered the privacy arena. This is most conspicuous in the United States. The expression by the Supreme Court of 'unenumerated rights' such as privacy since its seminal decisions in *Griswold v Connecticut* and *Roe v Wade* (which supported a constitutional right of privacy in respect of contraception and abortion, respectively) has resulted in privacy being equated with the liberty of personal choice: the freedom to pursue various activities, albeit normally in a private place. In other words, the concept of privacy includes the right to control access to and use of bodies. Moreover, since laws regulating abortion and certain sex acts profoundly affect both individual privacy and government power, it may be useful to recognize the category as incorporating the capacity to make personal decisions, what is called 'decisional privacy'.

Incursions into the home, office, or 'private space' have also spawned the idea of 'locational privacy' – an inelegant phrase that captures that feature of privacy invaded by assaults – overt or covert – on the personal domain.

A definition?

An acceptable definition of privacy remains elusive. Westin's ubiquitous and influential idea conceives of privacy as a claim: the 'claim of individuals, groups, or institutions to determine for themselves when, how, and to what extent information about them is communicated to others'. To regard privacy as a claim (or, the more so, as a right) not only presumes the value of privacy, but fails to define its content. It would, moreover, include the use or disclosure of *any* information about an individual. A similar criticism may be levelled at those conceptions of privacy as an 'area of life' or a psychological state.

Westin's definition has, however, exerted even greater influence in respect of its description of privacy in terms of the extent to which an individual has *control* over information about himself or herself. For control over information to be equated with privacy, an individual would have to be said to have lost privacy if he or she is prevented from exercising this control, even if he or she is unable to disclose personal information. This means that the value of privacy is presumed.

Similarly, if I knowingly and voluntarily disclose personal information, I do not thereby lose privacy because I am exercising – rather than relinquishing – control. But this sense of control does not adequately describe privacy, for although I may have control over whether to disclose the information, it may be obtained by other means. And if control is meant in a stronger sense (namely that to disclose information, even voluntarily, constitutes a loss of control because I am no longer able to curtail the dissemination of the information by others), it describes the *potential* rather than the *actual* loss of privacy.

Consequently, I may not attract any interest from others and therefore my privacy will receive protection whether or not I desire it! There is a distinction between my controlling the flow of information about myself, and my being known about in fact. In order to establish whether such control actually protects my privacy, according to this argument, it is also necessary to know, for instance, whether the recipient of the information is bound by restrictive norms.

Furthermore, if privacy is regarded as an aspect of broad-spectrum control (or autonomy), it is assumed that what is at issue is my freedom to choose privacy. But, as suggested above, you may choose to abandon your privacy; the control-based definition therefore relates to the question of which choices you exercise rather than the manner in which you exercise them. It is, in other words, a definition which presupposes the value of privacy.

In view of these headaches, may the answer lie in attempting to describe the characteristics of privacy? Again, however, considerable disagreement exists. One view is that privacy consists of 'limited accessibility' – a cluster of three related but independent components: *secrecy*: information known about an individual; *anonymity*: attention paid to an individual; and *solitude*: physical access to an individual.

A loss of privacy, as distinct from an infringement of a right of privacy, occurs, in this account, where others obtain information about an individual, pay attention, or gain access to him or her. The claimed virtues of this approach are, first, that it is neutral, facilitating an objective identification of a loss of privacy. Second, it demonstrates the coherence of privacy as a value. Third, it suggests the utility of the concept in legal contexts (for it identifies those occasions calling for legal protection). And fourth, it includes 'typical' invasions of privacy and excludes those issues mentioned above which, though often thought to be privacy questions, are best regarded as moral or legal issues in their own right (noise, odours, prohibition of abortion, contraception, homosexuality, and so on).

Yet even this analysis presents difficulties. In particular, to avoid presuming the value of privacy, the analysis rejects definitions that limit themselves to the *quality* of the information divulged. It therefore dismisses the view that, to constitute a part of privacy, the information concerned must be 'private' in the sense of being intimate or related to the individual's identity. If a loss of privacy occurs whenever *any* information about an individual becomes known (the secrecy component), the concept is severely diluted.

It is a distortion to describe *every* instance of the dissemination of information about an individual as a loss of privacy. To the extent, however, that privacy is a function of information or knowledge about the individual, this seems to be inescapable. In other words, in so far as the question of information about an individual is concerned, some limiting or controlling factor is required. The most acceptable factor is arguably that the information be 'personal'.

To claim that whenever an individual is the subject of attention or when access to him is gained he or she necessarily loses privacy is again to divest our concern for privacy of much of its meaning. Having attention focused upon you or being subjected to uninvited intrusions upon your solitude are objectionable in their own right, but our concern for the individual's privacy in these circumstances is strongest when he or she is engaged in activities which we would normally consider private. The Peeping Tom is more likely to affront our conception of what is 'private' than someone who follows us in public.

It is sometimes argued that by protecting the values underpinning privacy (property rights, human dignity, preventing or compensating the infliction of emotional distress, and so on), moral and legal discourse concerning privacy may be dispensed with. If true, this would undercut the conceptual distinctiveness of privacy. Second, even among those who deny the derivative character of privacy, there is little agreement concerning its principal defining features.

Worse, arguments about the meaning of privacy frequently proceed from fundamentally different premises. Thus, where it is described as a 'right', the issue is not seriously joined with those who regard it as a 'condition'. The former is usually a normative statement about the need for privacy (however defined); the latter merely makes a descriptive statement about 'privacy'. Moreover, claims about the desirability of privacy tend to confuse its instrumental and inherent value; privacy is regarded by some as an end in itself, while others view it as a means by which to secure other social ends such as creativity, love, or emotional release.

Privacy and personal information

Is there another way? Without undermining the significance of privacy as an essential value, could the answer lie in isolating the issues that give rise to individuals' claims? There is little doubt that originally the archetypal complaints in the privacy field related to what the American law calls 'public disclosure of private facts' and 'intrusion upon an individual's seclusion, solitude or private affairs'. More recently, the collection and use of computerized personal data, and other issues associated with our electronic society, have, of course, become major privacy concerns.

It seems clear that, at bottom, these questions share a concern to limit the extent to which private facts about the individual are respectively published, intruded upon, or misused. This is not to suggest that certain conditions (for instance, being alone) or certain activities (such as telephone-tapping) ought not to be characterized as privacy or invasions of privacy respectively.

In locating the problems of privacy at the level of personal information, two obvious questions arise. First, what is to be understood by 'personal' and, second, under what circumstances is a matter to be regarded as 'personal'? Is something 'personal' by virtue simply of the claim by an individual that it is so, or are there matters that are *intrinsically* personal? To claim that my political views are personal must depend on certain norms which prohibit or curtail inquiries into, or unauthorized reports of, such views. It may, however, suffice for me to invoke the norm that I am entitled to keep my views to myself.

These norms are clearly culture-relative as well as variable. As mentioned above, anthropological evidence suggests that primitive

Buying and selling privacy

You do not strike a deal about personal or private information. The law does not offer you a monopoly right in exchange for your publication of these facts. That is what is distinct about privacy: individuals should be able to control information about themselves. We should be eager to help them protect that information by giving them the structures and the rights to do so. We value, or want, our peace. And thus, a regime that allows us such peace by giving us control over private information is a regime consonant with public values. It is a regime that public authorities should support... (N)othing in my regime would give individuals final or complete control over the kinds of data they can sell, or the kinds of privacy they can buy. The P3P regime would in principle enable upstream control of privacy rights as well as individual control... (T)here is no reason such a regime would have to protect all kinds of private data... there may be facts about yourself that you are not permitted to hide; more important, there may be claims about yourself that you are not permitted to make ('I am a lawyer', or 'Call me, I am a doctor'). You should not be permitted to engage in fraud or to do harm to others.

Lawrence Lessig, *Code and Other Laws of Cyberspace* (Basic Books, 1999), pp. 162-3

societies have differential privacy attitudes. And it can hardly be doubted that in modern societies, conceptions of what is 'private' will fluctuate. There is certainly less diffidence in most modern communities with regard to several aspects of private life than characterized societies of even 50 years ago. Is there not a class of information that may plausibly be described as 'personal'? Normally it is objected that 'privateness' is not an attribute of the information itself; that the *same* information may be regarded as very private in one context and not so private or not private at all in another.

> **Anti-privacy moments**
>
> The last decade seems to have generated more than its share of what one might call 'anti-privacy moments' – moods in public opinion characterized by willingness to let more and more personal data slip out of individual control. The shock of mass terrorism in Europe and North America has been one impetus to such moods, though hardly the only one. What the last ten years do not seem to have yielded is more moments like Watergate or the revolt against excessive census demands in Germany – dramas that sharpen the public's immune reactions against privacy invasion, and consolidate the institutions and practices built upon such reaction.
>
> James B. Rule, in J. B. Rule and G. Greenleaf (eds.), *Global Privacy Protection: The First Generation* (Edward Elgar, 2008), pp. 272–3

Naturally, Jane may be more inclined to divulge intimate facts to her analyst or to a close friend than to her employer or partner. And her objection to the disclosure of the information by a newspaper might be expected to be even stronger. But the information remains 'personal' in all three contexts. What changes is the extent to which she is prepared to permit the information to become known or to be used. It is counter-intuitive to describe the information in the first context (the analyst) as 'not private at all' or even 'not so private'. We should surely want to say that the psychiatrist is listening to *personal* facts being discussed. Were the conversation to be surreptitiously recorded or the psychiatrist called upon to testify in court as to his patient's homosexuality or infidelity, we should want to say that *personal information* was being recorded or disclosed. The context has manifestly changed, but it affects the degree to which it would be reasonable to expect the individual to object to the information being used or spread abroad, not the *quality* of the information itself.

Any definition of 'personal information' must therefore include both elements. It should refer both to the *quality* of the information and to the *reasonable expectations of the individual concerning its use*. The one is, in large measure, a function of the other. In other words, the concept of 'personal information' postulated here is both descriptive and normative.

Personal information includes those facts, communications, or opinions which relate to the individual and which it would be reasonable to expect him or her to regard as intimate or sensitive, and therefore to want to withhold, or at least to restrict their collection, use, or circulation. 'Facts' are not, of course, confined to textual data, but encompass a wide range of information, including images, DNA, and other genetic and biometric data such as fingerprints, face and iris recognition, and the ever-increasing types of information about us that technology is able to uncover and exploit.

Greater clarity?

It might immediately be objected that, by resting the notion of 'personal information' on an *objective* determination of an individual's expectations, the definition is actually an exclusively normative one and therefore pre-empts enquiries concerning the desirability or otherwise of protecting 'personal information'. But any attempt to classify information as 'personal', 'sensitive', or 'intimate' entails an assumption that such information warrants special treatment.

To the extent that it is necessary to define the information by reference to some objective criterion, it is inevitable that the classification depends on what may legitimately be claimed to be 'personal'. Only information which it is reasonable to wish to withhold is likely, under any test, to be the focus of our concern, particularly if we are seeking its effective legal protection. An individual who regards information concerning, say, his automobile, as personal and therefore seeks to withhold details of the size of its engine will find it difficult to persuade anyone that his vehicle's registration document constitutes a disclosure of 'personal information'. An objective test of what is 'personal' will normally operate to exclude such species of information.

But this becomes more difficult where the individual's claim relates to information that affects her private life. It would not be unreasonable, for instance, for an individual to wish to prevent the disclosure of facts concerning her trial and conviction for theft. Applying the proposed definition of personal information as a first-order test of whether such information is personal may suggest that the claim is a legitimate one. But it is likely to be defeated on the ground that the administration of justice is an open and public process. The passage of time may, however, alter the nature of such events and what was once a *public* matter may, several years later, be reasonably considered as private.

Similarly, the publication of what was once public information garnered from old newspapers may several years later be considered an offensive disclosure of personal information. It does not therefore follow that the objective test pre-empts the balancing of the individual's right or claim to withhold personal information, on the one hand, against the competing interests of the community in, say, freedom of expression, on the other. By voluntarily disclosing or acceding to the use or dissemination of personal information, the individual does not relinquish his or her claim that he or she retains certain control over it. He or she may, for instance, allow the information to be used for one purpose (such as medical diagnosis), but object when it is used for another (such as employment).

With regard to opinions about an individual expressed by a third party, the existence of which the individual is *aware* (such as references sought for a job application), it would be reasonable to expect her to permit access to such material only by those who are directly concerned in the decision whether or not to employ her. Where she does *not* know that assessments have been made about her (where, for example, she is described as a 'bad risk' on the database of a credit reference agency) or that her communications have been intercepted or recorded, she may reasonably be expected to object to the use or disclosure (and in the case of surreptitious surveillance, to the actual acquisition) of the information, particularly if it is – actually or potentially – misleading or inaccurate *were she aware* of its existence.

It is true that on its own, an item of information may be perfectly innocuous, but when combined with another piece of equally inoffensive data, the information is transformed into something that is genuinely private. So Ms Wong's address is publicly available and, on its own, hardly constitutes 'private' information. Connect this with, say, her occupation, and the combination converts the data into vulnerable details that she has a legitimate interest in concealing.

An objective notion of personal information does not neglect the need to consider the complete context in which the data occur. In evaluating whether the information in question satisfies the threshold requirement of 'personal', the facts that are the subject of the individual's complaint will plainly need to be examined 'in the round'. It is hardly reasonable for victims to conceive of publicly accessible data (telephone numbers, addresses, number plates, etc.) as information whose disclosure or circulation they wish to control or curtail. In general, it is only when these data are rendered sensitive, for example by their linkage to other data, that a justifiable complaint could be said to materialize.

Reasonableness does not wholly exclude the operation of individual idiosyncrasy where its effect would be relevant to the circumstances of the case. Nor would an objective test deny the significance of such factors in determining whether it is reasonable for an individual to consider information as personal. The British, for example, are notoriously coy about revealing their salaries: Scandinavians far less so. Cultural factors will inevitably influence the judgement of whether it is reasonable to regard information as personal. And this is no less true within a specific society.

In any event, no item of information is – in and of itself – personal. An anonymous medical file, bank statement, or lurid disclosure of a sexual affair is innocuous until linked to an individual. Only when the identity of the subject of the information is revealed does it become personal. And this is no less true once this threshold is crossed; what is now personal information is worthy of protection only when it satisfies an objective test. But this does not occur in a conceptual or social vacuum; it must be evaluated by reference to the specific conditions.

Despite disagreement over the meaning, scope, and limits of privacy, there is little uncertainty about its significance and the threats to its preservation. Few doubt that the erosion of this fundamental value must be checked. The next chapter considers its recognition as a legal right.

Chapter 3
A legal right

Queen Victoria and Prince Albert were accomplished etchers. In 1849, the royal couple wanted copies made for their private use, and sent a number of plates of their etchings to the palace printer, one Strange. Several of the impressions somehow fell into the hands of a third party, Judge, who evidently obtained them through a 'mole' employed by Strange. In turn, Strange acquired them from Judge in the honest belief that they were to be publicly exhibited with the consent of Victoria and Albert. A catalogue was produced and they set about arranging the exhibition. When he learned that royal assent was nonexistent, Strange withdrew his participation from the exhibition, but decided to proceed with the printing of the catalogue. His proposal was to offer it for sale along with autographs of their regal artists.

The royal couple was not amused. The prince sought an injunction to prevent the exhibition and the intended circulation of the catalogue. It was, needless to say, granted, the court shamelessly acknowledging that 'the importance which has been attached to this case arises entirely from the exalted station of the Plaintiff...'.

Though the judgments in the case turn largely on the fact that the plates were the property of the prince, the court explicitly

9. The royal couple was not amused

recognized that this afforded a wider basis upon which the law 'shelters the privacy and seclusion of thoughts and sentiments committed to writing, and desired by the author to remain not generally known'.

The American genesis

This decision was a significant factor in the legendary article that in 1890 was to give birth to the legal recognition of privacy in its own right. Written by Samuel D. Warren and Louis D. Brandeis, their commentary was published in the influential *Harvard Law Review*. A few years before, the invention of the inexpensive and portable 'snap camera' by Eastman Kodak had changed the world. Individuals could be snapped at home, at work, or at play. The beginning of the end of privacy was nigh.

The two lawyers, Warren, a Boston attorney and socialite, and Brandeis, who would be appointed to the Supreme Court in 1916, angered by nascent media intrusion, so-called 'yellow journalism', wrote what is widely characterized as the most influential law review article ever published. It is often thought that the catalyst for their anger was that the press had snooped on Warren's daughter's wedding. But this seems unlikely since, in 1890, she was six years old! The more likely source of their irritation was a series of articles in a Boston high-society gossip magazine, describing Warren's swanky dinner parties.

In any event, the celebrated article condemned the press for their effrontery (foreshadowing also the threat to privacy posed by Kodak's new-fangled contraption), and contended that the common law implicitly recognized the right to privacy. Drawing upon decisions of the English courts relating to, in particular, breach of confidence, property, copyright, and defamation, they argued that these cases were merely instances and applications of a general right to privacy. The common law, they claimed, albeit under different forms, protected an individual whose privacy was invaded by the likes of a snooping journalist. In so doing, the law acknowledged the importance of the spiritual and intellectual needs of man. They famously declared:

10. The seminal 1890 article by Samuel Warren and his partner Louis Brandeis (above), who was later to become a distinguished member of the United States Supreme Court, expounded the claim that the common law protected the right of privacy

The intensity and complexity of life, attendant upon advancing civilization, have rendered necessary some retreat from the world, and man, under the refining influence of culture, has become more sensitive to publicity so that solitude and privacy have become more essential to the individual; but modern enterprise and invention have, through invasion upon his privacy, subjected him to mental pain and distress, far greater than could be inflicted by mere bodily injury.

The common law, they reasoned, has developed from the protection of the physical person and corporeal property to the protection of the individual's '[t]houghts, emotions and sensations'. But as a result of threats to privacy from recent inventions and business methods and from the press, the common law needed to go further. An individual's right to determine the extent to which his thoughts, emotions, and sensations were communicated to others was already legally protected but only in respect of authors of literary and artistic compositions and letters who could forbid their unauthorized publication. And though English cases recognizing this right were based on protection of property, in reality they were an acknowledgement of privacy, of 'inviolate personality'.

It was not long before their line of reasoning was put to the test. In 1902, the plaintiff complained that her image had been used without her consent to advertise the defendant's merchandise. She was portrayed on bags of flour with the dismal pun, 'Flour of the family'. The majority of the New York Court of Appeals rejected Warren and Brandeis's thesis, holding that the privacy argument had 'not as yet an abiding place in our jurisprudence, and... cannot now be incorporated without doing violence to settled principles of law...'. The minority, however, warmed to the idea, Gray J declaring that the plaintiff had a right to be protected against the use of her image for the defendant's commercial advantage: 'Any other principle of decision... is as repugnant to equity as it is shocking to reason.'

The iniquity of gossip

Gossip is no longer the resource of the idle and of the vicious, but has become a trade, which is pursued with industry as well as effrontery. To satisfy a prurient taste the details of sexual relations are spread broadcast in the columns of the daily papers. To occupy the indolent, column upon column is filled with idle gossip, which can only be procured by intrusion upon the domestic circle... Nor is the harm wrought by such invasions confined to the suffering of those who may be the subjects of journalistic or other enterprise. In this, as in other branches of commerce, the supply creates the demand. Each crop of unseemly gossip, thus harvested, becomes the seed of more, and, in direct proportion to its circulation, results in the lowering of social standards and of morality. Even gossip apparently harmless, when widely and persistently circulated, is potent for evil. It both belittles and perverts. It belittles by inverting the relative importance of things, thus dwarfing the thoughts and aspirations of a people. When personal gossip attains the dignity of print, and crowds the space available for matters of real interest to the community, what wonder that the ignorant and thoughtless mistake its relative importance. Easy of comprehension, appealing to that weak side of human nature which is never wholly cast down by the misfortunes and frailties of our neighbors, no one can be surprised that it usurps the place of interest in brains capable of other things. Triviality destroys at once robustness of thought and delicacy of feeling. No enthusiasm can flourish, no generous impulse can survive under its blighting influence.

Samuel D. Warren and Louis D. Brandeis, 'The Right to Privacy' (1890) 5 *Harvard Law Review* 196

The court's decision provoked general discontent. This led to the enactment by the State of New York of a statute that rendered the unauthorized use of an individual's name or image for advertising or trade purposes unlawful. But three years later, in a case involving similar facts, the Supreme Court of Georgia adopted the reasoning of Gray J. The Warren and Brandeis argument, 15 years after its publication, had prevailed. Most American states have since incorporated the 'right to privacy' into their law. Yet, despite the authors' heavy reliance on the judgments of English courts, no comparable development has occurred in England or in other common law jurisdictions.

Over the years, the American common law maintained its steady expansion of the protection of privacy. In 1960, Dean Prosser, a leading tort expert, expounded the view that the law now recognized not one tort, 'but a complex of four different interests... tied together by the common name, but otherwise [with] nothing in common'. He delineated their nature as follows:

> The first tort consists in intruding upon the plaintiff's seclusion or solitude or into his private affairs. The wrongful act is the intentional interference with the plaintiff's solitude or seclusion. It includes the physical intrusion into the plaintiff's premises and eavesdropping (including electronic and photographic surveillance, bugging, and telephone-tapping). Three requirements must be satisfied: (a) there must be an actual prying); (b) the intrusion must offend a reasonable man; (c) it must be an intrusion into something private.

The second tort is the public disclosure of embarrassing private facts about the plaintiff. Prosser distinguished three elements of the tort:

> (a) there must be publicity (to disclose the facts to a small group of people would not suffice); (b) the facts disclosed must be private facts (publicity given to matters of public record is not tortious); (c) the facts disclosed must be offensive to a reasonable man of ordinary sensibilities.

Third, he identified a tort that consists of publicity that places the plaintiff in a false light in the public eye. This is usually committed where an opinion or utterance (such as spurious books or views) is publicly attributed to the plaintiff or where his picture is used to illustrate a book or article with which he has no reasonable connection. The publicity must again be 'highly offensive to a reasonable person'.

Finally, Prosser distinguished the tort of appropriation, for the defendant's advantage, of the plaintiff's name or likeness. The advantage derived by the defendant need not be a financial one; it has, for instance, been held to arise where the plaintiff was wrongly named as father on a birth certificate. The statutory tort, which exists in several states, on the other hand, normally requires the unauthorized use of the plaintiff's identity for commercial (usually advertising) purposes. The recognition of this tort establishes what has been dubbed a 'right of publicity' under which an individual is able to decide how he or she desires to exploit his or her name or image commercially. The four forms of invasion of privacy, according to Prosser, were connected only in that each constituted an interference with the 'right to be let alone'.

This fourfold segregation of the right to privacy is regarded by some as misconceived because it undermines the Warren and Brandeis axiom of 'inviolate personality' and neglects its moral basis as an aspect of human dignity. The classification has nevertheless assumed a prominent place in American tort law, although, as predicted by one legal scholar, Harry Kalven, it has to a large extent ossified the conception into four types:

> [G]iven the legal mind's weakness for neat labels and categories and given the deserved Prosser prestige, it is a safe prediction that the fourfold view will come to dominate whatever thinking is done about the right of privacy in the future.

The vicissitudes of these four torts have been charted in an immense torrent of academic and popular literature. Nor has this development been restricted to the United States. Virtually every advanced legal system has, to a greater or lesser extent, sought to recognize certain aspects of privacy. These include Austria, Canada, China and Taiwan, Denmark, Estonia, France, Germany, Holland, Hungary, Ireland, India, Italy, Lithuania, New Zealand, Norway, the Philippines, Russia, South Africa, South Korea, Spain, Thailand, and the majority of Latin American countries.

A constitutional right

These four torts remained the effective means by which the American law protected privacy. And they marked, more or less, the confines of the constitutional protection of privacy as well. The principal concern of Warren and Brandeis was, of course, what we would now call media intrusion. Several years later, however, Justice Brandeis (as he now was) delivered a powerful dissent in the case of *Olmstead v United States* in 1928. He declared that the Constitution conferred 'as against the Government, the right to be let alone', adding, 'To protect that right, every unjustifiable intrusion by the Government upon the privacy of the individual, whatever the means employed, must be deemed a violation of the Fourth Amendment.' That view was adopted by the Supreme Court in *Katz v United States*. Since then privacy as the right to be let alone has repeatedly been invoked by the Supreme Court.

The most significant – and controversial – development came in 1965 with the Supreme Court's decision in *Griswold v Connecticut*. It declared unconstitutional a Connecticut statute prohibiting the use of contraceptives – because it violated the right of marital privacy, a right 'older than the Bill of Rights'. The Constitution makes no mention of the right of privacy. Yet in a series of cases the Supreme Court has – via the Bill of Rights (particularly the First, Third, Fourth, Fifth, and Ninth Amendments) – recognized, amongst other privacy rights, that of 'associational privacy', 'political privacy', and 'privacy of counsel'. It has also set the limits of protection against eavesdropping and unlawful searches.

By far the most divisive 'privacy' decision that the Court has decided is the case of *Roe v Wade* in 1973. It held, by a majority, that the abortion law of Texas was unconstitutional as a violation of the right to privacy. Under that law, abortion was criminalized, except when performed to save the pregnant woman's life. The Court held that states may prohibit abortion to protect the life of the foetus only in the third trimester. The judgment, which has been described as 'undoubtedly the best-known case the United States Supreme Court has ever decided', is concurrently welcomed by feminists, and deplored by many Christians. It is the slender thread by which the right of American women to a lawful abortion hangs. There appears to be no middle ground. The jurist Ronald Dworkin forthrightly depicts the intensity of the skirmish:

> The war between anti-abortion groups and their opponents is America's new version of the terrible seventeenth-century European civil wars of religion. Opposing armies march down streets or pack themselves into protests at abortion clinics, courthouses, and the White House, screaming at and spitting on and loathing one another. Abortion is tearing America apart.

Another 'privacy' judgment of the Court that generated a hullabaloo was *Bowers v Hardwick* in 1986, in which a bare majority held that the privacy protections of the due process clause did not extend to homosexual acts between consenting adults in private: 'No connection between family, marriage, or procreation on the one hand and homosexual conduct on the other has been demonstrated.'

This decision was explicitly overruled in *Lawrence v Texas* in which, by 6 to 3, the Supreme Court decided that it had construed the liberty interest too narrowly. The majority held that substantive due process under the Fourteenth Amendment entailed the freedom to engage in intimate consensual sexual conduct. Its effect is to nullify all legislation throughout the United

11. The United States Supreme Court's decision of *Roe v Wade* in 1973 sparked a controversy that persists to this day

States that purports to criminalize sodomy between consenting same-sex adults in private.

The American experience is both influential and instructive. Other common law jurisdictions continue to wrestle with the intractable problems of definition, scope, and reconciling privacy with other rights, especially freedom of expression. It is fair to say, as a generalization, that the preference of the common law is interest-based, while the continental tradition of civil law jurisdictions tends to be rights-based. In other words, while the English law, for example, adopts a pragmatic case-by-case approach to the protection of privacy, French law conceives of privacy as a fundamental human right. This disparity has nevertheless been attenuated by the impact of the European Convention on Human Rights and other declarations and directives emanating from Brussels. The intensity of this side-wind is most conspicuously

Map of surveillance societies around the world

Some safeguards but weakened protections
Systemic failure to uphold safeguards
Extensive surveillance societies
Endemic surveillance societies

12. Privacy is accorded differential protection across the globe

evident in the adoption by the United Kingdom in its Human Rights Act of 1998, as will become clear below.

Common law tribulations

It is not only the law of England and Wales that still grapples with the predicament of privacy. Australia, New Zealand, Ireland, Canada, Hong Kong, and other common law jurisdictions languish in a quagmire of indecision and hesitancy.

The English law, despite several commissions, committees, and attempts at legislation, remains uncertain and ambiguous. In 1972, the Younger Committee rejected the idea of a general right of privacy created by statute. It concluded that it would burden the court 'with controversial questions of a social and political character'. Judges would be likely to encounter problems balancing privacy with competing interests such as freedom of expression. The committee recommended the creation of a new crime and tort of unlawful surveillance, a new tort of disclosure or other use of information unlawfully acquired, and the consideration of the law on breach of confidence (which protects confidential information entrusted by one party to another) as a possible means by which privacy could be safeguarded. Similar reports have been produced in other common law jurisdictions.

In recent years, a spate of celebrity litigation has presented the courts with an opportunity to examine whether, in the absence of explicit common law privacy protection, the remedy of breach of confidence might provide a makeshift solution. These are best considered in Chapter 4. They demonstrate how a right of privacy is slouching towards the highest court to be born. One such case, involved the publication of photographs taken surreptitiously of the wedding of movie stars Michael Douglas and Catherine Zeta-Jones, and is also discussed in Chapter 4. Lord Hoffmann has declared in the House of Lords that the:

coming into force of the Human Rights Act 1998 weakens the argument for saying that a general tort of invasion of privacy is needed to fill gaps in the existing remedies. Sections 6 and 7 of the Act are in themselves substantial gap fillers; if it is indeed the case that a person's rights under Article 8 have been infringed by a public authority, he will have a statutory remedy. The creation of a general tort will.... pre-empt the controversial question of the extent, if any, to which the Convention requires the state to provide remedies for invasions of privacy by persons who are not public authorities.

The impact of this Act (which incorporates into English law Article 8 of the European Convention on Human Rights) cannot be overstated. It provides for the protection of the right to respect for family life, home, and correspondence. This measure, at least in the mind of one senior judge, gives 'the final impetus to the recognition of a right of privacy in English law'. Though his conviction may not be shared by all members of the judiciary, the analysis of privacy exhibited in recent cases suggests that the effect of Article 8 is to supply, at least, the potential for the horizontal application of the rights in this Article. Indeed, it is not unreasonable to identify in a number of recent judgments a willingness to allow Article 8 to thwart the birth of a full-blown privacy tort. One can almost hear the clank of the sword being returned to its scabbard.

As in Britain, deliberations about the need for legal protection have preoccupied law-reform commissions at both state and federal level in Australia. Nor have the courts been idle. In a significant decision in 2001, a majority of the High Court of Australia tilted gingerly towards the recognition of a privacy tort. In *Australian Broadcasting Corporation v Lenah Game Meats Pty Ltd*, the court, acknowledging the inadequacy of Australian law, expressed its support for the judicial development in common law jurisdictions of a common law action for invasion of privacy. In specifying what

13. Despite attempts to conduct their wedding in private, surreptitious photographs of the Douglases were taken, and became the subject of protracted and significant litigation in England

might constitute an unwarranted invasion of privacy, the court stated:

> Certain kinds of information about a person, such as information relating to health, personal relationships, or finances, may be easy to identify as private; as may certain kinds of activity, which a reasonable person, applying contemporary standards of morals and behaviour, would understand to be meant to be unobserved. The requirement that disclosure or observation of information or conduct would be highly offensive to a reasonable person of ordinary sensibilities is in many circumstances a useful practical test of what is private.

The decision, though inconclusive on the central issue, does suggest that the High Court, when presented with a more deserving plaintiff (this one was an abattoir whose cruel practices the Australian Broadcasting Corporation wished to expose), may recognize that a privacy tort may not be entirely unthinkable.

In 2005, the New Zealand Court of Appeal took a significant step towards recognizing a common law tort of privacy. In the case of *Hosking v Runting*, the defendants took pictures of the plaintiffs' 18-month-old twin daughters in the street, being pushed in their buggy by their mother. The father is a well-known television personality. The couple sought an injunction to prevent publication. The trial court held that New Zealand law did not recognize a cause of action in privacy based on the public disclosure of photographs taken in a public place. But, though the Court of Appeal dismissed the plaintiffs' appeal, it decided (by 3 to 2) that a case had been made out for a remedy for 'breach of privacy by giving publicity to private and personal information'. This view was based principally upon its interpretation of the English courts' analysis of the remedy for breach of confidence, as well as the fact that it was consistent with New Zealand's obligations under the ICCPR and the United Nations Convention on the Rights of the Child. The court also considered that their judgment facilitated the reconciliation of competing values, and enabled New Zealand to draw upon the extensive experience of the United States.

In their judgments, Gault P and Blanchard J specified two essential requirements for a claim to succeed. First, the plaintiff must have a reasonable expectation of privacy; and second, there must be publicity given to private facts that would be considered highly offensive to an objective reasonable person.

The Privacy Act of 1993 provides that any person may complain to the Privacy Commissioner alleging that any action is or appears to be 'an interference with the privacy of an individual'. If the Privacy Commissioner finds that the complaint has substance, he may refer it to the Proceedings Commissioner appointed under the Human Rights Act 1993, who may in turn bring proceedings in the Complaints Review Tribunal. The Tribunal may make an order prohibiting a repetition of the action complained of or requiring the interference to be rectified. It has the power to award damages.

While Ireland does not explicitly recognize a general right to privacy at common law, the courts have fashioned a constitutional right to privacy out of Article 40.3.1 of the Constitution under which the State guarantees to respect, defend, and vindicate the personal rights of the citizen. So, for example, in 1974 the majority of the Supreme Court held that privacy was included among these rights. Succeeding judgments have indicated that the Article extends to some invasions of privacy by interception of communications and surveillance.

Other approaches

The continental attitude to privacy is based on the concept of the 'right of personality'. In Germany, this right is guaranteed by the Basic Law. Article 1 imposes on all state authorities a duty to respect and protect 'the dignity of man'. Article 2(1) provides that 'Everyone shall have the right to the free development of his personality in so far as he does not violate the rights of others or offend against the constitutional order or the moral code.' These two articles combine to establish a general right to one's own personality; and the right to respect for one's private sphere of life is an emanation of this personality right.

In addition, the courts protect privacy as part of the right of personality under the Civil Code. They also employ the law of delict to provide a remedy against conduct injurious to human dignity such as the unauthorized publication of the intimate details of a person's private life, the right not to publish medical reports without the patient's consent; the right not to have one's conversation recorded without one's knowledge and consent; the right not to have one's private correspondence opened – whether or not it is actually read; the right not to be photographed without consent; the right to a fair description of one's life; and the right not to have personal information misused by the press.

The German courts recognize three spheres of personality: the 'intimate', the 'private', and the 'individual' spheres. The 'intimate sphere' covers one's thoughts and feelings and their expression, medical information, and sexual behaviour. Given its particularly private nature, this species of information enjoys absolute protection. The 'private sphere' includes information which, while neither intimate nor secret (such as facts about one's family and home life), is nevertheless private and therefore attracts qualified protection; disclosure might be justified in the public interest. The 'individual sphere' relates to an individual's public, economic, and professional life, one's social and occupational relations. It attracts the lowest degree of protection.

Privacy is zealously protected in France. Though it is not explicitly mentioned in the French Constitution, the Constitutional Council in 1995 extended the concept of 'individual freedom' in Article 66 to the right to privacy. Privacy was thus elevated to a constitutional right. In addition, Article 9 of the French Civil Code provides that 'Everyone has the right to respect for his private life...'. This has been interpreted by the courts to include a person's identity (name, date of birth, religion, address, and so on) and information about a person's health, matrimonial situation, family, sexual relationships, sexual orientation, and his or her way of life in general. It is also a criminal offence to encroach intentionally upon a private place by taking a photograph or by making a recording. Damages may be awarded for violations.

The Italian Constitution protects the right to privacy as a constituent of an individual's personality. Thus an invasion of privacy may give rise to a claim under the Civil Code, which provides that a person who intentionally or negligently commits an act that causes unreasonable harm to another is liable to compensate the latter. The Civil Code declares also that the publication of a person's image may be restrained if it causes prejudice to his dignity or reputation.

Article 10 of the Dutch Constitution guarantees the right to privacy, but it is a right subject to qualification; though the Supreme Court has held that the right to freedom of speech does not excuse an infringement of privacy, it will consider all circumstances in a privacy action, and a journalist may demonstrate that the publication in question was reasonable. Article 1401 of the Civil Code imposes a general liability for causing wrongful harm to others; it has been interpreted to include harm caused by publishing injurious private information without justification. The criminal law punishes trespassing into a person's home, eavesdropping on private conversations, and the unauthorized taking of photographs of individuals on any private property, and publishing the photograph so acquired.

While neither the Canadian Constitution nor its Charter of Rights and Freedoms include an explicit reference to privacy, the courts have filled the gap by construing the right to be secure against unreasonable search or seizure (Section 8 of the Charter) to embody an individual's right to a reasonable expectation of privacy. There is no common law right of privacy along American lines, but the lower courts have shown a willingness to stretch existing causes of action, such as trespass or nuisance, to protect the privacy of the victim. The common law deficiency has been resolved in a number of Canadian provinces by the enactment of a statutory tort of invasion of privacy. In British Columbia, Manitoba, Newfoundland, and Saskatchewan, the tort of 'violation of privacy' is actionable without proof of damage. The precise formulation of the tort differs in each province.

Quebec, as a civil law jurisdiction, has developed its remedy through the interpretation of general provisions of civil liability in the former Civil Code. The present protection, however, is explicitly incorporated in the new Civil Code. It provides that every person has a right to the respect of his reputation and privacy, and that no-one may invade the privacy of another person except with the consent of the person or his heirs, or unless it is authorized by law. The forms of privacy-invading conduct specified cover a fairly wide range of conduct. In addition, Section 5 of the Quebec Charter of Human Rights and Freedoms declares that every person has a right to respect for his private life. This provision is directly enforceable between citizens. The 1994 Uniform Privacy Act clarifies and augments the existing provincial statutes.

The international dimension

A fairly generous right to privacy is an acknowledged human right, and is recognized in most international instruments. So, for example, Article 12 of the United Nations Declaration of Human Rights and Article 17 of the International Covenant on Civil and Political Rights (ICCPR) both provide:

(1) No one shall be subjected to arbitrary or unlawful interference with his privacy, family, home or correspondence, nor to unlawful attacks on his honour and reputation.
(2) Everyone has the right to the protection of the law against such interference or attacks.

Article 8 of the European Convention on Human Rights (ECHR) declares,

(1) Everyone has the right to respect for his private and family life, his home and his correspondence.

(2) There shall be no interference by a public authority with the exercise of this right except such as is in accordance with the law and is necessary in a democratic society in the interests of national security, public safety or the economic well-being of the country, for the prevention of disorder or crime, for the protection of health or morals, or for the protection of the rights and freedoms of others.

The European Court of Human Rights in Strasbourg has had its hands fairly full adjudicating complaints from individuals seeking redress for alleged infractions of Article 8. Their grievances have exposed deficiencies in the domestic law of several European jurisdictions. For example, in *Gaskin v United Kingdom*, the Court held that the right to respect for private and family life imposed a duty to provide an individual with personal information about himself or herself held by a public authority. In *Leander v Sweden*, the court had ruled that such access could legitimately be denied to an applicant where the information related to national security, for example, for the purpose of vetting an individual for a sensitive position, provided there is a satisfactory process by which the decision not to provide the information may be reviewed. Two of the court's leading decisions in regard to telephone-tapping are discussed below.

Intrusion

Today's spy no longer relies on his unaided eyes and ears. As we saw in Chapter 1, an array of electronic devices renders his task relatively simple. And in the face of these technological advances, the traditional physical or legal means of protection are unlikely to prove particularly effective; the former because radar and laser beams are no respecters of walls or windows; the latter because, in the absence of an encroachment upon the individual's property, the law of trespass will not assist the beleaguered victim of electronic surveillance. The interest protected is the plaintiff's property rather than his privacy.

Physical intrusions into private premises raise similar questions to those generated by the interception of private conversations and correspondence, electronic or otherwise. No civilized society can permit the unauthorized entry and search of a person's home without a valid warrant issued in advance, normally by a court. The prevention, detection, and prosecution of criminal conduct frequently require searches of private premises by the police and other law enforcement authorities. This is a matter that raises deeper questions of policy that extend beyond the protection of privacy. It is nevertheless clear, especially in a modern industrialized society, that electronic surveillance, interception of correspondence, and telephone-tapping call for systematic and fairly elaborate legislative machinery to control, in particular, the circumstances under which the law will permit the use of such devices, and their legitimate application in the pursuit of offenders and the administration of criminal justice.

The laws of many democratic countries regulate the exercise of covert surveillance by a judicial authority. Normally a court order sets out the restrictions, including time limits, on the exercise of this power which is especially pernicious since it involves monitoring not only what the subject says, but also those to whom he or she speaks. Most are likely to be wholly innocent interlocutors.

Surveillance and terrorism

A powerful weapon in the so-called 'war on terror' is the wiretap. Its use has predictably intensified since the attacks of 11 September 2001. Within six weeks of this date, the United States Congress had enacted the United and Strengthening America by Providing Appropriate Tools Required to Intercept and Obstruct Terrorism

Act (USA PATRIOT Act). This was merely one of several measures that have been introduced to authorize the surveillance of a wide range of activities, including telephone calls, email, and Internet communications, by a number of law-enforcement officials. The provisions of a series of pre-11 September statutes – such as the Wiretap Statute, the Electronic Communications Privacy Act (ECPA), and the Foreign Intelligence Surveillance Act (FISA) – have been substantially amended, significantly diminishing their privacy safeguards.

Privacy advocates and civil libertarians have condemned numerous features of the legislation. Among their concerns is the fact that it reduces the judicial oversight of electronic surveillance by subjecting private Internet communications to a minimal standard of review. The Act also permits law-enforcement authorities to obtain what is, in effect, a 'blank warrant'; it authorizes 'scattershot' intelligence wiretap orders that do not need to specify the place to be searched or require that only the target's conversations be listened to.

Another disquieting feature of the statute is the power it affords the FBI to use its intelligence authority to evade judicial review of the 'probable cause' requirement of the Fourth Amendment which requires that search warrants specify the place to be searched. It prevents abuses such as random searches of the homes of innocent persons based on a warrant obtained to search someone else's home. In other words, in the case of electronic surveillance, the specificity requirement of the Fourth Amendment obliges law-enforcement officers applying for a court order to specify the telephone they wish to tap.

In its celebrated 1967 decision in *Katz v United States*, the Supreme Court held that a listening device placed outside a public telephone booth constituted an unlawful search. The government argued that since the bug was not actually inside the booth, no invasion of the plaintiff's privacy had occurred. Rejecting this view, the Court declared that 'the Fourth Amendment protects people, not places'. Though it has since retreated somewhat from this position, its judgment that protection should turn on whether in the circumstances the individual had a 'reasonable expectation of privacy' remains the hook on which to hang the claim that similar protection ought to apply to communications on the Internet. For the moment, however, the PATRIOT Act, its more recent incarnation, and related measures, place questions such as this on ice.

Prior to its enactment, investigators in terrorism and espionage cases were required to return to the court every time a suspect changed telephones or computers and obtain a fresh warrant.

The Act allows 'roving wiretap' warrants from a secret court to intercept a suspect's phone and Internet conversations, without identifying a specific phone or the suspect. In other words, when the target of a roving wiretap order enters another person's home, law-enforcement agents can tap the homeowner's telephone.

Are these legislative inroads into privacy really necessary? According to the American Civil Liberties Union:

> The FBI already has broad authority to monitor telephone and Internet communications. Current law already provides, for example, that wiretaps can be obtained for the crimes involved in terrorist attacks, including destruction of aircraft and aircraft piracy. Most of the changes to wiretapping authority contemplated in the USA PATRIOT Act would apply not just to surveillance of people suspected of terrorist activity, but to investigation of other crimes as well. The FBI also has authority to intercept communications without probable cause of crime for 'intelligence purposes under the Foreign Intelligence Surveillance Act ('FISA')'. The standards for obtaining a FISA wiretap are lower than those for obtaining a criminal wiretap.

Pen registers and trap-and-trace devices electronically screen telephone or Internet communications. So, a pen register monitors all numbers dialled from a telephone line or all Internet communications are recorded. The PATRIOT Act authorizes a federal judge or magistrate in one area to issue a pen register or a trap-and-trace order that does not specify the name of the Internet Service Provider (ISP) upon which it can be served. Indeed, it can be served on an ISP anywhere in the United States. The judge simply issues the order and law-enforcement agents fill in the locations at which the order can be served, thereby further curtailing the judicial function.

Modes of approval

Long before the current spate of anti-terrorist measures, the United States had enacted several statutes, both at federal and state level, which set standards to be satisfied before government interception was permitted. Before a warrant is issued under the Electronic Communications Privacy Act 1986 (ECPA), the law-enforcement officer must indicate the nature of the offence under investigation, the interception point, the types of conversations to be intercepted, and the names of the likely targets. He needs to demonstrate probable cause, and that normal investigative techniques are ineffective. Court orders under the Act authorize surveillance for up to 30 days (with the possibility of a 30-day extension). A report must be made to the court every 7 to 10 days.

It is a federal crime to wiretap or to use a machine to capture the communications of others without court approval, unless one of the parties has given their prior consent. It is also a federal offence to use or disclose any information acquired by illegal wiretapping or electronic eavesdropping. Legislation also provides protection against the interception of email and the surreptitious use of telephone-call-monitoring practices. These arrangements include a procedural mechanism to afford limited law-enforcement access to private communications and communications records under conditions consistent with the dictates of the Fourth Amendment that guarantees the right to be free of unreasonable search and seizure, and provides that no warrant shall be issued, save on probable cause.

A solution?

There is no perfect system. But, at the very least one would expect democratic societies to regulate this highly intrusive form of surveillance in a manner that ensures that the legitimate and reasonable expectations of its citizens are respected. In deciding whether to grant an application for a warrant to carry out covert surveillance, a court ought to satisfy itself that the proposed intrusion has a legitimate purpose. It should ensure that the means of investigation are proportionate to the immediacy and gravity of the alleged offence, balancing the need for the surveillance against the intrusiveness of the activity on the subject and others who may be affected by it. There must be a reasonable suspicion that the target is involved in the commission of a serious crime. It should also be satisfied that information relevant to the purpose of the surveillance is likely to be acquired, and that such information cannot reasonably be obtained by less intrusive means.

In reaching its decision, one would be entitled to assume that a judicial officer would have regard to the immediacy and gravity of the serious crime or the threat to public security, the place where the intrusion will occur, the method of intrusion to be employed, and the nature of any device to be used.

A court should consider the 'reasonable expectation of privacy' in the particular circumstances of the case. In respect of wiretapping, the suggestion is sometimes heard that a telephone user's reasonable expectation of privacy may be vindicated when the eavesdropper turns out to be a private individual, but not when it is the police acting under lawful authority. This is said to be based on an acceptance of risk, but it is difficult to see how such a distinction can be legitimately drawn. If I am entitled to assume that my private conversation will not be overheard by a private individual, why should that assumption be any less strong when the eavesdropper turns out to be the police?

A further recurring difficulty concerns the standards to be applied in the case of 'non-consensual surveillance' as opposed to 'participant monitoring'. The former occurs where a private conversation is intercepted by a person who is not a party to the conversation and who has not obtained the consent of any party to it. 'Participant monitoring' on the other hand, includes cases in which a party uses a listening device to transmit the conversation to one who is not a party, or where a party to the conversation records it without the consent of the other party. It is frequently argued that, while non-consensual surveillance ought to be legally controlled, participant monitoring – especially when used in law enforcement – is justifiable. But this neglects the distinctive interests that underpin the concern to protect the content and, perhaps even more importantly, the manner in which conversations are conducted. Moreover, though participant monitoring is a useful aid in the detection of crime, and arguably constitutes less of a risk to privacy than its non-consensual counterpart, 'the party to the conversation who secretly makes a recording can present matters in a way that is entirely favourable to his position because he controls the situation. He knows he is recording it.'

Europe

The European Court of Human Rights has been particularly energetic in this area. It is instructive briefly to compare two of its important decisions, one relating to Germany, the other to the

United Kingdom. The telephone-tapping in *Klass v Federal Republic of Germany* complied with the German statute. In *Malone v United Kingdom*, however, it was conducted without a comprehensive legislative framework. Although both involved analogue telephones, the principles expressed are sufficiently general to apply to digital telephony, as well as to the interception of written correspondence, and perhaps also to other forms of surveillance.

German law sets out stringent restrictions on interception including the requirement that applications be made in writing, that a basis exists in fact for suspecting a person of planning, committing, or having committed certain criminal or subversive acts, and that the surveillance may cover only the specific suspect or his presumed contact persons: exploratory or general surveillance is therefore not permitted. The law provides also that it must be shown that other investigatory methods would be ineffective or considerably more difficult. The interception is supervised by a judicial officer who may reveal only information that is relevant to the inquiry; he must destroy the remainder. The intercepted information must itself be destroyed when no longer required, nor may it be used for any other purpose.

The law requires that the interception must be immediately discontinued when these requirements have ended, and the subject must be notified as soon as this is possible without jeopardizing the purpose of the interception. He or she may then challenge the lawfulness of the interception in an administrative court and may claim damages in a civil court if prejudice is proved.

In addition, the German Basic Law protects secrecy of the mail, posts, and telecommunications. The court therefore had to decide whether interference was justified under Article 8(2) of the European Convention as being 'in accordance with the law' and necessary in a democratic society 'in the interests of national security...or for the prevention of disorder or crime'. While the court acknowledged the need for legislation to protect these interests, it held that the question was not the need for such provisions, but whether they contained sufficient safeguards against abuse.

The applicants contended that the legislation violated Article 8 of the European Convention because it lacked a requirement that the subject of the interception be 'invariably' notified following the termination of the surveillance. The Court held that this was not inherently incompatible with Article 8, provided that the subject was informed after the termination of the surveillance measures as soon as notification could be made without endangering the purpose of those measures.

In *Malone v United Kingdom*, the plaintiff, who, at his trial on a number of charges relating to handling stolen property, learned that his telephone conversations had been intercepted, issued a writ against the police. He argued in vain, first, that telephone-tapping was an unlawful infringement of his rights of privacy, property, and confidentiality; second, that it contravened Article 8 of the European Convention on Human Rights; and, third, that the Crown had no legal authority to intercept calls since no such power had been conferred by the law. He took his grievance to the European Court of Human Rights, where, not surprisingly, he succeeded. The Court unanimously held that the Convention had indeed been breached. As a result, the British Government acknowledged that a statute was required, and the Interception of Communications Act of 1985 was enacted. It establishes a fairly comprehensive framework, the centrepiece of which is the provision empowering the Secretary of State to issue warrants where he or she considers it necessary in the interests of national security, to prevent or detect serious crime, or safeguard economic wellbeing.

While wiretapping obviously assists in apprehending criminals and preventing crime and terrorism, the onus is on those who wish to employ this indiscriminate method of investigation to show that there is an overwhelming need to do so, that it is likely to be effective, and there are no acceptable alternatives. If this cannot be demonstrated, it becomes virtually impossible to justify the practice 'not because we wish to hamper law enforcement, but because there are values we place above efficient police work'.

A prudent approach to the problem would ensure that where the surveillance materials have been acquired in a seriously unconscionable manner, such that it would gravely undermine public confidence in the administration of justice, the information obtained should not be admitted in evidence in court.

Chapter 4
Privacy and free speech

Supermodel Naomi Campbell was photographed leaving a meeting of Narcotics Anonymous. The British tabloid newspaper *The Daily Mirror* published the pictures, together with articles claiming that she was receiving treatment for her drug addiction. She had denied publicly that she was an addict, and sued the newspaper for damages. The trial court and the Court of Appeal found against her. They held that by mendaciously asserting to the media that she did not take drugs, she had rendered it legitimate for the media to put the record straight. But her appeal to the House of Lords succeeded, and she was awarded compensation for a violation of her privacy.

Photographs of the wedding of Michael Douglas and Catherine Zeta-Jones were surreptitiously taken, notwithstanding explicit notice having been given to all guests forbidding 'photography or video devices at the ceremony or reception'. The couple had entered into an exclusive publication contract with *OK!* magazine, but its rival, *Hello!*, sought to publish these pictures. The stars reached for their lawyers, and won.

The European Court of Human Rights has, on a number of occasions, revealed the inadequacy of European domestic legal protection of privacy. One decision is particularly instructive.

14. Celebrities like supermodel Naomi Campbell are vulnerable to incessant pursuit by paparazzi

Princess Caroline of Monaco complained that paparazzi employed by several German magazines had photographed her while she was engaged in a variety of quotidian activities, including eating in a restaurant courtyard, horse riding, canoeing, playing with her children, shopping, skiing, kissing a boyfriend, playing tennis, sitting on a beach, and so on. A German court found in her favour in respect of the photographs which, though captured in a public place, were taken when she had 'sought seclusion'.

But, while accepting that some of the pictures were sufficiently intimate to warrant protection (such as those of her with her children or in the company of a boyfriend sitting in a secluded section of a restaurant courtyard), the court dismissed her complaint in regard to the rest. She turned to the European Court, which acknowledged that Article 8 applied, but sought to balance the protection of the princess's private life against that of freedom of expression as guaranteed by Article 10 of the Convention. Taking and publishing photographs, it decided, was a subject in which the protection of an individual's rights and reputation assumed especial significance since it did not concern the dissemination of 'ideas', but of images containing personal, or even intimate, 'information' about that individual. Moreover, pictures published in the tabloid press were frequently snapped in an atmosphere of harassment that generated in the paparazzi's quarry a strong sense of intrusion, or even of persecution.

The critical factor in balancing the protection of private life against freedom of expression, the Court held, was the contribution that the published photographs and articles made to a debate of general interest. The pictures of the princess were, it found, of a purely private nature, taken without her knowledge or consent, and, in some instances, in secret. They made no contribution to a debate of public interest given that she was not engaged in an official function and the photographs and articles related exclusively to details of her private life. Furthermore, while the public might have a right to information, including, in special circumstances, about the private life of public figures, they did not have such a right in this instance. It had no legitimate interest in knowing Princess Caroline's whereabouts or how she behaved in her private life – even in places that could not always be described as secluded. In the same way as there was a commercial interest for the magazines to publish the photographs and articles, those interests had, in the Court's view, to yield to the applicant's right to the effective protection of her private life.

The English courts have recently been vigorously seeking to resolve the endless tussles between public figures and the media. Despite the absence of a privacy statute, the judges appear to have fashioned a remedy out of a cluster of analogous legal actions. This Band-aid is unlikely to yield a coherent or durable solution to the problem.

Courting publicity?

Celebrities – stars of screen, radio, television, pop music, sport, and the catwalk – are regarded as fair game by the paparazzi. Members of the British royal family – most conspicuously, and tragically, the Princess of Wales – have long been preyed upon by the media.

It is persistently claimed that public figures forfeit their right to privacy. This contention is generally based on the following reasoning. It is asserted that celebrities relish publicity when it is favourable, but resent it when it is hostile. They cannot, it is argued, have it both ways. Second, the opinion is heard that the media have the right to 'put the record straight'. So, in the case of Naomi Campbell, since she lied about her drug addiction, there is, the Court of Appeal held, a public interest in the press revealing the truth.

The first assertion, advanced, not surprisingly, by the media, is a specious application of the idiom: 'live by the sword, die by the

> **A bogus public interest?**
>
> The argument that adopting a public life forfeits a private life is ridiculous. So too is the argument that, it is reported, many journalists use to establish a public interest: '*anything* may be relevant to assessment of a person's character'. True, anything may be relevant to a person's character, but not everything relevant to a person's character is of public interest. The odious practice of outing homosexuals, for instance, has also been defended on the ground of public interest... Not all persons whose appearance differs from their reality are thereby hypocrites. A homophobe, whether homosexual or not, who acts hostilely towards homosexuals solely because they are homosexuals, is unjust. *That* is the public interest. But if the homophobe is himself also homosexual, to publicize that further fact is protected neither by the outer's freedom of expression nor the public's right to information. On the contrary, it is an outrageous infringement of the homophobe's right to privacy.
>
> James Griffin, *On Human Rights* (Oxford University Press, 2008), pp. 240–1

sword'. It would sound the death knell for the protection of most public figures' private lives. The fact that a celebrity courts publicity – an inescapable feature of fame – cannot be allowed to annihilate their right to shield intimate features of their life from public view.

Nor is the second argument wholly persuasive. Suppose that a celebrity were HIV-positive or suffering from cancer. Can it really be the case that a legitimate desire on his or her part to deny that he or she is a sufferer of one of these diseases may be extinguished by the media's right to 'put the record straight'? If so, the protection of privacy becomes a fragile reed. Truth or falsity should not block the reasonable expectations of those who dwell in the glare of public attention.

But it is not only the rich and famous who have cause for complaint.

Ordinary people

Mr Peck was deeply depressed. One evening while walking down Brentwood High Street, he attempted to slash his wrists with a kitchen knife. He was unaware that he had been captured on CCTV by a camera installed by Brentwood Borough Council. The CCTV footage did not show him actually cutting his wrists. The operator was alerted only to the image of an individual in possession of a knife. The police were notified and arrived at the scene, where they seized the knife, provided Peck with medical assistance, and transported him to a police station, where he was detained under the Mental Health Act. After being examined and treated by a doctor, he was released without charge and taken home by police officers.

A few months later, the council published two photographs obtained from the CCTV footage to accompany an article headed: 'Defused – the partnership between CCTV and the police prevents a potentially dangerous situation.' Peck's face was not masked. The article described the circumstances as above. A few days afterwards, the *Brentwood Weekly News* used a photograph of the incident on its front page to illustrate an article on the use and benefits of CCTV. Again Peck's face was not concealed. Subsequently, another local newspaper published two similar articles, along with a picture of Peck taken from the CCTV footage, and stated that a potentially dangerous situation had been resolved. It added that Peck had been released without charge. Several readers recognized Peck from the picture.

Then extracts from the CCTV footage were included in a local television programme with an average audience of 350,000. This time, Peck's identity had been obscured, at the Council's oral request. A month or two later, Peck discovered from a neighbour that he had been filmed on CCTV, and that footage had been released. He took no action, as he was still suffering from severe depression.

The CCTV footage was also supplied to the producers of *Crime Beat*, a BBC series on national television with an average of 9.2 million viewers. The Council imposed several conditions, including that nobody should be identifiable in the footage. Nevertheless, trailers for an episode of the programme showed Peck's unmasked face. When friends informed him that they had seen him in the trailers, Peck complained to the Council. It contacted the producers, who confirmed that his image had been covered in the main programme. But when the programme was aired, despite the pixilation, he was recognized by friends and family.

His complaints to the Broadcasting Standards Commission and the Independent Television Commission (both now replaced by Ofcom, the Office of Communications) alleging, among other things, an unwarranted infringement of his privacy, were successful. His objection about the published articles to the Press Complaints Commission was, however, unproductive.

Peck then sought leave from the High Court to apply for judicial review concerning the Council's disclosure of the CCTV material. His application, and a further request for leave to appeal to the Court of Appeal, were both rejected. He therefore pursued his grievance in the European Court, which decided that the disclosure of the CCTV footage by the Council was a disproportionate interference with his private life, contrary to Article 8. The expression 'private life' in the Article was, it held, to be interpreted generously to include the right to identity and personal development.

Merely because the footage was taken on a public street did not render it a public occasion, since Peck was not attending a public event, nor was he a public figure, and it was late at night. Moreover, the disclosure of the footage to the media resulted in its being seen by a significantly larger audience than Peck could reasonably have foreseen. It was the extent of disclosure by the media that breached his Article 8 rights. The Court concluded that the Council could have obtained Mr Peck's consent prior to disclosure and it should have hidden his face.

The case is important authority for the proposition that merely because an individual is in a public place does not render his or her conduct public – except in so far as passers-by witness it. It was the extent of the further disclosure by various forms of media that breached Peck's Article 8 rights.

Intrusion and disclosure

The pursuit of information by the media frequently requires the use of intrusive methods: deception, zoom lenses, hidden devices, the interception of telephone conversations or correspondence, and the other forms of spying and surveillance described in Chapter 1. There is a tendency to conflate the intrusion practised by the prying journalist with the publication of the information thereby acquired. It is important that the two be kept separate.

This position was sensibly adopted in *Dietemann v Time, Inc.*, in which two reporters of *Life* magazine tricked the plaintiff into allowing them access to his home and there set up hidden surveillance devices to monitor the plaintiff, a virtually uneducated plumber who purported to diagnose and treat physical ailments. The resulting article certainly informed the public about a newsworthy topic – the unlicensed practice of medicine – but the court had to consider whether this would grant immunity to the reporters in respect of their surreptitious newsgathering techniques. On appeal, the judgment in the plaintiff's favour for invasion of privacy was upheld. In answer to the defendant's claim that the First Amendment's shield extended not only to publication but to investigation, the court remarked that the amendment 'has never been construed to accord newsmen immunity from torts or crimes committed during the course of newsgathering'.

Significantly, in its assessment of damages, the court took into account not only the nature and extent of the intrusive acts, but also the publication. It noted that 'there is no First Amendment interest in protecting news media from calculated misdeeds [thus] damages for intrusion [may] be enhanced by the fact of later publication'.

In respect of the First Amendment, though, the 'right to gather information is logically antecedent and practically necessary to any exercise of [the right to publish] and... cannot be given full meaning unless that antecedent right is recognized'. The common law denies the media a general privilege to gather information. Accordingly, the court correctly separated the two questions of intrusion and disclosure, assessing the reasonableness of the defendants' newsgathering techniques in the light of the common law principles developed under the former, and eschewing any First Amendment argument which would inevitably influence the latter.

The answer lies in the formulation of independent criteria by which to assess when an individual's seclusion may justifiably be violated, just as there are standards by which to test when the disclosure of private facts may be justified in the public interest.

Freedom of expression

We are all publishers now. The Internet has created hitherto unthinkable opportunities for freedom of expression. Bloggers proliferate at the rate of 120,000 a day. Social networking is the new form of community; Facebook has some 300 million members,

15. Revealing personal information is often hard to resist

MySpace around 100 million. Yet, these astonishing developments notwithstanding, the central question remains the same. How is privacy to be reconciled with freedom of expression?

The electronic age has still to address Warren and Brandeis's entreaty (discussed in Chapter 3) that the law ought to prevent the distress caused by the gratuitous publication of private information.

What are the justifications for free speech in a democratic society? They tend to be based either on the positive consequences fostered by the exercise of the freedom, or on the protection of individuals' right to express themselves. The former – consequentialist – argument

> **Gossip online**
>
> Even if gossip in cyberspace never bubbles up into the traditional press, it is more widely broadcast and more easily misinterpreted than it is in real space, resurrecting all of the stifling intimacy of a traditional society without the redeeming promise of being judged in context. The fact that gossip in cyberspace is recorded, permanently retrievable, and globally accessible increases the risk that an individual's public face will be threatened by past indiscretions. Gossip published on an Internet chat group may, in the short run, reach an audience that is no bigger than gossip over the back fence in a small town. But because Internet gossip, unlike individual memories, never fades, it can be resurrected in the future by those who don't know the individual in question, and thus are unable to put the information in a larger context. And unlike gossip in a small town, Internet gossip is hard to answer, because its potential audience is anonymous and unbounded.
>
> Jeffrey Rosen, *The Unwanted Gaze: The Destruction of Privacy in America* (Random House, 2000), p. 205

usually draws on the case made for free speech by John Milton and John Stuart Mill. The latter – rights-based – argument conceives of speech as an integral part of an individual's right to self-fulfilment.

These principles tend invariably to be amalgamated, and even confused. So, for example, Thomas Emerson discerns the following four primary justifications which include both sorts of claim: individual self-fulfilment; attainment of the truth; securing the participation by members of society in social, including political, decision-making; and providing the means of maintaining the balance between stability and change in society.

Champions of privacy, on the other hand, rely almost exclusively on rights-based arguments, as outlined in Chapter 2. But the extent to which the law may legitimately curtail speech that undermines an individual's privacy is often presented as a contest between these two heavyweights: freedom of speech versus privacy. But this may be mere shadow boxing. Why? Because 'at most points the law of privacy and the law sustaining a free press do not contradict each other. On the contrary, they are mutually supportive, in that both are vital features of the basic system of individual rights.'

A better approach?

The mist begins to clear once we focus our attention on the essential nature of privacy. When it is recognized that our core concern is the protection of personal information, the real character of the debate is illuminated. Happily (though all too rarely), from within the dark depths of the voluminous literature, shafts of light appear. For example, after a detailed discussion of the public disclosure tort, one writer concludes:

> Privacy law might be more just and effective if it were to focus on identifying (preferably by statute) those exchanges of information that warrant protection at their point of origin, rather than continuing its current, capricious course of imposing liability only if the material is ultimately disseminated to the public at large... [A] careful identification of particularly sensitive situations in which personal information is exchanged, and an equally careful delineation of the appropriate expectations regarding how that information can be used, could significantly curtail abuses without seriously hampering freedom of speech. At the very least, this possibility merits considerably more thought as an alternative to the Warren and Brandeis tort than it has received thus far.

And even Thomas Emerson suggests that there might be '[a]nother approach, and one that seems to me to be more fruitful' that would:

> place more emphasis on developing the privacy side of the balance. It would recognise the first amendment interests but it would give primary attention to a number of factors which derive ultimately from the functions performed by privacy and the expectations of privacy that prevail in contemporary society.

The first such factor is:

> [T]he element of intimacy in determining the zone of privacy. Thus so far as the privacy tort [of public disclosure] is concerned, protection would be extended only to matters related to the intimate details of a person's life: those activities, ideas or emotions which one does not share with others or shares only with those who are closest. This would include sexual relations, the performance of bodily functions, family relations, and the like.

There are some positive signs therefore that the quest for the elusive equilibrium between privacy and free speech has produced some scepticism about the conventional approach that languishes in an incoherent concept of privacy.

Whose freedom?

Does freedom of speech protect the interests of the speaker or the listener? Or, to put it more portentously, is the justification individual- or community-based?

The former is rights-based, and argues for the interests in individual autonomy, dignity, self-fulfilment, and other values that the exercise of free speech safeguards or advances. The latter is community-based, and is consequentialist or utilitarian. It draws on democratic theory or the promotion of truth to support free speech as facilitating or encouraging the unfettered exchange of ideas, the dissemination of information, and other means of enlarging participation in self-government.

Freedom of speech and privacy are often regarded as rights or interests of the individual, and – sometimes in the same breath – as rights or interests of the community as a whole. And, even more troubling, free speech is regarded as one, and privacy the other, thereby rendering any 'balancing' of the two somewhat problematic! In respect of the interests of the individual, they generally share the same concerns. Indeed, the social functions of privacy are difficult to distinguish from those of freedom of expression, as mentioned above. To treat them both as individual rights would seem to be an important step towards simplifying the issue.

Policy and principle

Theories of freedom of expression that seek to protect the audience are generally arguments of policy, based on the importance of that freedom to the community. Those that advance the interests of the speaker, on the other hand, are generally arguments of principle which give primacy to the individual's self-fulfilment over the interests of the community. The jurist Ronald Dworkin has suggested that free speech is likely to receive stronger protection when it is regarded as safeguarding, as a matter of principle, the rights of the speaker. And privacy is, in its broad sense, also rights-based rather than goal-based. If this is correct, it would at least facilitate a greater symmetry in the balancing exercise.

Unfortunately, the matter is more complex. At first blush, this strategy would provide a logical basis for claiming that publications that harm other individuals cannot seriously be said to advance the speaker's or publisher's interest in self-fulfilment. Who is 'fulfilled' by the disclosure that a supermodel is a drug addict? And who is to say whether certain forms of speech are instrumental in achieving this object?

Moreover, the argument 'suffers from a failure to distinguish intellectual self-fulfilment from other wants and needs, and thus fails to support a distinct principle of free speech'. It is also founded on the principle of the free dissemination of *ideas* rather than *information*, which reduces its utility in the present context. And, most embarrassingly, the argument is hard to deploy in defence of *press* freedom, which appears to rest almost entirely on the interests of the community, rather than the individual journalist, editor, or publisher.

What of the speaker's motives? It would not be unduly disingenuous to suggest that profit may be of some interest to newspaper editors and proprietors. And, as Eric Barendt remarks, 'a rigorous examination of motives to exclude speech made for profit would leave little immune from regulation'. Nor does the audience necessarily care; a good read is a good read whether its author is moved by greed or edification.

Truth

John Stuart Mill's celebrated argument from truth is based on the idea that any suppression of speech is an 'assumption of infallibility' and that only by the unrestricted circulation of ideas can the truth be revealed. But when taken to its logical conclusion, this would prevent any inroads being made into the exercise of the right to speak – at least truthfully. Apart from Mill's dubious supposition that there is an objective 'truth' out there, and his confidence in the dominance of reason, his theory makes the legal regulation of disclosures of personal information (as well as several other forms of speech that cause harm) extremely difficult to justify. It asserts that freedom of expression is a social good because it is the best process by which to advance knowledge

> **Truth versus falsehood**
>
> And though all the winds of doctrine were let loose to play on the earth, so Truth be in the field, we do injuriously by licensing and prohibiting misdoubt her strength. Let her and Falsehood grapple; who ever knew Truth put to the worse in a free and open encounter?
>
> I cannot praise a fugitive and cloistered virtue, unexercised and unbreathed, that never sallies out and sees her adversary, but slinks out of the race, where that immortal garland is to be run for, not without dust and heat.
>
> John Milton, *Areopagitica* (1644) (MacMillan, 1915)

and discover truth, starting from the premise that the soundest and most rational judgment is arrived at by considering all facts and arguments for and against. And, according to Emerson, this free marketplace of ideas should exist irrespective of how pernicious or false the new opinion appears to be 'because there is no way of suppressing the false without suppressing the true'.

But is the argument from truth really relevant to the protection of privacy? Frederick Schauer doubts whether truth is indeed ultimate and non-instrumental; does it not secure a 'deeper good' such as happiness or dignity? If truth is instrumental, then whether more truth causes a consequential strengthening of this deeper good is a question of fact and not an inexorable, logical certainty from definition. For Schauer, the argument from truth is an 'argument from knowledge'; an argument that the value in question is having people believe that things are in fact true.

Democracy

Free speech performs an essential function in promoting and maintaining democratic self-governance. This is an extension of the argument from truth, as the American political theorist Alexander Meiklejohn puts it:

> The principle of the freedom of speech springs from the necessities of the program of self-government. It is not a Law of Nature or Reason in the abstract. It is a deduction from the basic American agreement that public issues shall be decided by universal suffrage.

Yet, as in the case of the argument from truth, it must be queried how self-government is facilitated or advanced by the revelation of intimate private facts about, say, an individual's sexual proclivities? Is it 'speech' at all?

In some cases, such information may be relevant to self-government. Where, for instance, people acting through their democratically elected government consider a certain action to be sufficiently antisocial to constitute a criminal offence, then it is in the interest of self-governance that offenders are apprehended and punished. Similarly, where an individual holds a public office, and thereby actually acts on behalf of the people, representing and implementing their political opinions, any activity of that person which pertains directly to his or her fitness to perform that function is a legitimate interest of the community. Sadly, there are all too many examples of politicians championing 'family values', who are then exposed as adulterers or worse. A public interest test is capable of supporting freedom of expression in these cases. The argument from democracy should not be taken to justify unlimited freedom of speech in the privacy arena.

Press freedom

Arguments from democracy are in full flower here. For Milton and Blackstone, it was the prior restraint of the press that represented the most sinister threat to freedom of speech. Sir William Blackstone, the 18th-century jurist, declared:

> The liberty of the press is indeed essential to the nature of a free state; but this consists in laying no previous restraints upon publications and not in freedom from censure for criminal matter when published. Every free man has an undoubted right to lay what sentiments he pleases before the public: to forbid this, is to destroy the freedom of the press: but if he publishes what is improper, mischievous, or illegal, he must take the consequence of his own temerity.

Both the conception of the press and the boundaries of its freedom are, however, considerably wider today. Thus the term 'press' normally extends beyond newspapers and periodicals, and includes a far wider range of publications media: television, radio, and the Internet. Nor is the scope of press freedom restricted to prohibitions against 'prior constraint'.

The political justification for free speech is an application of the argument from truth. Mill's second hypothesis, it will be recalled, is the 'assumption of infallibility' that specifies the conditions under which we are able to have confidence in believing that what we think is true, actually is true. The safest way to achieve this, the argument runs, is to accord individuals the freedom to debate ideas: to subject them to contradiction and refutation. Interference with this freedom diminishes our ability to arrive at rational beliefs.

This is a powerful idea, even if it may appear to be based on an idealized model of the political process in which there is active popular participation in government. A free press does have the potential to engender this awareness and to facilitate its exercise.

The appeal of the arguments from truth and from democracy is that they establish independent grounds for freedom of expression in a way that arguments based on the interests of the speaker do not. But the media publish much that, even by the most generous exercise of the imagination, is not remotely connected to these noble pursuits. Does this suggest that they are entitled to no special treatment? Arguments to support special treatment for the press tend to fall on stony judicial ground. A stronger case can plainly be made where, unlike the *Daily Mirror* in the Naomi Campbell case, the press offends decorum rather than the law. This argument may then be made to turn on the importance to the political process of the publication of a particular report. Accounts of the private lives of government ministers, officials, politicians, and even perhaps royalty, it could plausibly be claimed, warrant special treatment. Here, the nature of the message, and not the medium of its propagation, is the focal point of concern. This approach does not distinguish whether the freedom is exercised in the press or the pub. It has the additional merit of avoiding the problem of defining the 'press'.

The First Amendment

In the United States, the issue of freedom of expression is debated against the background of the First Amendment's injunction that 'Congress shall make no law... abridging the freedom of speech, or of the press'. American courts and commentators have developed several theories of free speech, both rights-based and consequentialist, which seek to account for the exercise of freedom of expression in all its protean forms. Nevertheless, though it would be artificial to conceive of the problems encountered by the efforts to reconcile privacy and free speech as a discrete matter, the American law does appear to have developed the contours of a privacy/free speech theory.

In particular, there is a tendency to adopt a purposive construction of the First Amendment. This asks: what forms of speech or publication warrant protection by virtue of their contribution to the operation of political democracy. It has been employed in several decisions that distinguish, with variable consequences, between public figures and ordinary individuals. Indeed, the

Supreme Court applied the principle adopted in the well-known libel case of *New York Times v Sullivan* to the privacy case of *Time, Inc. v Hill* (see below). In the former decision, the Court expressed its philosophy in unequivocal terms:

> [W]e consider this case against the background of a profound national commitment to the principle that debate on public issues should be uninhibited, robust and wide open, and that it may well include vehement, caustic, and sometimes unpleasantly sharp attacks on government and public officials.

The chief purpose of the First Amendment is, in this approach, the protection of the right of all citizens to understand political issues in order that they might participate effectively in the operation of democratic government. This formula allows considerable scope for actions by private individuals who have been subjected to gratuitous publicity. In practice, however, it is frequently those who are in the public eye that – for this very reason – attract the attention of the tabloids. The difficult question which the theory is then required to answer is the extent to which such public figures are entitled to protection of aspects of their personal lives. And this, in turn, involves a delicate investigation of what features of a public figure's life may legitimately be exposed – in the furtherance of political debate. His sex life? Her health? Their finances?

Although this theory seeks to distinguish between voluntary and involuntary public figures, its application, except as a general rationale for the existence of the freedom of speech itself, provides uncertain guidance as to the respective rights and obligations in cases involving unwanted publicity. In the absence of an attempt to define the kinds of information in respect of which all individuals might *prima facie* expect to receive protection (even if such protection is subsequently to be outweighed by considerations of the public interest), one of the central purposes of recognizing an individual's interest in restricting information – the trust, candour, and confidence it fosters – is diminished.

Balancing competing interests

Is it possible to formulate a coherent theory of free speech which is both sufficiently broad to capture the complexities of the exercise of the freedom, and sufficiently specific to account for its variable applications? The argument from democracy attracts greater support than the Millian or autonomy-based theories, but all provide at best only the most general guidance in respect of the legitimate controls on the public disclosure of personal information by the media.

An interest-based theory that specifies the particular interests of the parties involved in the disclosure raises numerous difficulties (not unlike the interest-based accounts of privacy). And, while it is useful to distinguish, say, the 'personality' interests involved when private facts are published from the 'reputational' interests affected by defamatory publications, or the 'commercial' interests affected by breaches of confidence, this approach fails to explain which species of information warrant protection in the face of the competing claims of free speech.

The American Supreme Court has, in mediating between the two interests, resorted to the process of 'balancing' by which the interest in free speech is weighed against other interests such as national security, public order, and so on. If such interests are found to be 'compelling' or 'substantial', or where there is a 'clear and present danger' that the speech will cause significant harm to the public interest, the Court will uphold the restriction of free speech.

The dynamics of limitation

Emerson uses this phrase to describe the proposition that the public interest in the freedom of expression must fit in to a 'more comprehensive scheme of social values and social goals'. So far,

I have touched on the inapplicability of certain free speech justifications; I have allowed the right of privacy to escape unscathed. Where there is a genuine conflict between the two values how is privacy to be protected? Or, in other words, why should free speech be subordinated to the protection of personal information?

In what circumstances might the absolute protection of free speech be moderated? Emerson suggests three. The first is where the injury is direct and peculiar to the individual, rather than one suffered in common with others. The second is when the interest is an intimate and personal one: embracing an area of privacy from which both the state and other individuals should be excluded. The third consideration is whether or not society leaves the burden of protecting the interest to the individual, by, for example recognizing that he or she has a legal cause of action.

In the first two circumstances, the harm is likely to be direct and irremediable. Moreover, if the individual has the burden of establishing his or her case, the resources of the state are less likely to be marshalled into a coherent apparatus for the restriction of free speech. He proposes that 'so long as the interest of privacy is genuine, the conditions of recovery clearly defined, and the remedy left to the individual suit, it is most unlikely that the balance will be tipped too far toward restriction of expression'.

Even against the background of the First Amendment, Emerson's approach is persuasive. And no less so in the context of the English law's constitutional silences as to safeguards for free speech. In the words of one senior judge:

> It cannot be too strongly emphasised that outside the established exceptions, or any new ones which Parliament may enact in accordance with its obligations under the Convention [for the Protection of Human Rights and Fundamental Freedoms], there is

no question of balancing freedom of speech against other interests. It is a trump card which always wins.

The court nevertheless acknowledged, that 'a right of privacy may be a legitimate exception to freedom of speech'. And other judges have recognized that there are 'exceptional cases, where the intended publication is plainly unlawful and would inflict grave injury on innocent people or seriously impede the course of justice'. Another declared that 'Blackstone was concerned to prevent government interference with the press. The times of Blackstone are not relevant to the times of Mr Murdoch.'

The public interest

When is a matter in the public interest? Courts have struggled to formulate rational criteria by which to make this controversial judgment. Among the considerations that would seem to be relevant are the following: To whom was the information given? Is the victim a public figure? Was he or she in a public place? Is the information in the public domain? Did the victim consent to publication? How was the information acquired? Was it essential for the victim's identity to be revealed? Was the invasion a serious one? What were the publisher's motives in disclosing the information?

In the United States, publishers need only to raise the defence of public interest or newsworthiness for it generally to demolish the protection against the gratuitous publication of private facts by the media. Thus in *Sidis*, the court declared that 'at some point the public interest in obtaining information becomes dominant over the individual's desire for privacy'. The privilege is defined in the *Second Restatement of Torts* as extending to information 'of legitimate concern to the public' – a conclusion which is reached by weighing the competing interests of the public's right to know against the individual's right to keep private facts from the public's gaze. This may be decided by the judge, as a matter of law or, more often, by the jury as a question of fact. The test embodied in the *Restatement*, reads as follows:

> In determining what comprises a matter of legitimate public interest, account must be taken of the customs and conventions of the community; and in the last analysis what is proper becomes a matter of the community mores. The line is to be drawn when the publicity ceases to be the giving of information to which the public is entitled, and becomes a morbid and sensational prying into private lives for its own sake, with which a reasonable member of the public, with decent standards, would say that he had no concern.

The categories of information which are newsworthy have steadily expanded as the courts have become increasingly conscious of the free speech implications of censoring accurate reporting. Sexual matters – understandably – dominate. This is illustrated by two Californian cases. In the first, an ex-marine became the subject of intense media interest when he foiled an assassination attempt on President Ford. The *San Francisco Chronicle* revealed that Sipple was a prominent member of the gay community, which indeed was true, but he brought an action under the tort of the public disclosure of private facts because he claimed that he had always kept his homosexuality private from his relatives. The court dismissed his action on two grounds. First, the information was already in the public domain, and, second, it held that the facts disclosed were newsworthy because the exposé was fuelled by the wish to combat the stereotyping of gays as 'timid, weak and unheroic', and to discuss the potential biases of the President (one newspaper had suggested that the President's reticence in thanking Sipple was on account of the latter's homosexuality).

In the other case, a newspaper article revealed that the first female student president of a Californian college, Diaz, was a transsexual. The court held that her transsexuality was a private fact and also that, although she was involved in a public controversy (in that she accused the college of misuse of student funds), the disclosure was irrelevant to that issue and, accordingly, not newsworthy. The court emphasized that the purpose of First Amendment protection was 'to keep the public informed so that they may make intelligent decisions on matters important to self-governing people'. It was further explained that 'the fact that she is a transsexual does not adversely reflect on her honesty or judgment. Nor does the fact that she was the first woman student body president, in itself, warrant that her entire private life be open to public inspection.'

How are these two decisions to be reconciled? The answer may lie in the tenor of the *Diaz* article. The newspaper argued that the report was intended to portray the 'changing roles of women in society', but it was clear from the tone of the article that the author's objective stopped at the 'stark revelation'. An important feature of both decisions is that the articles purported to portray alternative lifestyles. It is therefore arguable that, if the article about Diaz had seriously intended to portray the changing role of women in society, the court may have resisted calls for its censorship.

Celebrities

Our planet is star-struck. The most trivial item of gossip about a celebrity seems to excite huge interest and fascination. News stands are crammed with magazines devoted to the unremitting supply of these ephemeral, generally inane, facts. Does stardom extinguish privacy? Though the *American Restatement* comments that 'there may be some intimate details of her life, such as sexual relations, which even the actress is entitled to keep to herself', the decision in *Ann-Margret v High Society Magazine, Inc.* illustrates that this delicacy has not yet been embraced by the courts. In that case, the actress was denied relief in respect of the publication of a nude photograph of herself, partly because the photograph was of 'a woman who has occupied the fantasies of many movie-goers' and therefore 'of great interest to many people'.

It is often claimed that courts simply accept the judgment of the press as to what is newsworthy. One writer contends that 'deference to the judgment of the press may actually be the appropriate and principled response to the newsworthiness enquiry'. But this neglects the reason why the subject is contentious at all. She observes that 'the economic survival of publishers and broadcasters depends upon their ability to provide a product that the public will buy', and argues that marketplace competition breeds into the papers a 'responsiveness to what substantial segments of the population want to know to cope with the society in which they live'.

The concept of public interest all too easily camouflages the commercial motives of the media. Worse, it masquerades as the democratic exercise of consumer choice: we get the sensationalism we deserve. Both forms of cynical tabloidism neglect the consequences for individuals who happen to be public figures because they are unfortunate enough to be catapulted into the public eye.

A mores test

To evaluate what is 'highly offensive', the American courts have developed what has been called a 'mores test'. Thus, in *Melvin v Reid*, the plaintiff's past as a prostitute and defendant in a sensational murder trial was revealed in a film called *The Red Kimono* which was based on these events. She had, in the eight years since her acquittal, been accepted into 'respectable society', married, and moved in a circle of friends who were ignorant of her past. Her action for the invasion of her privacy caused by the defendant's truthful disclosures was sustained by the California court (which had not hitherto recognized an action for invasion of privacy).

In *Sidis v F.-R. Publishing Corporation*, on the other hand, the plaintiff, a former child prodigy who, at 11, lectured in mathematics at Harvard, had become a recluse and devoted his time to studying the Okamakammessett Indians and collecting streetcar transfers. The *New Yorker* published an article, 'Where Are They Now? April Fool' written by James Thurber under a pseudonym. Details of Sidis's physical characteristics and mannerisms, the single room in which he lived, and his current activities were revealed. The magazine article acknowledged that Sidis had informed the reporter who had tracked him down for the interview that he lived in fear of publicity and changed jobs whenever his employer or fellow workers learned of his past. The New York District Court denied his action for invasion of privacy on the ground that it could find no decision 'which held the "right of privacy" to be violated by a newspaper or magazine publishing a correct account of one's life or doings... except under abnormal circumstances which did not exist in the case at bar'. On appeal, the Second Circuit affirmed the dismissal of the privacy action, but appeared to base its decision on a balancing of the offensiveness of the article with the public or private character of the plaintiff.

In neither *Melvin* nor *Sidis* however, was there a proper attempt to consider the extent to which the information divulged was 'private'. The conceptually vague notions of 'community customs', 'newsworthiness', and the 'offensiveness' of the publication, render these and many other decisions concerning 'public disclosure' unhelpful in an area of considerable constitutional importance. And this is equally true of the efforts by the Supreme Court to fix the boundaries of the First Amendment in respect of publications which affect the plaintiff's privacy. For example, in *Time, Inc. v Hill* the Court held that the plaintiff's action for invasion of privacy failed where he (and his family) had been the subject of a substantially false report. The defendant had published a description of a new play adapted from a novel which fictionalized the ordeal suffered by the plaintiff when he and his family were held hostage in their home by a group of escaped prisoners.

Adopting the test that it had applied in respect of defamation, the Supreme Court held, by a majority, that unless there was proof of actual malice (i.e. that the defendant knowingly published an untrue report), the action would fail. Falsity alone did not deprive the defendant of his protection under the First Amendment – if the publication was newsworthy. And, since the 'opening of a new play linked to an actual incident is a matter of public interest', the plaintiff, because he was unable to show malice, failed. Yet it does seem that the decision was not really concerned with the public disclosure of private information—whether or not it was even a genuine libel action!

The future

There is no golden fleece. Enactment tomorrow anywhere of a comprehensive privacy statute would generate new problems for the judicial construction of victims' rights against unsolicited intrusions into private lives. Nor would these difficulties be diminished if the courts were to pursue a common law case-by-case route toward protection. The media would continue to be tested daily – with more concentrated minds perhaps – as to whether stories are in the 'public interest'.

The quest for a just equilibrium will never end. The key issue is whether, as often seems to be the case, the interests of the individual are to be sacrificed at the altar of a contrived public interest? Opponents of legal, or even non-legal, checks on unwanted public disclosure like to depict concern for the victim as quaint or prudish. This is distinguished from the vigorous pursuit of the truth by the media. In many cases, of course, newspapers, like all commercial institutions, are moved by the interests of their shareholders, who may be less concerned about what is published in the paper than what appears in its balance sheet. Nor, since the press frequently concedes that it should resist publishing insensitive disclosures of private facts, it is hardly in a position to characterize such apprehensions as pious or censorious.

Privacy advocates may well include enemies of free speech, but that is no more a legitimate argument against them than the contention that advocates of free speech include avaricious newspaper proprietors. The power of the press lobby can, however, never be underestimated. How many politicians, whose careers often hang by a slender thread, wish to invite the animosity of the tabloids by championing curbs on reporting of what has come to be called 'bonk journalism'? The press, while quick to condemn the exposure of private lives in the name of the public interest, inevitably closes ranks against legislation. Unhappily, while most tabloids preach family values, they often demonstrate little concern or respect for the families of their victims.

Chapter 5
Data protection

Information is no longer merely power. It is big business. In recent years, the fastest growing component of international trade has been the service sector. It accounts for more than a third of world trade – and continues to expand. It is a commonplace to identify, as a central feature of modern industrialized societies, their dependence on the storage of information. The use of computers facilitates, of course, considerably greater efficiency and velocity in the collection, storage, use, retrieval, and transfer of information.

The routine functions of government and private institutions require a constant stream of data about us in order to administer effectively the countless services that are an essential ingredient of contemporary life. The provision of health services, social security, credit, insurance, and the prevention and detection of crime assume the availability of a substantial quantity of personal data and, hence, a readiness by individuals to supply it. The computerization of this – often highly sensitive – information intensifies the risks of its misuse.

Or indeed its careless loss. For example, Britain has recently experienced a number of security scandals. In 2008, a computer memory stick containing information on thousands of criminals was lost. On another occasion documents relating to al-Qaeda in Pakistan and the security situation in Iraq were left on a train by a Cabinet Office intelligence official. In 2007, the Chancellor of the Exchequer confessed that computer disks holding personal information on 25 million individuals and 7.2 million families had disappeared.

Genesis

The dawn of information technology in the 1960s witnessed growing anxiety about the perceived threats posed by the uncontrolled collection, storage, and use of personal data. The fear of Big Brother provoked calls in several countries for the regulation of these potentially intrusive activities. The first data-protection law was enacted in the German Land of Hesse in 1970. This was followed by national legislation in Sweden (1973), the United States (1974), Germany (1977), and France (1978).

Out of this early chrysalis were born two key international instruments: the Council of Europe's 1981 Convention for the Protection of Individuals with regard to the Automatic Processing of Personal Data, and the 1980 Organization for Economic Cooperation and Development (OECD) Guidelines Governing the Protection of Privacy and Transborder Data Flows of Personal Data. These documents formulated explicit rules governing the complete process of managing electronic data. At the core of data-protection legislation, since the OECD guidelines, is the proposition that data relating to an identifiable individual should not be collected in the absence of a genuine purpose and the consent of the individual concerned (see box).

At a slightly higher level of abstraction, it encapsulates the principle of what the German Constitutional Court has called 'informational self-determination' – an ideal that expresses a fundamental democratic ideal.

The OECD principles

Collection Limitation Principle

There should be limits to the collection of personal data and any such data should be obtained by lawful and fair means and, where appropriate, with the knowledge or consent of the data subject.

Data Quality Principle

Personal data should be relevant to the purposes for which they are to be used, and, to the extent necessary for those purposes, should be accurate, complete and kept up-to-date.

Purpose Specification Principle

The purposes for which personal data are collected should be specified not later than at the time of data collection and the subsequent use limited to the fulfilment of those purposes or such others as are not incompatible with those purposes and as are specified on each occasion of change of purpose.

Use Limitation Principle

Personal data should not be disclosed, made available or otherwise used for purposes other than those specified in accordance with Paragraph 9 except:
a) with the consent of the data subject; or
b) by the authority of law.

Security Safeguards Principle

Personal data should be protected by reasonable security safeguards against such risks as loss or unauthorized access, destruction, use, modification or disclosure of data.

Openness Principle

There should be a general policy of openness about developments, practices and policies with respect to personal data. Means should be readily available of establishing the existence and nature of personal data, and the main purposes of their use, as well as the identity and usual residence of the data controller.

Individual Participation Principle

An individual should have the right:
a) to obtain from a data controller, or otherwise, confirmation of whether or not the data controller has data relating to him;
b) to have communicated to him, data relating to him

  (i) within a reasonable time;
  (ii) at a charge, if any, that is not excessive;
  (iii) in a reasonable manner; and
  (iv) in a form that is readily intelligible to him;

c) to be given reasons if a request made under subparagraphs (a) and (b) is denied, and to be able to challenge such denial; and
d) to challenge data relating to him and, if the challenge is successful to have the data erased, rectified, completed or amended.

Accountability Principle

A data controller should be accountable for complying with measures which give effect to the principles stated above.

OECD Guidelines on the Protection of Privacy and Transborder Flows of Personal Data, Part Two (adopted 23 September 1980)

Adherence to, or more precisely, enforcement of, this objective (and the associated rights of access and correction) has been mixed in the forty or so jurisdictions that have enacted data-protection legislation. Most of these statutes draw on the two international instruments mentioned above. Article 1 of the Council of Europe's Convention on the Protection of Individuals with Regard to Automatic Processing of Personal Data states that its purpose is to secure in the territory of each Party for every individual, whatever his nationality or residence, respect for his rights and fundamental freedoms, and in particular his right to privacy, with regard to automatic processing of personal data relating to him ('data protection').

The importance of these principles cannot be overstated. In particular, of the use limitation and purpose specification principles are crucial canons of fair information practice. Together with the principle that personal data shall be collected by means that are fair and lawful, they provide a framework for safeguarding the use and disclosure of such data, but also (in the fair collection principle) for limiting intrusive activities such as the interception of email messages. Personal data may be used or disclosed only for the purposes for which the data were collected or for some directly related purposes, unless the data subject consents. This key precept goes a long way towards regulating the misuse of personal data on the Internet. But it requires rejuvenation where it already exists and urgent adoption where it does so only partially (most conspicuously in the United States).

The enactment of data-protection legislation is driven only partly by altruism. The new information technology disintegrates national borders; international traffic in personal data is a routine feature of commercial life. The protection afforded to personal data in Country A is, in a digital world, rendered nugatory when it is retrieved on a computer in Country B in which there are no controls over its use. Hence, states with data-protection laws frequently proscribe the transfer of data to countries that lack them. Indeed, the European Union has in one of its several directives explicitly sought to annihilate these 'data havens'. Without data-protection legislation, countries risk being shut out of the rapidly expanding information business.

EU Directive on the processing of personal data

Article 3

1. This Directive shall apply to the processing of personal data wholly or partly by automatic means, and to the processing otherwise than by automatic means of personal data which form part of a filing system or are intended to form part of a filing system.
2. This Directive shall not apply to the processing of personal data: in the course of an activity which falls outside the scope of Community law, ... and in any case to processing operations concerning public security, defence, State security (including the economic well-being of the State when the processing operation relates to State security matters) and the activities of the State in areas of criminal law, by a natural person in the course of a purely personal or household activity.

Article 6

1. Membering States shall provide that personal data must be:
(a) processed fairly and lawfully;
(b) collected for specified, explicit and legitimate purposes and not further processed in a way incompatible with those purposes. Further processing of data for historical, statistical or scientific purposes shall not be considered as incompatible provided that Member States provide appropriate safeguards;
(c) adequate, relevant and not excessive in relation to the purposes for which they are collected and/or further processed;
(d) accurate and, where necessary, kept up to date; every reasonable step must be taken to ensure that data which are inaccurate or incomplete, having regard to the purposes for which they were collected or for which they are further processed, are erased or rectified;

> (e) kept in a form which permits identification of data subjects for no longer than is necessary for the purposes for which the data were collected or for which they are further processed. Member States shall lay down appropriate safeguards for personal data stored for longer periods for historical, statistical or scientific use.
>
> Directive of the European Parliament and Council of 24 October 1995

The essentials of data protection

At the heart of any data-protection law lies the principle that personal data shall be collected by means that are 'lawful and fair in the circumstances of the case', to use the language of Hong Kong's Personal Data (Privacy) Ordinance of 1995 that will serve as a paradigm here. In respect of the use and disclosure of such data, they may be used or disclosed for the purposes for which the data were collected or for some directly related purposes, unless the data subject consents.

These provisions are buttressed by six 'data-protection principles' which are, in effect, the main cog of the legislative machinery. Briefly, the first principle prohibits the collection of data unless they are collected for a lawful purpose directly related to a function or activity of the data user who is to use the data, and that are adequate but not excessive in relation to that purpose. Personal data may be collected only by lawful and fair means. This requires a data user to inform the data subject of the purpose for which the data are to be used, the classes of persons to whom the data may be transferred, whether it is obligatory or voluntary for the data subject to supply the data, the consequences of failure to supply the data; and that the data subject has the right to request access to and correction of the data.

The second principle requires data users to ensure that the data held are accurate and up to date. If in doubt, the data user should discontinue using the data at once. It should not retain the data any longer than is necessary for the purpose for which they were collected. The third principle provides that without the prescribed consent of the data subject, personal data may not be used for any purpose other than the purpose for which the data were to be used at the time of their collection.

Fourth, data users are obliged to take appropriate security measures to protect personal data. They must ensure that they are adequately protected against unauthorized or accidental access, processing, erasure, or use by others lacking authority. The fifth principle relates to the publicity a data user is required to give to the kind of personal data it holds, and its policies and practices in respect of the handling of personal data. This is normally achieved by a 'privacy policy statement' that includes details of the accuracy, retention period, security, and use of the data, as well as measures taken regarding data access and data correction requests.

The final principle relates to the data subject's right to obtain access to personal data about him or her and to request a copy of such personal data held by that data user. Should the data turn out to be inaccurate, the data subject has the right to request the data user to correct the record.

A victim of intrusion or disclosure may complain to the Privacy Commissioner for Personal Data of a contravention of these principles. He or she has the power to issue an 'enforcement notice' to compel compliance with the law. Failure to comply with such a notice is an offence punishable on conviction by a fine and two years' imprisonment. The legislation provides also for compensation, including damages for injury to feelings.

A crucial element of the law is the power vested in the Privacy Commissioner to approve codes of practice to provide 'practical guidance' to both data users and data subjects. Those issued so far by the Commissioner are substantial documents that are a product of detailed and lengthy consultation with the appropriate parties. Moreover, while the statute provides that a failure by a data user to observe any part of a code shall not render it liable to civil or criminal proceedings, an allegation in such proceedings that a data user has failed to follow the code is admissible as evidence.

What are 'personal data'?

The starting point of any data-protection law is the concept of 'personal data' or, in some statutes, 'personal information'. The term has been used numerous times in this book, but what precisely does it include? Though there are differences between domestic statutes, they share a fairly broadly defined notion of the phrase. Article 2(a) of the European Union Directive employs the following formulation:

> [A]ny information relating to an identified or identifiable individual natural person ('data subject'); an identifiable individual is one who can be identified directly or indirectly, in particular by reference to an identification number or to one or more factors specific to his physical, physiological, mental, economic, cultural or social identity.

But what of data generated by cookies or RFID tags embedded in products or clothing? They do not necessarily refer to an individual, but since they facilitate decisions about a person, they warrant protection under the rubric of personal data.

Though the definition of personal data in existing legislation manifestly incorporates information the obtaining or disclosure of which would constitute what might properly be called an invasion of privacy, its wide sweep neglects these issues. My own view is that it is principally information that is intimate or confidential that warrants protection in the name of privacy. But while the Directive, and domestic data-protection legislation, neglects this species of information, it does not altogether ignore it, as we shall see.

Despite the fact that any data-protection regime extends well beyond the information of an essentially private kind, and their (perhaps inevitable) procedural, rather than substantive, nature, they provide useful signposts to the more effective resolution of the challenges, especially of electronic privacy.

Article 25 of the European Directive specifies that any transfer of personal data that are being processed or are to be processed after their transfer must attract an adequate level of protection by the jurisdiction to which they are sent. The adequacy of protection is to be evaluated by reference to the nature of the data, the purpose and duration of the proposed processing, the country of origin and of final destination, the general or sectoral regulation in the jurisdiction in question, and the nature and scope of security measures. This immediately endangered the future of business in the largest market on earth, the United States. I return to this difficulty below.

Sensitive data

Certain items of personal information are intrinsically more sensitive than others, and therefore warrant stronger protection. What might these types of information be? Article 8 of the European Directive requires Member States to prohibit the processing of personal data 'revealing racial or ethnic origin, political opinions, religious or philosophical beliefs, trade union membership, and the processing of data concerning health or sex life'. This restriction is, however, subject to a number of exceptions including, unless domestic legislation explicitly provides otherwise, the provision by the data subject of explicit consent to such processing. It is also permissible when necessary to protect the rights and duties of the controller in the field of employment law, or to protect the 'vital interests' of the data subject.

This is echoed in the legislation of other European jurisdictions. The United Kingdom's Data Protection Act of 1998 classifies as 'sensitive' information relating to the data subject's racial or ethnic origin, political opinions, religious or similar beliefs, membership of a trade union, physical or mental health, sexual life, the commission or alleged commission of any offence, or any proceedings for any offence committed or alleged to have been committed.

Any inventory such as these clearly requires interpretation. Data about the twisted ankle that sent you to the hospital is plainly less sensitive than your HIV-positive status. But a modest degree of common sense ought to ensure that distinctions such as this are drawn.

In view of their high sensitivity, preserving the privacy of medical records is particularly critical. A growing problem concerns the significant number of non-medical personnel who have access to patients' data. They are not always subject to a strict duty of confidence.

Recently the European Court of Human Rights penalized the government of Finland for its failure to protect medical patient data held by a hospital against the risk of unauthorized access. The judgment establishes a connection between the right to privacy under human rights law and the protection of personal information. It held that Article 8 includes a positive duty to ensure the security of personal data. The hospital's filing system contravened Finland's own law that requires hospitals to secure personal data against unauthorized access. The petitioner, a nurse at the hospital where she was being treated for HIV, suspected that her co-workers had discovered that she was HIV-positive by reading her confidential medical records. Although the hospital rules prohibited access to these files, save for purposes of treatment, in practice the records of patients were accessible to all hospital staff.

The Court held that the mere fact that the hospital had an insecure medical records system was sufficient to render it liable for the otherwise unexplained disclosure of the nurse's private medical data.

Equally troubling is the reckless loss of sensitive data stored on disks or memory sticks. In late 2008, for example, disks containing personal information on almost 18,000 National Health Service patients went missing from a North London hospital. The hospital admitted that the disks were lost when they were put in the post!

The records of AIDS patients or those who are HIV-positive are especially sensitive. A number of arguments have, however, been raised to justify the violation of these patients' medical confidentiality. It is urged, in particular, that in order to contain the spread of the disease it may be necessary for doctors to report cases to public health authorities. Indeed, in some jurisdictions, AIDS is a notifiable disease and therefore a legal duty arises to inform authorities of its appearance. The requirement of accurate information is plainly important if research into the causes and proliferation of AIDS is to be effectively conducted. But there is no compelling reason why such data cannot be anonymous. Given the traumatic consequences that their disclosure can produce, the onus should be on the health authority to demonstrate that the benefits outweigh patients' rights to confidentiality.

Indeed, the failure adequately to protect these data may well be counter-productive; many will simply be deterred from being tested for the virus. This will dry up sources of information and, at the same time, contribute indirectly to the further spread of the illness.

Other elementary failures in the security of medical data inspire little confidence in the proper enforcement of the Data Protection Act. A recent survey by two doctors at a top London hospital revealed that three-quarters of them carried unsecured memory sticks with confidential data. Hospital doctors routinely carry memory sticks containing names, diagnoses, X-rays, and treatment details. Of the 105 doctors at their hospital, 92 held memory sticks, with 79 of them containing confidential information. Only 5 of those were protected by passwords.

Digital data

The ubiquity of computers and computer networks facilitates almost instant storage, retrieval, and transfer of data – a far cry from the world of manual filing systems. More spectacularly, efforts to control the Internet, its operation or content, have been conspicuously unsuccessful. Indeed, its anarchy and resistance to regulation are widely vaunted as its very strength and appeal. Apart from the problem of when it is reasonable to expect that one's conversations are private, the nature of communication on the Internet generates different issues and expectations, and, hence, the need for different solutions.

While the monitoring of digital telephone systems (described in Chapter 1) may appear to be similar to the sending and receiving of email, the use of the Internet poses intractable challenges to regulation. For example, while it is simple to monitor my telephone calls or intercept my letters, the culture of the Internet encourages a range of activities whose observation presents irresistible opportunities for those who wish to supervise or control the private and the sensitive.

Data protection and privacy

But, you are entitled to ask, what does data protection have to do with privacy? The relationship between the two is not immediately obvious. They plainly overlap; indeed, the latter is routinely invoked as the interest that animates the former. But – even in our information society – it is not always individual privacy that is violated by the collection, use, storage, or transfer of personal data. This is not merely because 'personal data' is widely defined in data-protection statutes to include information about a 'person'

"We have to be forthright with the public. We have to have their confidence. We have to convince them we're working for the common good. *Then* we can invade their privacy."

16. The collection and use of personal data is readily – and often disingenuously – justified as being in the public interest

that is not necessarily 'private'. The simple answer is that in seeking to protect this class of data, information of a genuinely private nature is willy-nilly caught in the net.

Indeed, it is not wholly implausible to suggest that a number of the problems of defining privacy that we have encountered might be more practically resolved under the data protection umbrella.

Think of the cases of *Peck* and Princess Caroline that were discussed in Chapter 4. The European Court of Human Rights considered them under the rubric of Article 8's privacy clause in the European Convention. The central issue was the lawfulness of surreptitious photography in a public place. Data-protection statutes are not fashioned to provide comprehensive protection for individual privacy, but they routinely stipulate that personal data must be collected by means that are both lawful and fair. Such legislation thus affords incidental protection to privacy.

The American enigma

Despite – or perhaps because of – the magnitude of its information market, the United States has resisted the adoption of data-protection legislation along European lines – at least in the private sector. Its approach of self-regulation is in stark contrast to the comprehensive approach of the European Union model. This is, in part, attributable to a political culture that eschews vigorous regulatory bodies – a situation all too evident in the context of the credit crisis of 2008. It is hard to visualize the approval of the appointment of an independent Federal privacy commissioner.

To avoid a trade war with Europe, the United States created the tranquil-sounding 'Safe Harbor' framework. The scheme was designed to satisfy the EU that US companies endorsing the scheme would offer adequate privacy protection as defined by the European Union data-protection directive (see box). This compromise was approved by the European Union in 2000.

The scheme has attracted a disappointingly small number of American companies, as they dislike the perceived burden it imposes upon them. The EU Commission has observed that a number of US companies fail to abide by the requirement, stating in their publicly available privacy policy that they comply with the seven principles. In addition, these privacy statements do not

The Safe Harbor principles

1. NOTICE: An organization must inform individuals about the purposes for which it collects information about them, how to contact the organization with any inquiries or complaints, the types of third parties to which it discloses the information, and the choices and means the organization offers to the individuals for limiting its use and disclosure.
2. CHOICE: An organization must offer individuals the opportunity to choose (opt out) whether and how personal information they provide is used or disclosed to third parties (where such use is incompatible with the purpose for which it was originally collected or with any other purpose disclosed to the individual in a notice).
3. ONWARD TRANSFER: An organization may only disclose personal information to third parties consistent with the principles of notice and choice.
4. SECURITY: Organizations creating, maintaining, using or disseminating personal information must take reasonable measures to assure its reliability for its intended use and reasonable precautions to protect it from loss, misuse and unauthorized access, disclosure, alteration and destruction.
5. DATA INTEGRITY: Consistent with these principles, an organization may only process personal information relevant to the purposes for which it has been gathered. To the extent necessary for those purposes, an organization should take reasonable steps to ensure that data is accurate, complete, and current.
6. ACCESS: Individuals must have reasonable access to personal information about them that an organization holds and be able to correct or amend that information where it is inaccurate.
7. ENFORCEMENT: Effective privacy protection must include mechanisms for assuring compliance with the safe harbor principles, recourse for individuals to whom the data relate affected by non-compliance with the principles, and consequences for the organization when the principles are not followed.

> **Unsafe harbour?**
>
> Perhaps because of its very lack of teeth, Safe Harbor is today regarded as tantamount to a dead letter. Most organizations importing personal data into the United States... appear simply to disregard the measure. One consultant who advises corporate clients on privacy issues told me that he recommends that they do exactly this – on the assumption that enforcement is so lax that noncompliance is unlikely to bring any sanctions.
>
> J. B. Rule, *Privacy in Peril* (Oxford University Press, 2007), p. 138

generally include all the principles or they translate them incorrectly.

A significant deficiency in the implementation of the 'Safe Harbor' policy is the absence of a complaint enforcement mechanism by those companies that have adopted the system.

Protecting personal data online

The future is here. The digital world we have created will soon comprise a fibre-optic network that carries – in digital bits – an almost infinite number of television channels, home shopping and banking, interactive entertainment and video games, computer databases, and commercial transactions. This broadband communications network will link households, businesses, and schools to a plethora of information resources. When personal information assumes the form of bits, its vulnerability to misuse, particularly on the Internet, is self-evident.

We have produced a multifunctional telecommunication network that links all existing networks that previously were independent. Moreover, what used to be uni-functional, immobile, and large hardware is now multifunctional, portable, and diminutive: my iPhone allows me to send and receive email, buy and sell, watch television, read newspapers, and so on.

The capacity of computers grows at an astonishing velocity; according to so-called 'Moore's Law', the capacity of a computer is doubled every 18 months, while its price is unaffected. In other words, after a period of 15 years, the processing and storage capabilities of our computers are increased by a factor of 1,000.

Anonymity and identity

Anonymity is, as was discussed in Chapter 1, an important value. But it is not necessarily absolute anonymity that I seek. Instead, it is what Yves Poullet, Director of the CRID (*Centre de Recherches Informatique et Droit*), calls 'functional nonidentifiability' in respect of my message to a certain individual. The notion of anonymity should perhaps therefore be replaced by 'pseudonymity' or 'nonidentifiability'. This right cannot, of course, be absolute. A balance must be struck with the demands of national security, defence, and the detection and prosecution of crime. This is possible by the use of 'pseudo identities' furnished to individuals by specialist service providers who may be required to reveal a user's actual identity when required by the law.

Conventional accounts – understandably – neglect the value and importance of anonymity as a feature of the 'new privacy'. The instability of the subject is a central theme of postmodernism. The Internet appears as a living testament to the ideas of the absence of a universal, unitary truth, and the contingency and diversity of the self that emerge in the writings of postmodernist icons such as Jacques Lacan.

The fluidity of identity on the Internet is among its chief attractions, but there may be increasing pressure to establish who the sender is, especially for commercial purposes. Digital authentication is likely to grow in importance as more business is conducted online.

The future of data protection

The current data-protection regime sketched above is no panacea. It is ill-equipped to cope with the countless challenges to privacy by the Internet and technological advances in RFID, GPS, mobile telephony, and so on. These developments are admirably described by Poullet, who postulates a new suite of principles to manage these frequently unsettling developments.

The ubiquity and multi-functionality of electronic communication service environments, as well as their interactivity, the international character of networks, services, and equipment producers, and the absence of transparency in terminal and network functioning jeopardize online privacy. Poullet accordingly proposes a number of 21st-century principles that include the principle of encryption and reversible anonymity. This is of critical importance in providing protection against access to the content of our communications. Encryption software has become affordable to the ordinary computer user.

Another principle is that of encouraging technological approaches compatible with or improving the situation of legally protected persons. This could involve requiring that both software and hardware provide the necessary tools to comply with data-protection rules. They ought to include maximum protective features as standard.

This obligation also applies to those who process personal data to select the most appropriate technology for minimizing the threat to privacy. The development of the privacy-enhancing technologies (PETs) described in Chapter 1, ought to be encouraged and subsidized, voluntary certification and accreditation systems established, and PETs made available at reasonable prices.

Hardware should operate transparently; users should have complete control over data sent and received. They ought, for example, to be able to ascertain easily the extent of chattering on their computers, what files have been received, their purpose, and their senders and recipients. Anyone who has attempted to block pop-up windows will know how frustratingly difficult this process can be. Omitting to activate a cookie suppressor cannot be construed as *carte blanche* consent to their installation.

Our online lives warrant protection equivalent to the consumer laws that we enjoy in the material world. Why should surfers be expected to tolerate profiling, spamming, differential access to services, and so on? Online consumer protection legislation could open the door to a range of services, including the specification of the duties of ISPs, search engines, databases, as well as measures to prevent unfair competition and commercial practices. Moreover, as Poullet argues, why should product liability for hardware and software not extend beyond physical and financial harm to incorporate infringements of data-protection norms?

The advent of Web 2.0 has generated a massive explosion in social networking sites such as Facebook and MySpace, video-sharing sites like YouTube and Flickr, for the sharing of photographs, and Wikipedia, the online encyclopaedia written by its users. There are plainly privacy costs to be incurred. The members of social networks may be blissfully unaware of the consequences of the widespread dissemination of their personal information. Providers should, of course, inform them how to restrict access to these data. They ought to offer opt-out for general profile data and opt-in for sensitive data. Users need to know there is little or no protection against the copying of their personal data, whether or not these data relate to themselves or to others.

17. Proposals by the British government to introduce a central database of fingerprints and other personal data have attracted considerable opposition

There are other privacy perils. Facebook, for example, allows users to add gadgets to their profiles and play with third-party applications without leaving the Facebook site. But this gives rise to privacy problems. When a user installs a Facebook application, the application can see anything that the user can see. The application may therefore request information about the user, his or her friends, and fellow network members. There is nothing to stop the owner of the application from collecting, viewing – and misusing – this personal information. The Facebook terms of use agreement urges application developers to refrain from doing this, but Facebook had no way of discovering or preventing them from engaging in these activities. Though under pressure from the Canadian Privacy Commissioner, it has recently amended its privacy policy so that applications cannot access users' friends' profile information without the express permission of each friend. Users generally regard their profiles on social networking sites as a form of self-expression, but they have commercial value to marketing companies, competing networking sites, and identity thieves. Data mining has serious privacy implications: it exposes information that might otherwise be hidden. It is the process of analysing data from different perspectives and summarizing it into information that may be used to increase income, reduce costs, or both. Data-mining software permits users to analyze data from multiple perspectives, categorize it, and evaluate the relationships identified. In other words, it searches for correlations or patterns among numerous fields in large relational databases.

While it is extremely valuable in commercial, medical, or scientific contexts, data mining does create risks to privacy. In the absence of patterns, bits of raw data are largely worthless. But when mining the data reveals a configuration of behaviour that would otherwise be innocuous, the privacy threat is swiftly evident.

Chapter 6
The death of privacy?

'Privacy is dead. Get over it.' Thus spake Scott McNealy, CEO of Sun Microsystems. He is not alone; the demise of privacy has been pronounced by an expanding posse of pessimists and soothsayers. A requiem is, however, premature. The invaders are at the gate, but the citadel will not fall without a battle.

Vital signs

For many privacy advocates, however, privacy still lives and breathes, but requires urgent regeneration. Groups such as Privacy International, the Electronic Frontier Foundation (EFF), the Electronic Privacy Information Center (EPIC), and several others continue to wage a gruelling campaign against the seemingly inexorable conquest of Big Brother. The crusade has become especially challenging since the events of 11 September 2001.

Examples abound. Fears of comprehensive 24-hour monitoring by CCTV were raised in early 2009 by the announcement that to safeguard security at the 2012 Olympic Games in London, the British government has appointed EADS, a defence company, to develop a system, known as DYVINE, that would allow a central police control room to tap in remotely to any CCTV network in London and plot the information on a detailed 3D map. It would include vehicle number-plate recognition cameras as well as private networks, such as those operating in shopping centres and car parks. This will facilitate the tracking of suspects throughout the city. Advanced computer intelligence systems would assist officers by filtering out all but the most relevant CCTV feeds entering the control room, thereby cutting the time normally spent scrambling from one camera to the next.

The anxiety generated by systems such as this focuses on the dangers posed to privacy by the manifold forms of electronic and other forms of monitoring and intrusion discussed in Chapter 1. But there is the equally disconcerting onslaught perpetuated by the media in pursuit of sensationalist gossip discussed in Chapter 4. Both warrant a few brief concluding remarks here.

Memories are made of bits

Moore's Law and the World Wide Web have changed everything. The world is a very different one from the Cold War world. McLuhan's global village has finally arrived, and our business is everyone's business. Changes in technology allied to changes in ideology and a lack of deference to authority mean that transparency has increased dramatically, and we will not be able to return to opacity in the foreseeable future. If people are aware of the ramifications of what they do, and if they remember that the memory of an action will outlast the moment, and that the audience for a story is much wider than the immediate group of hearers or readers, then they will be able to do what people do so well – negotiate a nuanced set of strategies for disclosing information depending on the context. But they need to be fully aware that the online context is somewhat different from the offline world, in particular with digital 'memories' lasting far out into the future.

K. O'Hara and N. Shadbolt, *The Spy in the Coffee Machine* (Oneworld, 2008), p. 230

Technology and tranquillity

The pace of technological innovation will continue to increase. This will be accompanied by new and more insidious forms of encroachment on our private lives. But privacy is too fundamental a democratic value for it to be vanquished without a struggle. It is true that, especially in the face of real or perceived threats, many are disposed to trade their privacy for safety or security – even when it is demonstrated, for example, that the proliferation of CCTV cameras has achieved only limited success in curbing crime.

The erosion of privacy therefore tends to occur by quiescent accretion: through apathy, indifference, or tacit support for measures that are packaged as essential or appear innocuous. And we should not pretend that in our digital world the regulation of privacy-invading conduct will be unproblematic; far from it. Online privacy is bound to continue to be vulnerable to a wide range of attacks. Yet cyberspace is prone to some degree of control, not necessarily by law, but through its essential make-up, its 'code': software and hardware that constitutes cyberspace. That code, it is argued by Lessig, can either produce a place where freedom prevails or one of oppressive control. Indeed, commercial considerations increasingly render cyberspace decidedly susceptible for regulation; it has become a location in which conduct is more strongly controlled than in real space. In the end, he maintains, it is a matter for us to determine; the choice is one of architecture: what sort of code should govern cyberspace, and who will control it. And in this respect, the central legal issue is code. We need to choose the values and principles which should animate that code.

Our defences against these depredations will require also the political will to enact – and actively enforce – appropriate legislation and codes of conduct. Existing data-protection laws, where they exist, need constant revision and rejuvenation, and urgent enactment where they do not. The office of privacy or information commissioner requires adequate funding to facilitate the effective oversight of legislative and other threats to privacy, and the proper regulation and provision of advice and information. An appropriately funded, supported, and competent privacy commissioner can play an indispensable role as guardian of our personal data.

The collaboration of software and hardware manufacturers, service providers, and computer users, along with advice and information about how best to safeguard personal information, are critical components of any privacy protection strategy.

The importance of the privacy-enhancing technologies (PETs) to counter privacy-invading technologies (PITs) – described in Chapter 1 – cannot be over-emphasized. Humans create technology. It can therefore both impair and improve our privacy. Firewalls, anti-hacking mechanisms, and other means are the first line of defence. Expressing one's privacy preferences through, for example P3P (see Chapter 1) is another vital tool in safeguarding our vanishing privacy. How does it work? The privacy preference settings panel of 'Privacy Bird', for example, allows you to configure your personal privacy preferences. When it encounters a website that does not match your privacy preferences, a red warning icon appears in your browser title bar. There are three pre-configured settings: low, medium, and high. When you select a setting, a tick or check mark materializes next to the specific items that will trigger warnings under that setting. The low setting generates a warning only at websites that may use health or medical information, or keep marketing or mailing lists from which you cannot be removed. The medium setting includes additional warnings when sites may share your personally identified information, or if a site does not permit you to establish what data they hold about you. The high setting triggers the maximum number of warnings, including at most commercial websites.

Technological methods to facilitate such preferences are emerging, along with instruments by which data collectors are able to acquaint themselves with their responsibilities.

Pressure groups, non-governmental organizations, lobbyists, and privacy advocates of every stripe perform a vital function in raising consciousness of the relentless assaults on privacy.

While the extraordinary capacity of databases and the Web to collect, store, transfer, monitor, link, and match an incalculable amount of our personal information plainly poses considerable risks, technology is simultaneously our adversary and our ally.

Pursuing paparazzi

The appetite for tittle-tattle is unlikely to decline. It will continue to be fed – both offline and online – by unauthorized disclosures of personal information. The media in their print and digital manifestations, blogs, social networking sites, and other online purveyors of private facts, both voluntary and unsolicited, present intractable challenges to any form of regulation or control.

18. The photographers arrested after pursuing the vehicle in which Princess Diana was killed

The power of the paparazzi shows few signs of diminishing. Though their intrusive conduct is often conflated with the publication of its fruits, there is a widespread recognition that the law is inadequate on both counts.

At least four possible solutions have been advanced. The first seeks to criminalize the activities of invasive journalists and photographers. So, for example, the state of California (whose constitution explicitly protects privacy) enacted an 'anti-paparazzi' law that creates tort liability for 'physical' and 'constructive' invasions of privacy through photographing, videotaping, or recording a person engaging in a 'personal or familial activity'.

A second line of attack attempts to cajole or compel the media to adopt a variety of forms of self-regulation. The protracted efforts, especially in Britain, to achieve this compromise, and so avert legislative controls, have met with little success.

A third approach is legislation along the lines of the American tort of intentional intrusion upon the plaintiff's seclusion or solitude, or into his private affairs. Liability is distinct from that which may attach to the public disclosure, if any, of the information acquired as a result of the intrusion.

A fourth innovative strategy is to hit the paparazzi where it hurts – in their pockets. By denying them copyright in their pictures, the urge both to snoop and publish might be resisted – the images will not be theirs to sell. Thus if a tabloid could re-publish a surreptitiously obtained photograph of a pop star, without having to shell out a fee, the market for such images would plummet significantly. Paparazzi would go to the wall.

There is already a thin, but rather quaint, line of authority in common law jurisdictions that denies copyright to immoral, deceptive, blasphemous, or defamatory material, but it is unlikely to be invoked today. This proposal would enlarge the scope of turpitude that might induce a court to deny protection. But the idea is artificial, unwieldy, and conceptually problematic. If privacy is to be subsumed by copyright, what the law would in most cases be protecting is less the right of privacy than the plaintiff's right of publicity: the right to control the circumstances under which one's image may be bought and sold. The attraction of this propriety approach to the paparazzi problem is understandable; indeed property interests were among the midwives at the birth of the legal idea of privacy. As described in Chapter 3, the first American judgment to recognize that the common law protected privacy involved the tort of appropriation of name or likeness: the use for the defendant's commercial benefit – usually for advertising purposes – of the plaintiff's identity.

But privacy warrants protection in its own right; backdoor remedies will, in the end, be counterproductive. The ideal answer is explicit, carefully drafted legislation that creates civil and criminal sanctions for seriously offensive, intentional, or reckless intrusion into an individual's solitude or seclusion, and the unauthorized publication of personal information. The latter is, of course, always to be balanced against freedom of speech, as discussed in Chapter 4.

Neither at work nor at home are we entitled to assume that our online applications are safe. We must look to both technology and the law to provide shelter. Technology, it has been frequently stated, generates both the malady and part of the cure. And while the law is rarely an adequate tool against the dedicated intruder, the advances in protective software along with the fair information practices adopted by the European Directive, and the laws of several jurisdictions, afford a rational and sound normative framework for the collection, use, and transfer of personal data. It offers a pragmatic analysis of the uses to which personal information is actually put, the manner of its collection, and the legitimate expectations of individuals. These are the questions that will dominate the discussion of privacy long into our uncertain future. How we address them may determine whether or not we live privately ever after.

Annex

Global Privacy Standards for a Global World
The Civil Society Declaration
Madrid, Spain, 3 November 2009

Affirming that privacy is a fundamental human right set out in the Universal Declaration of Human Rights, the International Covenant on Civil and Political Rights, and other human rights instruments and national constitutions;

Reminding the EU member countries of their obligations to enforce the provisions of the 1995 Data Protection Directive and the 2002 Electronic Communications Directive;

Reminding the other OECD member countries of their obligations to uphold the principles set out in the 1980 OECD Privacy Guidelines;

Reminding all countries of their obligations to safeguard the civil rights of their citizens and residents under the provisions of their national constitutions and laws, as well as international human rights law;

Anticipating the entry into force of provisions strengthening the Constitutional rights to privacy and data protection in the European Union;

Noting with alarm the dramatic expansion of secret and unaccountable surveillance, as well as the growing collaboration between governments and vendors of surveillance technology that establish new forms of social control;

Further noting that new strategies to pursue copyright and unlawful content investigations pose substantial threats to communications privacy, intellectual freedom, and due process of law;

Further noting the growing consolidation of Internet-based services, and the fact that some corporations are acquiring vast amounts of personal data without independent oversight;

Warning that privacy law and privacy institutions have failed to take full account of new surveillance practices, including behavioral targeting, databases of DNA and other biometric identifiers, the fusion of data between the public and private sectors, and the particular risks to vulnerable groups, including children, migrants, and minorities;

Warning that the failure to safeguard privacy jeopardizes associated freedoms, including freedom of expression, freedom of assembly, freedom of access to information, non-discrimination, and ultimately the stability of constitutional democracies;

Civil Society takes the occasion of the 31st annual meeting of the International Conference of Privacy and Data Protection Commissioners to:

(1) Reaffirm support for a global framework of Fair Information Practices that places obligations on those who collect and process personal information and gives rights to those whose personal information is collected;

(2) Reaffirm support for independent data protection authorities that make determinations, in the context of a legal framework, transparently and without commercial advantage or political influence;

(3) Reaffirm support for genuine Privacy Enhancing Techniques that minimize or eliminate the collection of personally identifiable information and for meaningful Privacy Impact Assessments that require compliance with privacy standards;

(4) Urge countries that have not ratified Council of Europe Convention 108 together with the Protocol of 2001 to do so as expeditiously as possible;

(5) Urge countries that have not yet established a comprehensive framework for privacy protection and an independent data protection authority to do so as expeditiously as possible;

(6) Urge those countries that have established legal frameworks for privacy protection to ensure effective implementation and enforcement, and to cooperate at the international and regional level;

(7) Urge countries to ensure that individuals are promptly notified when their personal information is improperly disclosed or used in a manner inconsistent with its collection;

(8) Recommend comprehensive research into the adequacy of techniques that "deidentify" data to determine whether in practice such methods safeguard privacy and anonymity;

(9) Call for a moratorium on the development or implementation of new systems of mass surveillance, including facial recognition, whole body imaging, biometric identifiers, and embedded RFID tags, subject to a full and transparent evaluation by independent authorities and democratic debate; and

(10) Call for the establishment of a new international framework for privacy protection, with the full participation of civil society, that is based on the rule of law, respect for fundamental human rights, and support for democratic institutions.

References

Chapter 1: The assault

'It was reported in early 2009...': *Sunday Times*, 4 January 2009.
'Free conversation is often characterized...': L. B. Schwartz, 'On Current Proposals to Legalize Wiretapping' (1954) 103 *University of Pennsylvania Law Review* 157, p. 162.
Examples of characteristics on which biometric technologies can be based: drawn from Roger Clarke, 'Biometrics and Privacy', http://www.anu.edu.au/people/ Roger.Clarke/DV/Biometrics.html
'[A] bit more invasive than a security guard...': L. Lessig, *Code and Other Laws of Cyberspace* (New York: Basic Books, 1999), p. 194.
'Imagine if a hacker put together information...': E. G. Lush, 'How Cyber-Crime Became a Multi-Billion-Pound Industry', *The Spectator*, 16 June 2007.
Platform for Privacy Preferences (P3P) Project: http://www.w3.org/P3P/
'It is a complex and confusing protocol...', and 'Simple, predictable rules...': Electronic Privacy Information Center (EPIC), http://www.epic.org/reports/prettypoorprivacy.html

Chapter 2: An enduring value

My attempt to address the intractable problem of defining privacy draws on my serial endeavours to grasp this nettle; some of these works are listed in the section on 'Further reading'.

'The closer people come...': R. Sennett, *The Fall of Public Man* (Harmondsworth: Penguin, 1974), p. 338.
'In ancient feeling...': H. Arendt, *The Human Condition* (Chicago: University of Chicago Press, 1958), p. 38.
'[L]iberalism may be said largely...': S. Lukes, *Individualism* (Oxford: Basil Blackwell, 1973), p. 62.
'One of the central goals...': M. Horwitz, 'The History of the Public/Private Distinction' (1982) 130 *University of Pennsylvania Law Review* 1423, p. 1424.
'[T]he sole end...': J. S. Mill, *On Liberty* (London: Longman, Roberts & Green, 1869), p. 9.
'On any given day...': A. F. Westin, *Privacy and Freedom* (New York: Atheneum, 1967), pp. 34–5.
'[A]n air of injured gentility': H. Kalven, 'Privacy in Tort Law: Were Warren and Brandeis Wrong?' (1966) 31 *Law and Contemporary Problems* 326, p. 329.
The 'claim of individuals, groups...': A. F. Westin, *Privacy and Freedom* (New York: Atheneum, 1967), p. 7.
Privacy consists of 'limited accessibility': R. Gavison, 'Privacy and the Limits of Law' (1980) 89 *Yale Law Journal* 412.
'To the extent that people conceal...': R. Posner, 'The Right of Privacy' (1978) 123 *Georgia Law Review* 393, p. 401.

Chapter 3: A legal right

Prince Albert v Strange (1849) 1H. & W. 1. 64 E.R. 293. On appeal: (1849) 1 Mac. & G. 25, 41 E.R. 1171.
S. D. Warren and L. D. Brandeis, 'The Right to Privacy' (1890) 5 *Harvard Law Review* 196.
'Flour of the family': *Roberson v Rochester Folding Box Co.* 171N.Y. 538; 64N.E. 442 (1902).
Supreme Court of Georgia: *Pavesich v New England Life Insurance Co.*, 122 Ga. 190; 50S.E. 68 (1905).
W. L. Prosser, 'Privacy' (1960) 48 *California Law Review* 383.
Its moral basis as an aspect of human dignity: E. J. Bloustein, 'Privacy as an Aspect of Human Dignity: An Answer to Dean Prosser' (1964) 39 *New York University Law Review* 962.
H. Kalven, 'Privacy in Tort Law: Were Warren and Brandeis Wrong?' (1966) 31 *Law and Contemporary Problems* 326.
Olmstead v United States 277 U.S. 438 (1928).

Katz v United States 398 U.S. 347 (1967).
Griswold v Connecticut 381 U.S. 479 (1965).
Roe v Wade 410 U.S. 113 (1973).
'[U]ndoubtedly the best-known case...': R. Dworkin, *Life's Dominion: An Argument about Abortion and Euthanasia* (London: Harper Collins, 1993) pp. 4 and 103.
Bowers v Hardwick 478 U.S. 186 (1986).
Lawrence v Texas 539 U.S. 558 (2003).
Report of the Committee on Privacy (Chairman: K. Younger), Cmnd 5012 (1972) Para. 653.
Douglas v Hello! Ltd [2007] 2 W.L.R. 920 (H.L.).
Lord Hoffmann: *Wainwright v Home Office* [2003] U.K.H.L. 53, Para. 34.
The 'final impetus to the recognition of a right of privacy...': *Douglas v Hello! Ltd* [2005] 1 Q.B. 967 at para 111, *per* Sedley LJ.
Australian Broadcasting Corporation v Lenah Game Meats Pty Ltd [2001] HCA 63.
Hosking v Runting and Pacific Magazines NZ Ltd [2004] CA 101.
Gaskin v United Kingdom (1989) 12 E.H.H.R. 36.
Leander v Sweden (1987) 9 E.H.R.R. 443.
Katz v United States 389 U.S. 347 (1967).
'[T]he party to the conversation...': *Privacy*, Australian Law Reform Commission No. 22, Para. 1128.
Klass v Federal Republic of Germany (1978) 2 E.H.H.R 214.
Malone v United Kingdom (1984) 7 E.H.R.R. 14.
'[N]ot because we wish to hamper...': S. M. Beck, 'Electronic Surveillance and the Administration of Criminal Justice' (1968) 46 *Canadian Bar Review* 643, p. 687.

Chapter 4: Privacy and free speech

Some of the discussion on the attempt to reconcile privacy and freedom of expression is based on my *Privacy and Press Freedom* (London: Blackstone, 1995).
Campbell v Mirror Group Newspapers Ltd [2004] 2A.C. 457 (H.L.)
Douglas v Hello! Ltd [2006] Q.B. 125; [2007] 2 W.L.R. 920 (H.L).
Von Hannover v Germany [2004] E.M.L.R. 379 (E.C.H.R).
Peck v United Kingdom [2003] E.M.L.R. 379 (E.C.H.R.).
Dietemann v Time, Inc. 449F. 2d 244 (1971).
T. L. Emerson, *The System of Freedom of Expression* (New York: Random House, 1970).

'[A]t most points the law...': T. L. Emerson (above), p. 331.
'Privacy law might be more just...': D. L. Zimmerman, 'Requiem for a Heavyweight: A Farewell to Warren and Brandeis's Privacy Tort' (1983) 68 *Cornell Law Review* 291, pp. 362-4.
'[A]nother approach, and one...': T. L. Emerson, 'The Right of Privacy and Freedom of the Press' (1979) 14 *Harvard Civil Rights-Civil Liberties Law Review* 329, p. 343.
'[S]uffers from a failure...': F. Schauer, *Free Speech: A Philosophical Enquiry* (Cambridge: Cambridge University Press, 1982), p. 56.
'[A] rigorous examination of motives...': E. Barendt, *Freedom of Speech*, 2nd edn. (Oxford: Oxford University Press, 2005), p. 24.
'The principle of the freedom of speech...': A. Meiklejohn, *Political Freedom: The Constitutional Powers of the People* (New York: Oxford University Press, 1965).
'The liberty of the press is indeed essential...': W. Blackstone, 4 *Commentaries on the Laws of England* (1769), pp. 151-2.
York Times v Sullivan 376 U.S. 254 at p. 270 per Brennan J (1964).
Time, Inc. v Hill 385 U.S. 374 (1967).
'[S]o long as the interest of privacy...': T. Emerson, *Towards a General Theory of the First Amendment* (New York: Vintage, 1966), p. 75.
'It cannot be too strongly emphasised...': *R v Central Independent Television PLC* [1994] Fam. 192 at p. 203 per Hoffmann LJ (as he then was).
'[E]xceptional cases, where the intended...': *Schering Chemicals Ltd v Falkman* [1982] 1 Q.B. 1 at p. 18 per Lord Denning M.R.
'Blackstone was concerned to prevent...': *Schering* (above), p. 39, per Lord Templeman.
'[A]t some point the public interest...': *Sidis v F-R Publishing Co.* 34F. Supp. 19 (S.D.N.Y., 1938); 113F. 2d. 806 at p 809 (1940).
Restatement (Second) of the Law of Torts, §652D (b) and comment h.
Sipple v Chronicle Publishing Co. 201 Cal. Rptr 665 (1984).
Diaz v Oakland Tribune Inc. 118 Cal. Rptr 762 at p. 773 (1983).
Ann-Margret v High Society Magazine, Inc. 498F. Supp. 401 at p. 405 (1980).
'[D]eference to the judgment...': D. L. Zimmerman, 'Requiem for a Heavyweight: A Farewell to Warren and Brandeis's Privacy Tort' (1983) 68 *Cornell Law Review* 291, p. 353.
Melvin v Reid 112 Cal. App. 285; 297P. 91 (1931).
Sidis v F.-R. Publishing Corporation Sidis v F-R Publishing Co. 34F. Supp. 19 (S.D.N.Y., 1938); 113F. 2d. 806.
Time, Inc. v Hill 385 U.S. 374, p. 388 (1967).

Chapter 5: Data protection

I v Finland Eur. Ct. H.R., No. 20511/03 (17 July 2008).
Eastweek Publisher Ltd v The Privacy Commissioner for Personal Data [2000] H.K.C. 692.

Chapter 6: The death of privacy?

L. Lessig, *Code and Other Laws of Cyberspace* (New York: Basic Books, 1999).
Platform for Privacy Preferences (P3P) Project: http://www.w3.org/P3P/
Privacy Bird: http://www.privacybird.org

Further reading

The subject of privacy has attracted the attention of scholars from a wide variety of disciplines, including philosophy, sociology, political science, and law. To avoid swamping the reader with an impossibly vast list of sources, I have restricted this inventory to reasonable – and accessible – proportions, omitting references to the prodigious quantity of periodical literature that grapples with this kaleidoscopic concept (the most essential of which are cited in the 'References' section).

Chapter 1: The assault

P. Agre and M. Rotenberg (eds.), *Technology and Privacy: The New Landscape* (Cambridge, MA: MIT Press, 1997).
K. Ball and F. Webster (eds.), *The Intensification of Surveillance: Crime, Terrorism and Warfare in the Information Age* (London: Pluto Press, 2003).
C. J. Bennett, *Privacy Advocates: Resisting the Spread of Surveillance* (Cambridge, MA: MIT Press, 2008).
C. J. Bennett and D. Lyon (eds.), *Playing the Identity Card: Surveillance, Security and Identification in Global Perspective* (London: Routledge, 2008).
A. Cavoukian and D. Tapscott, *Who Knows? Safeguarding Your Privacy in a Networked World* (Toronto: Random House, 1995).
S. Davies, *Big Brother: Britain's Web of Surveillance and the New Technological Order* (London: Pan Books, 1996).
W. Diffie and S. Landau, *Privacy on the Line: The Politics of Wiretapping and Encryption* (Cambridge, MA: MIT Press, 2007).

P. Fitzgerald and M. Leopold, *Stranger on the Line: The Secret History of Phone Tapping* (London: The Bodley Head, 1987).

D. Flaherty, *Protecting Privacy in Surveillance Societies: The Federal Republic of Germany, Sweden, France, Canada, and the United States* (Chapel Hill, NC: University of North Carolina Press, 1989).

D. Flaherty, *Protecting Privacy in Two-Way Electronic Services* (London: Mansell Publishing Limited, 1985).

J. Gibb, *Who's Watching You? The Chilling Truth about the State, Surveillance and Personal Freedom* (London: Collins & Brown, 2005).

J. Goldsmith and T. Wu, *Who Controls the Internet? Illusions of a Borderless World* (Oxford: Oxford University Press, 2006).

C. Jennings and L. Fena, *The Hundredth Window: Protecting Your Privacy and Security in the Age of the Internet* (New York: Free Press, 2000).

K. Laidler, *Surveillance Unlimited: How We've Become the Most Watched People on Earth* (Cambridge: Icon Books, 2008).

J. Losek, *The War on Privacy* (Westport, CT: Praeger, 2007).

D. Lyon, *The Electronic Eye: The Rise of Surveillance Society* (Minneapolis, MI: University of Minnesota Press, 1994).

D. Lyon, *Surveillance after September 11* (Cambridge: Polity Press, 2003).

D. Lyon (ed.), *Surveillance as Social Sorting: Privacy, Risk, and Digital Discrimination* (London and New York: Routledge, 2003).

D. Lyon, *Surveillance Society: Monitoring Everyday Life* (Buckingham: Open University Press, 2001).

D. Lyon, *Surveillance Studies: An Overview* (Cambridge: Polity Press, 2007).

D. Lyon, *Theorizing Surveillance: The Panopticon and Beyond* (Uffculme: Willan Publishing, 2006).

R. Mansell and S. Collins (eds.), *Trust and Crime in Information Societies* (Cheltenham: Edward Elgar Publications, 2005).

G. Marx, *Undercover: Police Surveillance in America* (Berkeley, CA, and London: University of California Press, 1992).

M. S. Monmonier, *Spying with Maps: Surveillance Technologies and the Future of Privacy* (Chicago, Ill: University of Chicago Press, 2002).

C. Norris and G. Armstrong, *The Maximum Surveillance Society: The Rise of CCTV* (London: Berg, 1999).

J. Parker, *Total Surveillance: Investigating the Big Brother World of E-spies, Eavesdroppers and CCTV* (London: Piatkus Books, 2000).

J. K. Petersen, *Understanding Surveillance Technologies: Spy Devices, Privacy, History and Applications* (Boca Raton, FL: Auerbach, 2007).
J. B. Rule, *Privacy in Peril* (New York: Oxford University Press, 2007).
J. B. Rule, *Private Lives and Public Surveillance* (London: Allen Lane, 1973).
B. Schouten, N. C. Juul, A. Drygajlo, and M. Tistarelli (eds.), *Biometrics and Identity Management* (Heidelberg: Springer, 2008).
D. J. Solove, *The Digital Person: Technology and Privacy in the Information Age* (New York: New York University Press, 2004).
D. J. Solove, M. Rotenberg, and P. Schwartz, *Privacy, Information, and Technology* (New York: Aspen, 2006).
C. J. Sykes, *The End of Privacy* (New York: St Martin's Press, 1999).
D. Thomas and B. B. Loader (eds.), *Cybercrime: Law Enforcement, Security and Surveillance in the Information Age* (London: Routledge, 2000).
R. Whitaker, *The End of Privacy: How Total Surveillance is Becoming a Reality* (New York: New Press, 1999).

Chapter 2: An enduring value

P. Birks (ed.), *Privacy and Loyalty* (Oxford: Oxford University Press, 1997).
S. Bok, *Secrets: On the Ethics of Concealment and Revelation* (New York: Pantheon, 1982).
A. Etzioni, *The Limits of Privacy* (New York: Basic Books, 1999).
D. Flaherty, *Privacy in Colonial New England* (Charlottesville, VA: University Press of Virginia, 1972).
O. Gandy, Jr, *The Panoptic Sort: A Political Economy of Personal Information* (Boulder, CO: Westview Press, 1993).
J. Griffin, *On Human Rights* (Oxford and New York: Oxford University Press, 2008).
R. F. Hixson, *Privacy in a Public Society: Human Rights in Conflict* (New York: Oxford University Press, 1987).
J. Inness, *Privacy, Intimacy and Isolation* (New York: Oxford University Press, 1992).
L. Lessig, *Code and Other Laws of Cyberspace* (New York: Basic Books, 1999).
L. Lessig, *Code: Version 2.0* (New York: Basic Books, 2006).
A. Moore, *Privacy Rights: Moral and Legal Foundations* (Philadephia, PA: University of Pennsylvania Press, 2009).

B. Moore, *Privacy: Studies in Social and Cultural History* (New York: M. E. Sharp, 1984).

E. Neill, *Rites of Privacy and the Privacy Trade: On the Limits of Protection for the Self* (Montreal and Kingston: McGill-Queen's University Press, 2001).

M. C. Nussbaum, *Hiding from Humanity: Disgust, Shame, and the Law* (Princeton, NJ: Princeton University Press, 2004).

J. Pennock and J. Chapman, *Privacy: Nomos XIII* (New York: Atherton Press, 1971).

J. Rosen, *The Naked Crowd: Reclaiming Security and Freedom in an Anxious Age* (New York: Random House, 2004).

F. Schoeman (ed.), *Philosophical Dimensions of Privacy: An Anthology* (Cambridge: Cambridge University Press, 1984).

F. Schoeman, *Privacy and Social Freedom* (Cambridge: Cambridge University Press, 1992).

R. Sennett, *The Fall of Public Man* (Harmondsworth: Penguin, 1974).

D. J. Siepp, *The Right to Privacy in American History* (Cambridge, MA: Harvard University Press, 1978).

D. J. Solove, *Understanding Privacy* (Cambridge, MA: Harvard University Press, 2008).

R. Wacks, *Law, Morality, and the Private Domain* (Hong Kong: Hong Kong University Press, 2000).

R. Wacks (ed.), *Privacy: The International Library of Essays in Law and Legal Theory*. Volume I: *The Concept of Privacy* (London, Dartmouth, New York: New York University Press, 1993).

A. F. Westin, *Privacy and Freedom* (New York: Atheneum, 1967).

A. F. Westin and M. A. Baker, *Databanks in a Free Society: Computers, Record-Keeping, and Privacy* (New York: Quadrangle, 1972).

J. Young (ed.), *Privacy* (New York: Wiley, 1978).

Chapter 3: A legal right

A. T. Kenyon and M. Richardson (eds.), *New Dimensions in Privacy Law: International and Comparative Perspectives* (Cambridge: Cambridge University Press, 2006).

J. L. Mills, *Privacy: The Lost Right* (New York: Oxford University Press, 2008).

P. Regan, *Legislating Privacy: Technology, Social Values and Public Policy* (Chapel Hill, NC: University of North Carolina Press, 1995).

J. B. Rule and G. Greenleaf (eds.), *Global Privacy Protection: The First Generation* (London: Edward Elgar, 2008).

R. Wacks, *Personal Information: Privacy and the Law* (Oxford: Clarendon Press, 1989).

R. Wacks (ed.), *Privacy: The International Library of Essays in Law and Legal Theory*. Volume II: *Privacy and the Law* (London, Dartmouth, New York: New York University Press, 1993).

R. Wacks, *The Protection of Privacy* (London: Sweet & Maxwell, 1980).

Chapter 4: Privacy and free speech

L. Alexander, *Is There a Right of Freedom of Expression?* (Cambridge: Cambridge University Press, 2005).

E. Barendt, *Freedom of Speech*, 2nd edn. (Oxford: Oxford University Press, 2007).

C. Calvert, *Voyeur Nation: Media, Privacy, and Peering in Modern Culture* (New York: Basic Books, 2004).

H. Jenkins, *Convergence Culture: Where Old and New Media Collide* (New York: New York University Press, 2008).

J. Rozenberg, *Privacy and the Press* (Oxford: Oxford University Press, 2005).

D. J. Solove, *The Future of Reputation: Gossip, Rumor, and Privacy on the Internet* (New Haven, CT: Yale University Press, 2007).

H. Tomlinson, *Privacy and the Media: The Developing Law* (London: Matrix Chambers, 2002).

R. Wacks, *Privacy and Press Freedom* (London: Blackstone Press, 1995).

Chapter 5: Data protection

C. Bennett, *Regulating Privacy: Data Protection and Public Policy in Europe and the United States* (Ithaca, NY: Cornell University Press, 1992).

C. Bennett and C. Raab, *The Governance of Privacy: Policy Instruments in Global Perspective*, 2nd edn. (Cambridge, MA: MIT Press, 2006).

M. Berthold and R. Wacks, *Hong Kong Data Privacy Law: Territorial Regulation in a Borderless World*, 2nd edn (Hong Kong: Sweet & Maxwell Asia, 2003).

L. Bygrave, *Data Protection Law: Approaching its Rationale, Logic and Limits* (The Hague: Kluwer Law International, 2002).

P. Schwartz and J. Reidenberg, *Data Protection Law: A Study of United States Data Protection* (Dayton: Michie, 1996).

Chapter 6: The death of privacy?

S. Garfinkel, *Database Nation: The Death of Privacy in the Twenty-First Century* (Sebastopol, CA: O'Reilly, 2000).

S. Gutwirth, *Privacy and the Information Age* (Lanham, MD: Rowman & Littlefield, 2002).

B. Kahin and C. Nesson (eds.), *Borders in Cyberspace: Information Policy and the Global Information Infrastructure* (Cambridge, MA: MIT Press, 1997).

G. Laurie, *Genetic Privacy: A Challenge to Medico-Legal Norms* (Cambridge: Cambridge University Press, 2002).

D. Lyon, C. Bennett, and R. Grant (eds.), *Visions of Privacy: Policy Choices for the Digital Age* (Toronto: University of Toronto Press, 1998).

K. O'Hara and N. Shadbolt, *The Spy in the Coffee Machine: The End of Privacy as We Know It* (Oxford: Oneworld, 2008).

J. Rosen, *The Unwanted Gaze: The Destruction of Privacy in America* (New York: Random House, 2000).

C. J. Sykes, *The End of Privacy* (London: St Martin's Press, 2000).

J. Zittrain, *The Future of the Internet: And How to Stop It* (London: Allen Lane, 2008).

Websites

Electronic Privacy Information Center (EPIC) http://www.epic.org

Privacy International http://www.privacyinternational.org

Privacy Rights Clearinghouse http://www.privacyrights.org

American Civil Liberties Union http://www.aclu.org/privacy

Roger Clarke's Dataveillance and Information Privacy Pages http://www.anu.edu.au/people/Roger.Clarke/DV

Electronic Frontier Foundation (EFF) http://www.eff.org

Health Privacy Project (HPP) http://www.healthprivacy.org

Anti-Phishing Working Group http://www.antiphishing.org

The Privacy Forum privacy@vortex.com

Institute for the Study of Privacy Issues (ISPI) http://www.PrivacyNews.com

Medical Privacy Coalition http://www.medicalprivacycoalition.org

People for Internet Responsibility (PFIR) http://www.pfir.org

Privacy News and Information http://www.privacy.org

World Privacy Forum http://www.worldprivacyforum.org

"牛津通识读本"已出书目

古典哲学的趣味	福柯	地球
人生的意义	缤纷的语言学	记忆
文学理论入门	达达和超现实主义	法律
大众经济学	佛学概论	中国文学
历史之源	维特根斯坦与哲学	托克维尔
设计，无处不在	科学哲学	休谟
生活中的心理学	印度哲学祛魅	分子
政治的历史与边界	克尔凯郭尔	法国大革命
哲学的思与惑	科学革命	丝绸之路
资本主义	广告	民族主义
美国总统制	数学	科幻作品
海德格尔	叔本华	罗素
我们时代的伦理学	笛卡尔	美国政党与选举
卡夫卡是谁	基督教神学	美国最高法院
考古学的过去与未来	犹太人与犹太教	纪录片
天文学简史	现代日本	大萧条与罗斯福新政
社会学的意识	罗兰·巴特	领导力
康德	马基雅维里	无神论
尼采	全球经济史	罗马共和国
亚里士多德的世界	进化	美国国会
西方艺术新论	性存在	民主
全球化面面观	量子理论	英格兰文学
简明逻辑学	牛顿新传	现代主义
法哲学：价值与事实	国际移民	网络
政治哲学与幸福根基	哈贝马斯	自闭症
选择理论	医学伦理	德里达
后殖民主义与世界格局	黑格尔	浪漫主义

批判理论　　　　德国文学　　　　儿童心理学
电影　　　　　　戏剧　　　　　　时装
俄罗斯文学　　　腐败　　　　　　现代拉丁美洲文学
古典文学　　　　医事法　　　　　卢梭
大数据　　　　　癌症　　　　　　隐私
洛克